SWAMP MUSIC

Gator Country's Musical Legacy

Michael Ray FitzGerald

SWAMP MUSIC: Gator Country's Musical Legacy
Hidden Owl, LLC.
Copyright © 2018 by Michael Ray FitzGerald

michaelrayfitzgerald.com
HiddenOwl.com

Designed by Michael Ray FitzGerald and Richard Levine

ISBN: 978-0-9962371-1-6

Printed in the United States

For Larry Steele, who kept the memories.

Table of Contents

Preface

When Tom Register and I sat down to discuss his memoir (which Joe Black and I developed into a movie script) we marveled over how many acts—more than 100 national-label signings—have emerged from the Northeast Florida area.

We reminisced about the good-old days when there were literally hundreds of gigs and even more bands to fill them. My journalistic curiosity kicked in, and I started asking questions: Why did this happen? What was behind all this? Why was Jacksonville such a booming music town? There had to be reasons.

After an hour of brainstorming, we came up with a plausible explanation.

Of course there is never one cause for an event or series of events. It's usually a combination of factors. One of the big ones was the baby-boom generation—a "demographic bulge" of massive proportions—reaching its teenage years and having some discretionary income. The "teen market," as it was then called, was reaching critical mass. It must have looked to our parents as if kids were taking over the world—and we were.

Then there were the young entrepreneurs—hustlers like Register, Joe Giles and Sidney Drashin, who capitalized on this market with their teen dances.

But the catalyst—what made the Jacksonville music scene take off like a rocket—was the disk jockeys at the local radio stations. Television had a hand in this, but radio led the way. The Jacksonville-area music boom seems to have begun with a handful of DJs who made extra money by promoting local and regional shows. Radio and concerts were symbiotic industries, and besides, while disk-jockeying was a glamorous gig, it didn't pay much. DJs had to augment their paltry paychecks.

Our story begins in the 1950s, when local DJs like Marshall Rowland, Frank Thies, and Glenn Reeves were involved in promoting live shows by big-name, national acts who were already getting airplay. Getting the DJs involved was simply a way for signed acts to keep them playing their records (however, after the 1959 payola investigations, this sort of tie-in with radio stations became a risky business).

WQIK owner Rowland and his sometimes-partner Mae Axton, often acting as subcontractors for Col. Tom Parker and singer Hank Snow, brought in some big-name Nashville acts. The Hank Snow Jamboree, a package tour the pair brought to the Gator Bowl in 1955, included a 20-year-old Elvis Presley, who created pandemonium by jokingly inviting his screaming female fans backstage. This incident partly led to RCA's decision to purchase Presley's contract from Memphis-based Sun Records, which RCA had actually been considering for quite some time, regardless of Axton's oft-repeated claim to have expedited the deal (Atlantic Records also made an unsuccessful bid for Presley's contract).

Memphis is another example of a great music scene that exploded and then, like Jacksonville's, died. In the 1960s it was an even bigger phenomenon than Jacksonville, because it had recording studios and some record-business infrastructure. More importantly, however, airplay again was the key—local acts could get played on the radio, and airplay sold records. In 1954, Sun Records owner Sam Phillips was able to get Dewey Phillips (no relation) at R&B station WHBQ to play Presley's first recording, "That's All Right, Mama" only hours after the acetate was cut in Sun's studio. In the 1960s, Memphis' Stax Records became an R&B juggernaut in part because co-owner Jim Stewart had been canny enough to sign WDIA jock Rufus Thomas to the label, thereby ensuring sufficient amounts of airplay for Thomas's records as well as garnering recognition and credibility for the fledgling label (Thomas had previously recorded for Phillips' Sun Records).

In Jacksonville, DJs—and sometimes the station owners themselves—often doubled as promoters, bringing national acts to large venues. It was a perfect symbiosis: the station could present the show and at the same time hammer the acts' records, ensuring a full house plus lots of record sales—a conflict of interest, certainly, but a convenient one. Everyone was happy: the station, the act, the record label, the fans. Local and unknown acts could open for these national acts, filling out the bill for next to nothing.

Preface

The youth market was so music-hungry it would go for almost anything that catered to teen tastes. Dance-party TV shows like Dick Clark's *American Bandstand* or the *Lloyd Thaxton Show* were already popular on TV. Small-time local entrepreneurs like Joe Giles, who managed a black group called the J-Notes, realized something similar, on a smaller scale, could be done. Giles' genius was in using local bands to fill a small hall. The idea was similar to what used to be called "record hops" that featured DJ's playing the recent hits, but it used real, live singers and bands. It worked.

Another local hustler, Tom Register, had just graduated from Englewood High and landed a job at WAPE-AM, the biggest station in Jacksonville, doing sales and promotions. His ambition, however, was to be a jock, or "on-air talent." He took a six-week course at a technical school in Atlanta to get his first-class operator's license. He didn't land the DJ slot he coveted at "the Big Ape," but he did get hired at a small, 1,000-watter in Fernandina Beach, WTAP, owned by Marshall Rowland, who also owned WQIK.

Register had taken note of what Joe Giles was doing with the J-Notes. Black music was the real deal; even the rah-rah types knew that. White garage bands couldn't hold a candle to them. Frat boys like Phil Walden in Macon, Ga., and Tommy Couch in Jackson, Miss., made their fortunes booking black bands like the Mighty Panthers (with Otis Redding), Doug Clark and the Hot Nuts, and the Thirteen Screaming N***ers [*sic*] into frat parties and high-school dances.

Giles and Register had essentially privatized the high-school-dance concept, eliminating the high school. Halls were cheap, bands even cheaper—a promoter could rent a women's club or some other small hall for $200 and hire a local band to do a four-hour show for $100—and the kids would flock. Register already had his act: the Lemon Twisters, a black band featuring a young James Brown-style front man, Little Robert (Moore). Register signed the band to a management deal, but working with them was stressful: "They were late a lot," he says. Sometimes the take from the shows was disappointing, other times it was quite profitable. "We could take in $2,000 per night." Thus a roughly $300 investment could realize a 500-percent profit.

Having been in radio promotion and advertising, Register knew success depended on getting the word out. He printed up posters and stapled them to telephone poles next to high schools. He wanted to take the concept to the next level. Radio ads could pack his shows, but radio ads, especially on youth-oriented WAPE, would have eaten up too much of his capital. Still, Register had something his competitor Giles didn't: connections. He knew people in radio. He approached WAPE jocks Jack Mock and Cliff Hall Jr. He offered them a $25 fee for making brief appearances at his Lemon Twisters dances. Register didn't care how long the DJs performed as long as they "talked up" their appearances for a few days before the show—in fact, it didn't matter if they showed up at all. The point was the free advertising he would be getting on these very influential stations.

WAPE was a 50,000-watt powerhouse that beamed its signal straight up the East Coast and could be heard in every market from Daytona Beach to the Carolinas. It was one of the most powerful forces in the music biz. Airplay on the Big Ape ("The Mighty 690") could make or break a national act.

Local airplay had helped several acts move to the head of the line, so to speak, in terms of getting signed to major labels. For example, in 1955, Gainesville's Dream Weavers, which included two members from Jacksonville, got signed to Decca and developed a huge hit after getting their own show on college station WRUF in Gainesville. The Nightcrawlers' single "Little Black Egg" broke on WROD in Daytona in 1965. It got even bigger when Big Ape jock Dino Summerlin began playing it on WAPE a year later. Summerlin and partner Register had hired the Nightcrawlers to play one of their dances, so Summerlin began hammering their record on the Big Ape. Decca/MCA subsidiary Kapp Records jumped on it, and the record went to No. 85 on *Billboard*'s Top 100 and became a garage-band standard.

Summerlin earned extra cash on weekends making personal appearances at teen dances the Northside Youth Center for $20 per night. His job was to fill in during the bands' breaks. Register approached Summerlin and offered him $25. He didn't care how long Summerlin was onstage. "I told him he could just come in and say hello if he wanted."

Summerlin took him up on the offer, but when he realized how much money Register's dances were pulling in decided he wanted to become a partner in the venture, expanding it to include other acts. Register would find the acts. Summerlin would "talk up" the shows on the air, which would bring in the kids. Summerlin would entertain them between acts. The plan worked perfectly. Summerlin, who was making $85 per week as a WAPE jock, began making ten times that doing teen dances. He also began managing local bands, whose records he would play on his show and whom he would put on his and Register's teen dances. Summerlin even started his own record label, Kimberly-Ann Records, named after his daughter. Everyone was happy. The bands would get guaranteed airplay and full houses at their gigs. They made a paltry $50 or $100 per show but rarely if ever complained. "Most of the musicians didn't care about the money," Register explains. "They were happy having a taste of fame."

But wait—wasn't this illegal? Didn't having a financial interest in the acts whose records he was playing constitute a form of "payola" or "kickback"? Of course it did, and Summerlin apparently realized this at the time—he went so far as to christen his new boat "Payola." Payola no doubt paid for the boat. Since the payola scandals of the 1950s, which ruined Alan Freed's career (but left Dick Clark's surprisingly unscathed), radio stations had shied away from playing local acts, mostly for this very reason—it was too easy for DJs to extract kickbacks, often in indirect and imaginative schemes, from acts whose records they played.

Other Big Ape DJs saw what was going on and started doing the same thing. DJ Ron Wayne began promoting his own dances. Alan Facemire produced a record for a band he managed called the Second Coming, which of course he played on his Sunday-night radio show, *The Underground Circus*.

Station owner Bill Brennan should have had some idea about what was going on under his nose—someone at WAPE kept tabs of all the DJs' appearances and how much they were paid.

Brennan, who piloted his own Learjet, and two of his employees were killed in a 1968 crash, and suddenly it was all over for the Big Ape jocks. Brennan's wife and brothers decided to sell the station. The new owners came in and cleaned house, the entire staff was out. The DJs who had done so much to enrich the local scene—and themselves, of course —were gone.

Summerlin had already moved over to competitor WPDQ, by this point the No. 1 station in the market. But PDQ too would soon be sold, its format changed to R&B. Summerlin left town for a small station in Palatka and later for Texas, eventually returning to his home state of North Carolina.

All of this meant the end of airplay for local bands. Teen dances shrunk and disappeared. Times changed. "The music was different," Register says. "You couldn't dance to it. Kids would just sit on the floor and listen while the band jammed." What is more, promoters found out they would legally be liable if a kid got hurt, and the cost of insurance to cover this inevitability was prohibitive. Only a couple of promoters emerged who had the capital and the know-how to pull off local shows. One had been Register's fiercest competitor, Sidney Drashin of Jet Set Promotions. Register went back to work at his father's plant nursery.

Despite the disappearance of the teen dances, the market for local music had been galvanized by radio. Jacksonville became a bona fide "music town": there were thousands of fans who still appreciated live music and local acts. Radio had been the catalyst; local TV stations had followed their lead with music shows like *McDuff Hayride,* a country-music hoedown that featured a young Johnny Tillotson as a regular (when Dowdy got canceled, Tillotson got his own show). A show catering to teen tastes, *Shakin' Up Summer,* featuring Palatka band the Illusions, helped get that group signed to Columbia.

But radio was the leader. Pop radio tapped into the pulse of the youth market. Former WAPE jock "Honest John" Ferree told a reporter for the *Florida Times Union* that the youth culture of the 1960s "came about because of the big clear-channel radio stations [like WAPE]." Many jocks, such as WPDQ's Glenn Reeves, WAPE's Jim Shirah, and

WOBS's Dave Crawford and Willie Martin, were singers, musicians, and songwriters themselves. These hip, young DJs knew exactly what the kids would like—sometimes even before the kids themselves knew.

Musicians, singers and bands came from all over Florida and Georgia. A band called the Blues Messengers from Bradenton, Fla., moved to Jacksonville's hippie district, Riverside, in 1968. The band's leader, Dickey Betts, had been making forays to Jacksonville for years with his earlier band, the Jokers. The Blues Messengers changed their name to the Second Coming, and after Big Ape jock Alan Facemire became the band's manager and produced its first single, became the hottest act in town. A band from Daytona, the Allman Joys, frequently came to town to play Art Eisen's Comic Book Club. When Duane Allman landed a deal with Phil Walden's Capricorn Records in 1969, he came back to Jacksonville to recruit players from the Second Coming (Betts and Berry Oakley) and the 31st of February (Butch Trucks). The biggest and most famous Jacksonville band, Lynyrd Skynyrd, under an earlier name, also got airplay on WAPE in 1970. This local airplay had little or nothing to do with the band's getting signed in 1974, but it made its members confident enough to stick with it and make frequent sorties to Atlanta, where the band was signed by producer and label owner Al Kooper.

What happened in Jacksonville in the 1960s —and in Memphis—can probably never be repeated. It was a perfect storm of confluences. Thanks to deregulation, most stations nowadays are mere links in huge corporate chains (WAPE is now owned by Atlanta-based media giant Cox Communications). Gone are freewheeling owners like Bill Brennan and Marshall Rowland. Corporate stations are understandably reluctant to play local acts.

Local acts rarely get airplay, yet when they do, there is often a powerful reaction. For example, when Planet Radio (WPLA-FM, a Clear Channel outlet) began playing Limp Bizkit's version of "Faith" in 1994, it led to an immediate buzz in record-industry circles in Los Angeles, and the band was invited west to meet with label executives. In 1999, Rick Schmidt, a jock at WXSR (a Clear Channel outlet in Tallahassee), began hammering

Creed's demos, which led to a major deal and eventual sales of more than 30 million albums. In 2001, Jacksonville band Ten High (renamed Start Trouble) was signed to Columbia Records after Planet Radio jock Flounder played the group's recordings on *Native Noise,* a now-defunct local-music show.

But this power to break an act or to get a band signed is exactly what the media chains' legal departments worry about and why they shy away from it—radio programmers and DJs know full well the power they can bring to bear. Most of this power has been deliberately taken out of the hands of DJs and put into the hands of ostensibly more disinterested program directors (PDs) or outside consultants. Yet there are still imaginative kickback schemes than can be arranged. It's just too tempting.

So how does a new act catch a break these days? By marketing itself any way it can, creating a fan base and "buzz" via the Internet, the best bet being YouTube. Maybe the World Wide Web is the new radio.

Then again, who the hell knows?

Introduction: Jacksonville Blues

I got my first taste of North Florida music on the radio in early 1962. It was Ray Charles doing his version of an obscure country song, "I Can't Stop Loving You." His recording, which sailed to the top of the charts and stayed there for five weeks, was ubiquitous. I had no idea at the time, but this version encapsulated the intersection of R&B and country that embodied North Florida, where Charles had been raised.

In 1966, I took up the electric guitar, alongside many if not most of my male friends. One of the first things you needed to learn was the intro riff from "Little Black Egg," released a year earlier by Daytona's Nightcrawlers, already a garage-band standard.

In 1968 came "Spooky," a No. 3 nationwide hit by the Classics IV, a group from Jacksonville. I was 15, living on the world's largest naval air station in Lemoore, Calif. My father, an ordnanceman, loaded bombs onto fighter planes aboard the USS Oriskany.

Like many teens of my era, I had caught the music bug, but there wasn't much live-music action in Lemoore, just a tatty five-piece called the Leftovers I followed around. That band seemed to have disappeared after the lead singer got killed in a car crash. When my father got orders to NAS Jacksonville, a high-school friend who had lived in Jacksonville told me I would love it—it was "really happening."

Man, was he right.

On April Fool's Day six of us—my mom and dad, two brothers and a sister, plus the family dachshund—crammed ourselves into a Ford Falcon station wagon for four miserable days. Fortunately, the dog was on tranquilizers—and my mother should have been. When we finally arrived, we could smell the ocean—or was it the Glidden paint plant? My father missed the turnoff to U.S. 17 and went over the Fuller Warren bridge twice before finally asking a toll-taker for directions to the base.

It was a heady time for a Boston-born navy brat to be arriving in cracker country. Jacksonville was then—and pretty much still is—the capital of South Georgia. This was the Deeeeeep South. The bus station still had the corrugated fiberglass partitions that not long before had separated whites from blacks. We arrived on April 4, the day Martin Luther King got shot. I was sitting in the bathtub in the base hotel when the news from Memphis came over the radio.

My folks had gone to nearby Orange Park to look for a house. They wound up buying a cheap, cinderblock model exactly like thousands of other cheap cinderblock houses in Jacksonville. The total price was $12,900. Thanks to the V.A. Bill, they only put $10 down.

Duly ensconced at Orange Park High School, I was surprised to discover there were young bands all over the place. There were half a dozen rock groups at Orange Park Senior High alone: the Daybreakers, the Nu-Sounds, the Six Teens, the Sound Vibrations and more. The Daybreakers even had a hit single on 50,000-watt WAPE-AM, which could be heard from Daytona to North Carolina. Coincidentally, my new friends in the Daybreakers recorded at the same Edgewood Avenue studio, Sound Lab, the Classics had started their careers in.

Little of it made any sense to me: middle-class, white kids in penny-loafers—with no socks—in love with black music. Nonetheless, if you were a music lover, Jacksonville in the late 1960s was a great place to be. The music scene was hitting critical mass and was set to explode.

Being a rock musician in Jacksonville had its dangers. Having long hair in those days was an open invitation to having your ass kicked. Packs of rednecks—apparently with nothing better to do—cruised around town in muscle cars, looking for longhairs to terrorize. It was very much like in the movie *Easy Rider*. If you were hitchhiking and spotted a pickup truck or a car with its rear end jacked up, the best thing to do was make yourself scarce—quick. There was only one area where you could be left alone: Riverside, Jacksonville's answer to Greenwich Village, where rents were low and people were open-minded.

My dad had taken me to Paulus Music downtown and co-signed for my first professional guitar, a Gibson SG Standard, which we bought for the princely sum of $348.40—I'd wanted a Les Paul, like my buddy, Page, in the Daybreakers had, but it was out of my price range. I was to make the $22 monthly payments with wages I earned at the navy base, busing tables at the enlisted men's cafeteria for $1.65 an hour. I hated that job because the jarheads constantly hassled me about my hair, which was an inch—maybe—over the tops of my ears.

Despite setting me up with my new guitar, things got progressively worse between me and my military dad. Music was okay as a hobby—it kept me off the streets, my mom reasoned—but he thought I was an ignoramus to even dare think anyone could make a living at it. He didn't object when I moved in with my grandmother, who had moved down from Boston to get away from the gray slush. She bought a trailer and rented a lot in a nice, little trailer park close to school.

In the trailer park where my grandmother and I lived, there was another local legend: Paul Glass. His black, stringy hair was already fairly long. He had quit school a year before to become a rock musician with a band called Marshmellow Steamshovel. But he spent most of his days at home, shades drawn, practicing his Epiphone ES-335, like the one John Lennon used in *Let It Be*.

Skipping school, I brought my new SG by one day, hoping for some pointers. Never one for niceties, Glass sneered, "You don't deserve this guitar," as he fondled it. He wanted to borrow it, but of course I wouldn't let it out of my sight. So we struck a bargain: He'd bring me along on his gigs; I would let him use the guitar and in return I would get to meet his band mates and other musicians (like Jeff Carlisi, later of .38 Special, and Leon Wilkeson of Lynyrd Skynyrd). I might even get to "sit in" once in a while.

Glass became my mentor. As part of my instruction in guitar lore, he took me to see a Riverside band called the Second Coming, which featured a virtuoso picker from

Bradenton by the name of Dickey Betts. If Clapton was God, as the saying went, then Betts would have been Jesus—he could play Clapton's solo on "Crossroads" note-for-note, which Clapton himself could not replicate.

Betts' guitar playing was our drug. We hitchhiked all over Northeast Florida—as far as Ravine Gardens in Palatka—to hear Betts at every possible opportunity. One night, the two of us set out on a hitchhiking excursion into one of Jacksonville's toughest blue-collar neighborhoods. This was a risky proposition for semi-longhairs, but we braved our way to the Woodstock Youth Center on Beaver Street to get our regular dose of Betts' magic.

It was not the band's best performance. The group had a mystery guest that evening: Betts stood by as most of the solos were taken by a strange, diffident young man who looked like the Cowardly Lion and spent most of the show staring down at his Fender Stratocaster, stringy hair draped over his face.

We couldn't understand why Betts was letting this guy hog the solos. "We came to hear Dickey!" we shouted. "Dickey can play circles around this dude!" It would be months before we found out that this dude was Duane Allman, and that he was already famous.

Adding his younger brother, Gregg, to the lineup, Allman incorporated the foundations, the format and the fan base of the Second Coming. The new lineup played a couple of previously scheduled shows as "the Second Coming and guests." Fans had no inkling that this was the debut of the Allman Brothers Band.

Then they disappeared.

Later that year, another musician friend, guitarist-keyboardist Jesse Gay, and I were browsing at Hoyt Hi-Fi in Roosevelt Mall (right next to site of the old Scene nightclub, where the Second Coming had been the house band). In a display you couldn't miss was an album bearing a figure that looked a lot like Berry Oakley doing his best Jesus imitation. Here he was in a dark robe, standing with both arms outstretched, as if he were blessing the group of sinners below him—most of whom looked familiar.

Introduction

"Is that—?" I stammered as I pointed to the album. The store clerk, who had obviously been asked this question many times, interjected, "It sure is!"

There they were, the Second Coming, reincarnated as the Allman Brothers Band. The biggest surprise, though, was that the group had an album out on a major label, Atlantic.

Our necks snapped as my friend and I shot looks at each other. Suddenly anything was possible. Success in the music biz for local dudes was a reality, not just some pipe dream —as my dad had declared. As usual, the parents were wrong! Lynyrd Skynyrd, Blackfoot, .38 Special, Johnny Van Zant, Molly Hatchet, and others would follow in the ABB's path.

Leon Wilkeson of Lynyrd Skynyrd (who died of a heart attack in 2002) told author Lee Ballinger he'd had the same experience: "The Allman Brothers showed us that it would work, that it was worth pursuing—you know, putting your head on the chopping block." A band of Westsiders called One Percent were able to pick up a lot of loose fans as the Second Coming and its spin-off, the Load, left town. But being a big fish in small pond was never enough for Lynyrd Skynyrd.

To be successful, musicians must be nomads—ready to travel whenever and wherever the siren of success beckons. Betts and his compadres had bolted Tampa for Jacksonville and had just as quickly left Jacksonville for Macon. Glass and I chose to stay in Jacksonville, where the living is easy.

I often wonder why I stay here. I did a three-month stint in Los Angeles once, and I hated it so much I thought I might "go postal." I hated Atlanta, too. And Orlando. What is it about this place?

I'm guessing that pure laziness—the hallmark of any musician worth his salt—has a lot to do with it. Jacksonville had a good music scene, nice weather, the ocean—and it was cheap. Housing is relatively inexpensive, so I don't have to work that hard to pay my rent. Anywhere else, I'd have to get a real job to live this well.

The Denizens

"Musicians don't retire; they stop when there's no more music in them."

Louis Armstrong

Abrahams, Karen

Texas-born folk-blues-rocker, lived and performed in Jacksonville for 15 years. She returned to Texas, where she scored international airplay with a unique surf-rock/bluegrass remake of Jefferson Airplane's "White Rabbit." Based in Austin, Abrahams continues to tour the folk and Americana festival circuit in the U.S. and Europe.

Adderly, Julian ("Cannonball")

Famed alto saxophonist, originally from Tampa, graduate of Florida A&M in Tallahassee, where his parents were educators. He and brother Nat Adderly worked with Ray Charles in and around Tallahassee in the late 1940s. After completing his music degree, Adderley moved to Fort Lauderdale in 1948 to become band director at Dillard High School. He joined the U.S. Army and led an army band from 1951-1953 which included brother Nat on trumpet. In 1955 the Adderly brothers traveled to New York where they sat in with Oscar Pettiford at the Café Bohemia in Greenwich Village. Word hit the street that the new guys in town were hot properties. Cannonball worked with Pettiford for a while and then formed his own quintet with brother Nat in 1956. He put that project on hold to join Miles Davis' band in 1957 (alongside tenor man John Coltrane). Cannonball Adderly recorded

Julian and Nat Adderley

his own albums for Savoy, Riverside, EmArcy, and Capitol. In 1966, he landed a top-40 hit, "Mercy, Mercy, Mercy," written by pianist/sideman Joe Zawinul (who would later form Weather Report). He also worked with singer Nancy Wilson. Adderly died in 1975 at age 46 from complications of a cerebral hemorrhage.

Also see *Adderly, Nat.*

Adderly, Nat

Renowned jazz trumpeter, younger sibling of Julian "Cannonball" Adderly, also born in Tampa and a graduate of FAMU. Renowned vibrophonist Lionel Hampton had performed at a concert at FAMU in 1954; Adderly arranged to audition for him and got the gig. After a European tour with Hampton, Adderly left Florida for

New York City with brother Julian. Later worked with J.J. Johnson, the Woody Herman Orchestra and Cannonball Adderly's sextet; formed his own group after Cannonball's death. Recorded for Savoy, Riverside, EmArcy, Jazzland, Atlantic, Milestone, A&M, Prestige, Steeplechase and Galaxy Records. Died in Lakeland in 2000, age 68.

Also see *Adderly, Julian*; *Charles, Ray*.

Aleka's Attic

Gainesville rock band formed in 1987 by actor-singer River Phoenix and his sister Rain; early line-up included Josh McKay on bass and Josh Greenbaum on drums. The elder brother of successful actor Joachim Phoenix, River was born in Madras, Oregon. After moving about extensively, the Phoenix family relocated to Los Angeles in 1979, where River's mother took a job as an assistant to the head of casting at NBC. She brought River and Rain to agent Iris Burton, who landed River several spots in television commercials. River's first significant acting role

was in the 1982-83 season of CBS series *Seven Brides for Seven Brothers*.

In 1987, wanting to remove his family from the depredations of Hollywood, John Phoenix decided to relocate to the other side of the U.S., renting a house in Gainesville (River would later buy his family a 20-acre farm in Micanopy). After playing some music on the set of *A Night in the Life of Jimmy Reardon*, distributed by Island Pictures, Kim Buie of sister company Island Records signed River Phoenix that same year, whereupon he assembled Aleka's Attic. By this point he had appeared in approximately a dozen major motion pictures and would soon win an academy award for his supporting role in Sidney Lumet's *Running on Empty* (1988).

Aleka's attic recorded a set of demos, but Island executives became skeptical of the group's ability to tour due to River Phoenix's busy acting schedule, and due to his lack of participation the project was shelved (one song, "Too Many Colors," appeared in a 1991 Gus Van Sant film, *My Own Private Idaho*). Aleka's Attic decided to assemble its own independent release to be titled *Never Odd or Even*, but it too failed to materialize. The group disbanded in 1992, whereupon Phoenix formed a short-lived group called Blacksmith. He died a year later outside Johnny Depp's Los Angeles nightclub, the Viper Room, of a multiple-drug overdose. Phoenix was 23.

Two former members of Aleka's Attic, Josh Greenbaum and Tim Hankins, went on to form Gainesville band Seraphim. REM's Michael Stipe bought the rights to the Island recordings in 1997 and released them via the Internet.

Alpert, Herman ("Trigger")

Jazz bassist from Indianapolis; moved to NYC in late 1930s. Worked with Glenn Miller Band until drafted in early 1941. Rejoined Miller in Army Air Force Band during the war. Also worked with Tex Beneke and Benny Goodman. Later became prominent NYC session player, working with Ella Fitzgerald, Louis Armstrong, Frank Sinatra, and many others. Led his own band for Riverside Records in 1956. Alpert retired to Ponte Vedra Beach, where he died in 2013 at age 97.

Alias

Jacksonville-based rock group formed by guitarist Dorman Cogburn, vocalist Jimmy Dougherty and former Skynyrd backup singer Jo Billingsley. Recorded one album for Mercury, released in 1979.

Session players on the album included surviving members of Lynyrd Skynyrd Allen Collins, Gary Rossington, Leon Wilkeson and Billy Powell plus future Rossington-Collins Band singer-guitarist Barry Lee Harwood. According to an interview with Cogburn, the album sold about 100,000 units, but Mercury declined to exercise its option for a follow-up. A performing band was assembled and embarked on a brief tour with Skip Veahman on guitar, Chuck Hasley on keyboards, Steve Pratt on bass and Chuck Colby on drums.

In 1983, Dougherty became front man for the short-lived Allen Collins Band on MCA. Dougherty and Cogburn reunited in 1988 as Action Figures. Dougherty died in Jacksonville of a heart attack in January 2008 at age 56. Billingsley died in Cullman, Al., in 2012 after a long battle with cancer. She was 58. Cogburn continues to release material, both new and historic, on his own label, Streetfighter Records.

Also see *Dougherty, Jimmy; Billingsley, Jojo; Allen Collins Band.*

Allen Collins Band

An outgrowth of the Rossington Collins Band, formed after Rossington quit the group, this band, led by former Lynyrd Skynyrd guitarist and featuring Skynyrd members Leon Wilkeson and keyboardist Billy Powell recorded one album, *Here,*

11

There and Back in 1983 for MCA. Other members included drummer Derek Hess and singer-guitarist Barry Lee Harwood, who had both been in Rossington Collins, virtuoso guitarist Randall Hall and lead singer Jimmy Dougherty

After the ACB imploded in 1984, Collins tried forming a new lineup with various musicians including Robert Nix (drums), Andy Ward King (bass), Mike Owings (guitar), and later Steve Reynolds (drums), Michael Ray FitzGerald (vocals and guitar), and Phil Price (bass). Dougherty, Price, FitzGerald and King would later work with new-wave group Mike Angelo & the Idols.

Also see *Lynyrd Skynyrd; Rossington Collins Band; Dougherty, Jimmy; Harwood, Barry Lee; Owings, Mike; FitzGerald, Michael Ray, King, Andy.*

Allen, Bruce

This keyboardist came to Daytona Beach from East St. Louis, Ill., in the early 1990s to study at Bethune-Cookman University, where he met saxophonist and fellow divinity student Allen Wiggins. In 1994, the pair formed duo Allen & Allen, which soon signed to gospel label Light Records, a subsidiary of prominent Christian label Word Records. The duo's debut album reached No. 20 on *Billboard*'s gospel chart. The duo later recorded for CGI and Platinum Records. Bruce Allen moved to Jacksonville, where he became senior pastor at the Church Fellowship, while Wig-

gins returned to Orlando to take up the ministry founded by his parents. Allen has since relocated to Orlando.

Allman Brothers Band

Legendary rock-blues-jazz-country sextet formed in Jacksonville in 1969, featured Daytona natives Duane and Gregg Allman. The ABB also included members of Jacksonville-based bands the Second Coming (Dickie Betts and Berry Oakley) and the Bitter Ind (Jacksonville native Claude "Butch" Trucks). The ABB was the first act signed to Macon-based Capricorn Records; the group broke up in late 1970s; later re-formed and signed to Arista; later to Epic.

Betts was fired in 2000 and reformed his band, Great Southern, but retired from touring in 2015, although he does make appearances from time to time. In October 2014 the ABB announced it was disbanding and performed a farewell concert in New York. Drummer Butch Trucks formed the Freight Train Band; however, he committed suicide in his West Palm Beach home in January 2017. Gregg Allman died of liver cancer in May 2017.

Also see *Betts, Dickey; Second Coming; Trucks, Butch*

Allman, Duane

Born in Nashville, Tenn., Duane and his brother Gregg came to Daytona Beach with their widowed mother in 1959, where they fell in love with R&B and formed several bands. One of these was the All-man Joys, who toured the Southeast and signed to Buddy Killen's Nashville-based Dial Records, where they recorded one un-released album in 1966. The brothers briefly joined Butch Trucks' band, the 31ˢᵗ of February, who were signed to Vanguard Records. This lineup recorded an album's worth of demos for the label that were re-jected. The Allman Joys later morphed into Hourglass and were signed by Liberty

Records. Duane soon got fed up with living in Los Angeles while waiting on the label to promote the band, so in 1969 he bolted for Muscle Shoals, Ala., where he became a prominent session musician. Rick Hall, owner of Muscle Shoals' FAME Productions, also signed Allman as a solo artist. Atlantic executive Jerry Wexler acquired Allman's contract from Hall, whereupon he and manager Phil Walden formed a joint venture, Capricorn Records, to release Allman's as-yet-un-named project. Between sessions Allman made several sorties to Jacksonville to scout for musicians for his new band, one of whom was Second Coming bassist Berry Oakley, whom he had met at Jack-sonville's Comic Book Club during an All-man Joys gig. Allman was also acquainted with Second Coming guitarist Dickey Betts, whom he also recruited for the All-man Brothers Band. After successfully launching the band, Allman was killed in a motorcycle accident in Macon, Ga., in 1971.

Also see *Allman, Gregg; Oakley, Berry; Betts, Dickey; Trucks, Butch; 31ˢᵗ of Feb-ruary.*

Allman, Gregg

Born in Nashville in 1947, Allman relocated with his family to Daytona Beach, where he and his older brother, Duane, formed several bands, including popular touring act the Allman Joys, who were spotted in St. Louis by Nitty Gritty Dirt Band manager Bill McEuen. McEuen garnered the group a deal with Liberty Records in 1967, and the band changed its name to Hourglass. During this period Allman shared an apartment with singer-songwriter Jackson Browne, whose personal style of songwriting exerted an influence on Allman's own writing.

Already considered one of the premier blue-eyed-soul vocalists of his generation, Allman moved back to North Florida, and later to Macon, where he would serve as lead vocalist and organist for the influential Allman Brothers Band throughout most of its existence, writing much of the

band's material. He and Duane also briefly hooked up with drummer Butch Trucks in Trucks' band 31st of February, which included Jacksonville musicians Scott Boyer and David Brown. During the many breakups of the ABB, Allman would form his own bands, an early version of which included guitarist Boyer. Allman, who was married six times, wed pop singer Cher in 1975; the marriage lasted four years. Arguably as famous for his addictions as for his talent, he is the author of the 2012 autobiography *My Cross to Bear*. Allman died at his home in Richmond Hill, Ga. (outside Savannah) in 2017 from complications related to liver cancer.

Also see *Allman Brothers Band; Hourglass; Allman Joys; Boyer, Scott.*

Allman Joys

Group from Daytona Beach originally formed as the Escorts by teen siblings

Duane and Gregg Allman. In 1966 songwriter John D. Loudermilk spotted the band in a club called the Briar Patch and was impressed with their style. Loudermilk introduced them to Nashville executive Buddy Killen, who signed them to his label, Dial Records. Other members included Mabron McKinney on bass and Maynard Portwood on drums. A single of Willie Dixon's song "Spoonful" was released on Dial and sold modestly. An album's worth of material was recorded but remained shelved.

The Allman Joys also enjoyed a stint as backing band for a Pensacola-based girl group called the Sandpipers. The brothers Allman also worked briefly with Butch Trucks' band the 31st of February, signed to New York's Vanguard Records.

While doing an extended engagement in Pensacola in 1967, a rival group, Alabama's the Five Men-Its, had lost singer Eddie Hinton (originally from Jacksonville, Florida) and bassist Fred Styles. Other Men-Its members included keyboardist Paul Hornsby and drummer Johnny Sandlin. Since the Allman Joys had lost their drummer, the remaining members of both groups joined forces, dubbing themselves Hour Glass. McKinney would be replaced by Daytona bassist/guitarist Pete Carr. This amalgamation was playing an extended engagement in St. Louis when they were spotted by Nitty Gritty Dirt Band manager Bill McEuen,

who brought them to Los Angeles and landed them a deal with Liberty Records.

Also see *Allman Brothers Band; Allman, Duane; Allman, Gregg; Carr, Pete; Hinton, Eddie; Trucks, Butch; 31st of February.*

Alter Bridge

In 2004, three former members of Tallhassee band Creed, Mark Tremonti, bassist Brian Marshall, and drummer Scott Phillips, joined with former Mayfield Four guitarist-vocalist Myles Kennedy to form Alter Bridge, based in Orlando. The group at first stayed with Creed's label, Wind-Up Records, and its first release was certified gold. However, Alter Bridge has made several label switches since then, including Republic and Roadrunner, ultimately forming its own UMG-distributed label. Alter Bridge has released five albums. In 2009, Tremonti, Marshall and Phillips reunited with singer Scott Stapp for a short-lived Creed reunion; however, they are again touring as Alter Bridge, whose record sales do not even begin to approach that of Creed's. Tremonti also formed a solo project with bassist Wolfgang Van Halen, Eddie Van Halen's son.

Amaru, Bobby

Original drummer for Jacksonville rock band Burn Season; later formed own group named Amaru. Since 2012, Amaru has served as lead singer for Memphis-based rock band Saliva.

Also see *Burn Season.*

Ande, Bill

Guitarist from South Florida, toured with teen group the Ardells, who in addition to playing their own dances served as a backing band for many major artists. Affiliated with Henry Stone's Miami-based Sherlyn Music, Ande co-wrote a song for the Legends, "Don't Be Ashamed," which was released on Warner Bros. Records in 1964. In 1966, the Ardells changed their name to the Razor's Edge and released "Let's Call It a Day, Girl," on Pow Records. The song, which was owned by Dick Clark, peaked at No. 77 on *Billboard*'s Hot 100 and guaranteed the group spots on Clark's *American Bandstand* and *Where the Action Is.*

In the late 1960s Ande relocated to San Francisco, where he worked with a group of guys from Florida who called itself Osceola. Ande returned to Florida in the mid-1970s whereupon he joined southern-rock band the Tallahassee Band. Becoming more interested in the recording side, Ande managed and co-owned several studios including one in Jacksonville founded by former Roadshow Records executive Fred Frank, Coast to Coast Music, where he engineered recordings by Chill Deal, Mamado and many others. He also wrote a song for Jacksonville gospel singer Walter Ponder, "Your Precious Love," released on Frank's label, Coast to Coast Records. Ande moved to Orlando in early 1990s but now lives in Chicago, where he continues to perform.

APB (Artimus Pyle Band)

Jacksonville-based rock band led by former Lynyrd Skynyrd drummer Artimus Pyle after the group's 1977 plane crash decimated the band. The APB issued three albums on MCA and has at various times included bassist Allen Woody (later with Allman Brothers Band, now deceased), former Lynyrd Skynyrd and Rossington-Collins bassist Tim Lindsay (now with Molly Hatchet), and bluesmeister axe-man Greg Baril. Pyle rejoined Skynyrd in 1987 but had an acrimonious split with the band in 1991. Pyle independently released an album of new material in 2007. Pyle moved to North Carolina, where he assembled a new band.

Also see *Lynyrd Skynyrd; Molly Hatchet; Baril, Greg.*

Armstrong, Pat

Born in Atlanta, Armstrong came to Jacksonville with his family as a toddler. He got his first taste of the music business hiring local bands for teen dances. After earning a law degree at Mercer University in Macon, he became partners in a booking and talent-management agency with Alan Walden, brother of Capricorn Records founder Phil Walden. One of the agency's first clients was Jacksonville rock band Lynyrd Skynyrd; another was Gainesville-based Mudcrutch, which featured Tom Petty. After falling out with Walden in 1973, Armstrong rebounded with southern-rock band Molly Hatchet, who sold 4 million records for Epic. In the early 1980s, Armstrong moved to Orlando, where he managed the careers of Pat Travers, Quiet Riot and Stranger and built a state-of-the-art recording studio as well as a Sony-distributed label, PARC Records. His studio, which he sold to Full Sail, was host to clients like the Backstreet Boys, N'Sync, and Britney Spears. Besides the music business, Armstrong has interests in commercial real estate and banking.

Also see *Molly Hatchet; Lynyrd Skynyrd; China Sky; Mudcrutch.*

Attitudes

Jacksonville new-wave band, signed and produced by Capricorn Records A&R man Robert Nix in 1983. The group consisted of Frank Phillips on guitar and vocals, Danny Esposito, formerly of Johnny Van Zant's Austin Nickels Band, on lead guitar, Judd Shirley on bass, Michael Gossett on drums and Kent Mitchell on keyboards. Capricorn went bankrupt shortly after

signing the group, hence the group's debut album was never released. Phillips later hooked up with punk godfathers Stevie Stiletto. Esposito committed suicide in February 2008 at age 46. He was living in Athens, Ga., at the time.

Also see *Stiletto, Stevie; Nix, Robert.*

Audio Orange

See *3AE.*

Axe

Bobby Barth's Gainesville-based band, signed to MCA.

Also see *Barth. Bobby*; also see *Blackfoot.*

Axton, Hoyt

The son of songwriter-publicist Mae Axton, Hoyt Axton was born in Duncan, Oklahoma, in 1938. His father, John T.

Axton, a US Navy officer, was stationed in Jacksonville during World War II; the family settled in the Murray Hill area (on Dellwood Ave.) in 1949. John T. and Mae were both schoolteachers.

Hoyt Axton graduated from Lee High in 1956 and left town amidst a furor after burning down—as a prank—Knauer's Hardware on graduation night. He briefly attended Oklahoma State before joining the navy himself. He was discharged in 1961, and after a short stint in Nashville, where he recorded a single for the small Briar label, a song he co-wrote with mother Mae, he headed for San Francisco, where he became part of the local folk scene and hooked up with Steppenwolf's managers.

He signed with Horizon Records in 1962; his debut album included the original version of "Greenback Dollar," which became a hit for the Kingston Trio. Other songwriting successes included "The Pusher," covered by Steppenwolf, "Joy to the World" and "Never Been to Spain," both covered by Three Dog Night, and "The No-No Song," covered by Ringo Starr. Axton recorded for several other labels including A&M.

Axton also had a minor career as a film and television actor. His mother became his manager and ran his label, Bullfrog Records. He developed several health problems and at age 61 died of heart failure in his home in Montana in 1999, two

years after his mother drowned in her Hendersonville hot tub.

Also see *Axton, Mae.*

Axton, Mae

Born in Bardwell, Tex., in 1914, raised mostly in Oklahoma, Axton came to Jacksonville with her naval-officer husband in 1949, where she became an English teacher at DuPont and Paxon high schools. She also freelanced as a music journalist for *Country Song Roundup* and served as a regional publicist for Nashville-based concert promoter "Colonel" Tom Parker. In her 1960 autobiography-of-sorts, *Country Singers as I Know 'Em*, Axton claimed she introduced Parker to a 19-year-old Elvis Presley, and in addition hounded RCA's Nashville division head, Steve Sholes, to sign Presley (other sources indicate that RCA had been keeping an eye on Presley long before this). In 1955, she and local musician Tommy Durden co-wrote Presley's first million seller, "Heartbreak Hotel," although WQIK owner Marshall Rowland and others have said the song had been written and performed by Durden before he even met Axton. In any case, she wrote or co-wrote more than 90 songs for various (mostly country-western) singers, even one for Perry Como. She also helped develop Jacksonville singers Merlene Garner and Johnny Tillotson. After moving to Nashville, she did promotional and public-relations work for Eddy Arnold, Tanya Tucker and others and managed her son Hoyt's record label, Bull-frog Records. She died in 1997, drowning in her hot tub in her home in Henderson-ville.

Also see *Axton, Hoyt; Tillotson, Johnny; Garner, Merlene.*

Bailey, Debbie

This versatile vocalist and songwriter toured as background singer with Lynyrd Skynyrd from 1991 to 1994. Still lives and performs in Jacksonville as Debra Rider.

Bales, Kevin

Originally from Atlanta, winner of 1993 Great American Jazz Piano Competition in Jacksonville. For 10 years he was a profes-sor of jazz studies at University of North Florida in Jacksonville. In 1999, he recorded and performed with fellow UNF alumnus Marcus Printup on Blue Note Records. Bales has also worked with the likes of Wynton Marsalis, Louie Bellson, Eddie Daniels, James Moody, Ben Tucker, Ira Sullivan, Sam Rivers, Nat Adderley, Bunky Green and Nathen Page. Bales re-turned to Atlanta in 2004, where he teaches at Georgia State University.

Also see *Printup, Marcus.*

Balsamo, Terry

Jacksonville guitarist who temporarily re-placed Wes Borland in Limp Bizkit in 1995, later added to the lineup of rock band Cold, one of Bizkit leader Fred Durst's proteges. Balsamo was with Cold from 1999 to 2004. He went on to join Ar-kansas-based rock band Evanescence, for whom Cold had served as opening act. In 2015, Balsamo left Evanescence, rejoining Cold a year later and is still touring with the group.

Also see *Limp Bizkit; Cold.*

Baril, Greg

Hot-shot guitarist in the style of Stevie Ray Vaughan, originally from Connecti-cut; moved to Jacksonville in late 1980s. Baril's band has included former Lynyrd Skynyrd and Rossington Collins members Tim Lindsay (now bassist with Molly Hatchet), former Outlaws bassist Buzzy Meekins, former Rossington-Collins Band drummer Derek Hess, former Lynyrd Skynyrd drummer Artimus Pyle, and fu-ture Allman Brothers Band guitarist Derek Trucks.

Also see *APB; Trucks, Derek; Lindsay, Tim; Meekins, Buzzy.*

Barlow, Von

Jazz drummer who has worked with Mose Allison, Lou Rawls, Ray Charles, Eddie Harris, Bobby Hutcherson, Bunky Green, Roy Ayers, Etta James and Longineu Par-sons. Still lives and performs in Jack-sonville.

Barth, Bobby

Born 1952 in Kansas, guitarist/vocalist Barth had already performed in several bands before moving to Gainesville in the late 1970s, where he fronted rock band Alien, which signed with Curb Records, distributed by MCA. After changing its name to Axe, Barth's group released two albums. Axe left Curb/MCA in 1982 and signed to Atco, where it released two albums.

Barth joined Jacksonville band Blackfoot, also signed to Atco, in 1984 until the group's breakup two years later. In 2004, Barth rejoined Blackfoot sans Rick Medlocke, who had become a permanent member of Lynyrd Skynyrd, and stayed with them till 2010. Axe was resurrected for a reunion show in 2012. Barth has since retired.

Also see *Blackfoot*.

Beggar Weeds

Jacksonville new-wave band, formed in 1986 by guitarists Scott Leuthold and Adam Watson along with drummer Alan Cowart. After performing in Athens, Ga., REM's Michael Stipe took an interest in the band and produced some tracks, which were released on an independent EP.

Betts, Dickey

Vocalist-guitarist and founding member of the Allman Brothers Band. Born in West Palm, raised in Bradenton, where he formed the Jokers with guitarist Joe Dan Petty; he later formed the Blues Messengers in Sarasota with bassist Berry Oakley, drummer John Meeks, guitarist Larry Reinhardt and keyboardist Reese Wynans.

The Blues Messengers relocated to Jacksonville in 1968, changing their name to the Second Coming. Duane Allman, who already had a deal with the newly formed Capricorn Records, came to Jacksonville to recruit Oakley for his project. Sitting in with the Second Coming, Allman became so impressed with Bett's guitar work he decided to add him to the mix. The new group was dubbed the Allman Brothers Band.

A pioneer in the country-rock fusion of the 1970s, Betts wrote and sang the ABB's biggest hit, "Ramblin' Man," which went to Number Two on the *Billboard* Hot 100 in September 1973. Since leaving the ABB (more than once) Betts has led several bands of his own, including the Dickey Betts Band (on Epic), Great Southern (Arista), and BHLT, which included Jimmy Hall of Wet Willie, Chuck Leavell of Sea Level and Butch Trucks of the ABB.

In 2000, Betts was dismissed from the ABB and began performing sporadically as Dickey Betts and Great Southern. Betts had a comeback tour scheduled for 2018 but suffered some health issues including a severe head injury and was sidelined in-definitely.

Also see *Allman Brothers Band; Second Coming; Oakley, Berry; Reinhardt, Larry; Wynans, Reese.*

Billingsley, JoJo

Born Deborah Jo Billingsley in Memphis in 1952, nicknamed "JoJo" by Ronnie Van Zant, joined Lynyrd Skynyrd's backing-vocal group, the Honkettes, in 1975, work-ing alongside Leslie Hawkins and Cassie Gaines. After Skynyrd's 1977 plane crash and subsequent demise (she was not on the plane), she joined the group Alias for which she sang lead alongside Jimmy Dougherty. Alias released an unsuccessful album on Mercury but was notable for participation by several former Skynyrd

members. She also did some session work with the Atlanta Rhythm Section and later began singing Christian music, along with occasionally working with former Skynyrd members in various projects. Billingsley moved to Cullman, Ala., with her husband in 1986, where she became a gospel singer and minister. She died of cancer at age 58.

Also see *Lynyrd, Skynyrd; Hawkins, Leslie; Alias; Dougherty, Jimmy.*

Bitter Ind

Jacksonville-based folk-rock group formed in 1965 by drummer Butch Trucks and bassist David Brown while students at Florida State University in Tallahassee. Both had been students at Jacksonville's Englewood High School. After adding 12-string guitarist and vocalist Scott Boyer, the group attained a modicum of regional success and was featured on an area TV show titled *Let's Go.* In 1968, the Bitter Ind changed its name to Tiffany System to release a single on Minaret Records, a cover of Dino Valenti's "Let's Get To-gether" (which became a huge hit for The Youngbloods). The group did some recording in Miami and landed an album deal with New York-based Vanguard Records. A year or so later they returned to Miami with new members Duane and Gregg Allman, whom they had met in Daytona Beach, to record some new demos (including Gregg Allman's song "Melissa") with producers Steve Alaimo and Brad Shapiro in an unsuccessful effort

21

to garner a second release. Those recordings were later released by Alaimo on a TK Records subsidiary under the title *Duane and Greg Allman* [sic]. Trucks would soon join Duane and Gregg in the Allman Brothers Band; Brown would become a sought-after session player based in Miami. He moved to San Francisco to join Boz Scaggs' band. Boyer later reunited with former Bitter Ind cohort Scott Boyer in Cowboy, who signed to Capricorn Records thanks to a recommendation from Duane Allman. Members of Cowboy, including Boyer and Brown, would become the backbone of the Gregg Allman Band.

Also see *Allman Brothers Band; 31st of February; Brown, David; Cowboy.*

Blackfoot

Originally known as Fresh Garbage (after the Spirit song of the same title), this Jacksonville rock band was formed in 1970 by singer-guitarist Rickey Medlocke. However, at this time Medlocke served as the group's drummer. Other members included guitarist Charlie Hargrett, bassist Greg T. Walker, drummer Jakson Spires and virtuoso keyboardist Ron Sciabarasi.

Medlocke and Walker left 1971 to join a pre-fame incarnation of Lynyrd Skynyrd, with whom they recorded one aborted album, later released as *Skynyrd's First and Last*, in Muscle Shoals, Ala. Medlocke was Skynyrd's backup drummer and alter-

nate vocalist (he sang two songs on the album).

Re-forming Blackfoot in 1972, the band sent some demos to producer Jimmy Johnson at Muscle Shoals, who landed the band a deal with Island Records, releasing its debut album, *No Reservation*s, in 1975. Island soon dropped the group, but a year later Blackfoot landed a deal with Epic, where it released another unsuccessful album, *Flying High*, also produced by Johnson. In 1978 the members briefly served as backup band for singer Ruby Starr. After opening for Detroit band Brownsville Station in 1978, singer Cub Coda introduced Blackfoot to his manager, music-store owner Al Nalli.

Nalli landed Blackfoot a deal with Atco (a division of Atlantic Records) in 1979, where they scored hits "Train, Train" and "Highway Song," their album, *Blackfoot Strikes*, earning platinum status. In 1983, Blackfoot added British keyboardist Ken Hensley, formerly of Uriah Heep, and a year later added guitarist-vocalist Bobby Barth, formerly with Gainesville rock band Axe. Blackfoot recorded a couple more albums before disbanding in 1986, whereupon Medlocke continued to record as Rickey Medlocke and Blackfoot, releasing the album *Medicine Man* in 1990 on Nalli Records and *After the Reign* on Wildcat Records in 1994.

In 1996, Medlocke was invited to rejoin Skynyrd, this time as a guitarist and vocalist.

After touring with the Southern Rock All-Stars for several years, Walker, Hargrett and Spires re-formed Blackfoot in 2004 with Barth as front man; however, drummer Spires died of an aneurysm in 2005 and was replaced by Christoph Ullmann and later Mark McConnell of the Southern Rock All-Stars. In 2006, Jimmy Johnson's son Jay joined the group on guitar and vocals, replacing Barth. This incarnation lasted until 2010.

In 2012, Medlocke took control of the trademark, organized an all-new Blackfoot lineup and produced an album titled *Southern Native.* Walker and Hargrett regrouped as Fired Guns.

Also see *Lynyrd Skynyrd; Barth, Bobby; Medlocke, Rickey.*

Black Kids

Everything seems to have gone right for this young band formed in 2006 by siblings Reggie Youngblood (guitar and vocals) and Ali Youngblood (keyboard) along with former *Folio Weekly* staff writer Owen Holmes (bass and vocals). After performing around Jacksonville for a year, the group garnered a slot at the Athens, Ga., Popfest and got rave reviews in national and international music mags, including England's *New Musical Express*

(NME). *Rolling Stone* included the band in one of its "artists to watch" listings.

The group was signed by London-based Quest Management and commenced to touring the UK. Black Kids' debut album *Partie Traumatic*, was produced by Suede guitarist Bernard Butler and released in 2008 on UK-based Almost Gold Records. It was picked up for U.S. distribution by Columbia and entered *Billboard*'s Top 200 chart at No. 127. The group released a follow-up EP in 2009 titled *Cemetery Lips* also on Columbia. The Black Kids' song "I'm Not Gonna Teach Your Boyfriend How to Dance with You" is included on the soundtrack of the 2009 movie *Jennifer's Body.*

The band toured in 2013 and worked on an album that was never released. In 2017, Black Kids reunited and completed an album titled *Rookie*, but the group appears to have no recording contract as of this writing.

Blair, Ron

A navy brat born in San Diego in 1948, Blair attended high school in Jacksonville in the early 1960s. Moving to Gainesville about 1968 to attend University of Florida, he played bass with local band RGF. He also spent some time in Macon (his sister was married to Gregg Allman).

In the early 1970s he headed west to pursue a musical career in Los Angeles, where he was invited to work on some demos for keyboardist Benmont Tench. Tom Petty heard this ensemble and recruited its members to serve as his new band. Blair worked with Tom Petty & the Heartbreakers from 1975 until 1982, when he was replaced by Del Shannon's bassist Howie Epstein. After leaving the Heartbreakers, Blair worked with Stevie Nicks, Del Shannon, the Tremblers and Mike Campbell's side project, the Dirty Knobs. Blair rejoined the Heartbreakers in 2002, replacing his replacement, Epstein, who was having serious addiction issues and later died of a heroin overdose.

Also see *Tom Petty & the Heartbreakers; Lynch, Stan; Campbell, Mike.*

Blake, Blind

Born Arthur Phelps in Jacksonville ca. 1890s, Blake became a nationally-renowned blues artist in the 1920s for Chicago-based Paramount Records, for which he sold literally millions of "race records." Blake seems to have utterly disappeared at the height of his success around 1932—some historians believe he was murdered; others think he went into hiding, and another thinks he stumbled in front of a Chicago streetcar.

Blues Messengers

Sarasota rock band that became the Second Coming—one of the most influential bands in North Florida—after moving to Jacksonville in 1969. The group changed its name at the suggestion of nightclub owner Leonard Renzler, who offered them a house gig at the Scene, because he thought bassist Berry Oakley looked like Jesus.

The band also included guitarist-vocalist Larry Reinhardt and Dickey Betts, Betts' wife, Dale on vocals and keyboards, and drummer-singer John Meeks. Meeks died in a house fire in 1976. Reinhardt died from liver disease in 2012. Singer Dale Betts married drummer Joe English and lives in North Carolina. Betts and Oakley became founding members of the Allman Brothers Band.

Also see *Second Coming; Allman Brothers Band; Betts, Dickey; Oakley, Berry; Reinhardt, Larry; Wynans, Reese.*

Bonds, Gary "U.S."

Born Gary Anderson in Jacksonville in 1939, son of an Edward Waters College professor. He and his mother relocated to Norfolk, Va., while Anderson was a child. He was discovered in the late 1950s singing on a Norfolk street corner, by Frank Guida of Legrand Records. Guida re-named him "U.S. Bonds" without consulting him. Bonds soon scored a string of hits, including "Quarter to Three" and "New Orleans."

In the early 1980s, after a long fallow period, Bonds recorded two albums for EMI-America with producer Bruce Springsteen.

Bonds lives on Long Island and still tours regularly. He has also done some acting, appearing in the Netflix series *Lilyhammer*.

Bonds, Johnny

Bass player from Live Oak; joined the Stanley Brothers' band in 1961. Died in 2003.

Also see *Stanley Brothers*.

Bonnie Gringo Band

Southern-rock band formed in Jacksonville in the late 1970s by brothers Tim and David Briggs, both featured on guitars and vocals. It also included keyboardist David Gum from MacClenny, bassist Clinton Carver, and drummer John "Jay" Wasley from Winterhaven. David Briggs had left the group by the time it recorded its first and only album for Daytona Beach-based Auric Records in 1979. Later members included guitarists Jim Harrison, who was in turn replaced by Steve Wheeler, and bassist Brady Green. Harrison went on to work with Richfield, who released one single on Capitol, and Wheeler worked with the Danny Joe Brown Band and China Sky, both signed to Epic Records. Briggs spent eight years as a member of Alabama's touring band.

Also see *Briggs, Tim; Wheeler, Steve; Danny Joe Brown Band; Richfield*.

Boone, Pat

Charles Eugene "Pat" Boone claims descent from Daniel Boone. His father, Archie Boone, studied architecture at the University of Florida in Gainesville, where he met Jacksonville native Margaret Pritchard. The couple settled in Jacksonville, where Pat was born in 1934. The Boones had been hoping for a girl, whom they intended to name Patricia; when Eugene was born, they nicknamed him Pat.

After a short time in Jacksonville, Archie Boone was offered a job by his uncle in Nashville; the Boones moved there when Pat was 3. At 19, Pat Boone married Shirley Lee Foley, the daughter of country music star Red Foley. The couple eloped to Denton, Texas, where Boone attended North Texas State College. While in Denton, Boone won first prize at a talent show. This success led to a spot on Ted Mack's *Amateur Hour*, which in turn led to a regular stint on the *Arthur Godfrey Show*. Boone signed to Republic Records in 1954, which released his first single, "Two Hearts, Two Kisses." Boone's version was a cover of an R&B record that was toned down for white listeners, a modus operandi Boone would capitalize upon with great success. In 1955, he brought his winning formula to Randy Wood's Nashville-based Dot Records, where he scored several huge hits, including a cover of Fats Domino's "Aint That a Shame." Boone also re-did two Little Richard tunes, "Tutti Frutti" (which Elvis Presley covered as well) and "Long Tall Sally." An ardent admirer of Bing Crosby, Boone conveyed a clean-cut image designed to appeal to both teens and parents; his white-buck shoes became a trademark of sorts.

While appearing in many movies and hosting his own network TV show (*The Pat Boone Show*, ABC, 1957-1960), he stayed in college, graduating *summa cum laude* from Columbia University in 1958. Boone also wrote the theme for the 1960 Charlton Heston epic *Exodus*.

After the British Invasion made Boone's white bucks seem hopelessly dated, Boone regrouped with his family and began touring as a gospel act, the Boone Family (daughter Debby would go on to score a couple of pop hits in the 1970s).

In the 1980s, he hosted a syndicated gospel show on radio. In the 1990s, Boone returned as host of a Christian-music TV show on Trinity Broadcasting Network, which was unceremoniously canceled after he released an album of hard-rock and heavy metal covers (*In a Metal Mood*, Hip-O Records, 1997)—performed tongue-in-cheek as big-band arrangements. To promote the album, Boone made a tandem appearance at the American Music Awards alongside Alice Cooper. Boone was inducted into the Nashville-based Gospel Music Hall of Fame in 2003. He keeps busy and recently celebrated his 63rd year in show business.

Borland, Wes

Original guitarist for Limp Bizkit; Borland formed Big Dumb Face as a side project. BDF released an album on Fred Durst's Flawless Records (distributed by Inter-

scope). In 2001, after leaving LB, Borland and his brother, Scott (LB's keyboardist), formed the short-lived Eat the Day with former Filter singer Richard Patrick. Borland also toured with Marilyn Manson and served a short stint in Nine Inch Nails. After a brief reunion with Bizkit in 2004, Borland left again and formed Black Light Burns, signed to former LB producer Ross Robinson's new label. Borland returned to LB again in 2009. He also performs with Queen Kwong, fronted by his wife, Carré Calloway. The couple lives in Detroit, where they are building a studio in their home.

Also see *Limp Bizkit; Durst, Fred.*

Boyce, Richard

Bassist and vocalist from Plainfield, N.J., original member of the Parliaments' backing band, formed in 1964, later named Funkadelic. He left the group in 1966 and enlisted in the army. Boyce moved to Jacksonville in the late 1990s, where he has performed with several R&B and rock groups.

Boyer, Scott

Born in upstate New York in 1947, this guitarist/vocalist put together folk-rock trio the Bitter Ind while a student at Florida State University in Tallahassee. Other members were drummer Butch Trucks and bassist David Brown. He later formed Capricorn Records acts Cowboy and became a member of the Gregg

Allman Band. Boyer and Talton briefly re-formed Cowboy in 2010. In February 2018 Boyer died in Muscle Shoals, where he'd resided for 30 years.

Also see *Bitter Ind, Cowboy, Brown, David.*

Briggs, Tim

Originally from Indiana, this guitarist/drummer/singer came to Jacksonville in the mid-1970s, where he and brother David formed the Eagles-influenced Bonnie Gringo Band, which released one album on Daytona Beach's Auric Records in 1979.

In 1987 he formed the group Briggs, which was spotted at a gig by Alabama member Teddy Gentry, who liked the group and wanted to produce an album. This led to an offer to join Alabama's road band, with which Briggs performed for eight years. He also performed with Alabama on the song "Sweet Home, Alabama" included in *Skynyrd Frynds*, a tribute to Lynyrd Skynyrd released on MCA Records in 1994. In 1997, Briggs recorded a solo album in Nashville which was released by Intersound Records. He lives in Los Angeles.

Also see *Bonnie Gringo Band.*

Bristow, Carol

Blue-eyed-soul vocalist; sang background with .38 Special, Lynyrd Skynyrd and the Outlaws and was featured singer in Jack-

sonville Beach band Synergy alongside former Atlantic artist (and future Creed producer) John Philip Kurzweg and future Lynyrd Skynyrd guitarist Randall Hall.

Also see *.38 Special; Lynyrd Skynyrd; Synergy; Kurzweg, John.*

Brown, David

Born in Shreveport, raised in Jacksonville. In 1966, while students at Florida State University in Tallahassee, bassist Brown and Jacksonville drummer Butch Trucks formed the Bitter Ind with guitarist/vocalist Scott Boyer. The group did some recording in Miami, which led to their signing with Vanguard Records and a name change to the 31st of February. Daytona musicians Duane and Gregg Allman joined the group in an effort to salvage its Vanguard deal. The new line-up recorded some demos at TK Studios in Hialeah under the auspices of producer Steve Alaimo. Vanguard, however, declined to release the album, and these tracks were eventually released by TK subsidiary Bold Records under the title *Duane and Greg* [sic] *Allman.*

With not much happening for the band, Brown stayed in Hialeah to focus on session work. As a member of TK Records' studio band, the Zoo, Brown backed Wilson Pickett, Betty Wright, Latimore, Mercy and others.

In 1970 he moved to San Francisco to join Boz Scaggs' band. In 1973, Brown relocated, to Macon, Ga., to join his former Bitter Ind cohort Boyer in Cowboy. In addition to recording four albums for Capricorn, members of Cowboy also served as the nucleus for the early Gregg Allman Band. Brown continued his session work, playing bass for the likes of Al Kooper, Charlie Daniels, Martin Mull, Elvin Bishop, Kitty Wells and Arthur Conley. In 1977, he returned to San Francisco and spent five years with RSO act Mistress and after that did a two-year stint with Commander Cody. In 1985 Brown joined R&B rockers Norton and the Knockouts and continues to work with them. Not to be confused with Bay Area bassist David Brown who worked with Santana and died in 2000.

Also see *Bitter Ind; Cowboy; Trucks, Butch.*

Brown, Danny Joe

This Jacksonville native and Terry Parker High School graduate became front man for Molly Hatchet in 1974, a southern-rock band formed three years earlier by guitarist/vocalist Dave Hlubek and bassist Tim Lindsey. Under the auspices of manager/executive producer Pat Armstrong, Hatchet would sign to Epic Records, where it would garner no fewer than four platinum (million-selling) albums.

Brown left Hatchet in 1980 and formed the Danny Joe Brown Band with Bobby Ingram (guitar and vocals), Steve Wheeler (guitar and vocals), Kenny McVay

(guitar), John Galvin (keyboards and vocals), Buzzy Meekins (bass and vocals) and Jimmy Glenn (drums). This group released one album, *Danny Joe Brown and the Danny Joe Brown Band*, on Epic under the supervision of famed producer-engineer Glyn Johns. A single, "Nobody Walks On Me," written by Wheeler, was made into a video that garnered rotation on MTV. After a 1981 tour opening for fellow Jacksonville rockers Blackfoot, Brown's band members mutinied. Scrambling for a new backup band, Brown hired a South Carolina group named Revelation and finished the tour.

Brown returned to Hatchet in 1982, bringing keyboardist Galvin with him. He left Hatchet again in 1995 due to health problems and was replaced by Phil McCormack. Brown died of renal failure in 2005.

See *Danny Joe Brown Band;* also see *Molly Hatchet*

Bryant, Van

Front man for rap group 69 Boyz, whose single "Tootsee Roll" reached No. 8 on *Billboard*'s Hot 100 in 1994. Later became a DJ on Orlando's 102 JAMZ. In 1999, Bryant began performing under the name Thrill da Player. Bryant also operates HomeBass Records in Orlando.

Also see *69 Boyz; Chill Deal; McGowan, Johnny; Orange, Nathaniel; 95 South.*

Buie, Buddy

Born Perry Buie in Marianna in 1941 and raised in nearby Dothan, Ala., this guitarist, songwriter, producer and artist manager started out managing the Webs, a group from Dothan who became Roy Orbison's backing band, later known as the Candymen. The Webs also included future pop star Bobby Goldsboro. The Candymen hooked up with Atlanta's Lowery Organization, which also happened to handle Jacksonville's Classics IV.

Buie, along with Jacksonville guitarist J.R. Cobb, wrote the lyrics to the Classics' first hit, "Spooky," which was originally an instrumental tune by Atlanta saxophonist Mike Sharp (Shapiro). Buie and Cobb continued their collaboration, putting together the band that became known as the Atlanta Rhythm Section, for which Buie cowrote more songs with Cobb. Buie also managed the group. The ARS included Cobb on guitar and Jacksonville drummer Robert Nix.

Buie's songs have been recorded by many other artists including Garth Brooks and Wynonna Judd. "Spooky" was covered by Martha Reeves, Dusty Springfield, Andy Williams and among others. Buie retired to Dothan., where he died in 2015.

Also see *Classics IV; Cobb, J.R.; Nix, Robert; Goldsboro, Bobby.*

Burman, Ron

Burman moved to Jacksonville with his family from Philadelphia when he was 12.

He attended Wolfson High and the Bolles School. Burman ran student activities at FSCJ's South Campus, where he hired bands for college shows. He later worked at the campus radio station at Florida State University, WVFS, and was talent buyer for FSU's Student Government Productions. After graduating, he went to Norman, Oklahoma, where he briefly worked as an agent for Bulging Eye Booking but took off for Manhattan after a few months.

In New York, Burman worked for ABC Booking, where he handled Anita Baker, B.B. King, the O'Jays and other R&B as well as reggae acts. He was later hired by *College Music Journal* to expand its annual CMJ Music Marathon, an expo that presents up-and-coming acts to college talent buyers.

In 1997, Burman joined the staff of Dutch metal label Roadrunner Records with a mandate to bring in rock acts with more mainstream appeal. He signed Vancouver, B.C., neo-grunge band Nickelback, who sold more than 50 million units for Roadrunner (now co-owned by Warner Music Group and Universal Music Group). Burman was rewarded with a vice presidency.

In 2013 Burman moved to Dutch label Mascot Records as president of its North American operations. He lives in New York City.

Burn Season

After a protracted negotiation with Flawless's Fred Durst, this Jacksonville "nu-metal" band, formerly known as Smakt-Down, signed to Elektra Records in 2001. In 2004, Elektra's operations were discontinued; Burn Season was dropped before its debut album was released. The band snagged a new deal with Pompano Beach-based Bieler Bros. Records, which included four tracks from the Elektra recordings on its 2005 debut.

Burn Season disbanded in 2007. Drummer-vocalist Bobby Amaru formed his own short-lived band, Amaru, and in 2012 became lead singer for Memphis-based rock band Saliva. In 2010, guitarist-vocalist Damien Starkey joined multiplatinum Jacksonville-based band Puddle of Mudd as bassist (Puddle of Mudd's future appears uncertain as of this writing). Starkey also leads his own band, Society Red, and now focuses on writing for film and television. Other members of Burn Season included Adam Silk and Roger David on bass and guitarist Tim Nold.

Also see *Amaru; Starkey, Damien.*

Burrell, Auburn

Lead guitarist for Jacksonville's Dalton gang in the mid-1960s; replaced Mac Doss (who briefly replaced original member J.R. Cobb) in the Classics IV in 1968. In 1970 Burrell and singer Mylon LeFevre formed the Holy Smoke Doo-Dah Band, signed to Columbia Records. Became an in-demand session musician based in Atlanta and Los Angeles. Burrell has worked in that capacity with Joe South, Paul Davis, Pyramid, Frankie Miller, Leo Sayer, David Rea, David Blue, and Burton Cummings. Burrell also toured with Mac Davis. Now lives in Colorado.

Also see *Classics IV.*

Butler, Mike

Second-edition bassist for Jacksonville punk godfathers Stevie Stiletto & the Switchblades; the band relocated to San Francisco in the late 1980s. While the rest of the group decided to return home, Butler stayed in the Bay Area and by 1991 wound up working with heavy metal band Exodus, who signed to Capitol. From 2006 to 2009 he was with San Francisco band Jetboy. He currently plays with rock band American Heartbreak. Butler is also well known for his pod-based radio show *The Rock and Roll Geek Show* and operates his own multimedia production company.

Also see *Stiletto, Stevie Ray.*

Caddell, Freddie

Doo-wop singer, student at Jacksonville's DuPont High School. Fronted a group called the Twirls. Released three singles on the Memphis-based Ardent label in the early 1960s including "Gotta Big Fat Mama."

Campbell, Jo Ann

A Jacksonville Beach Fletcher High School cheerleader and drum majorette, Campbell did a stint in the USO in 1954, touring Europe as a dancer. She moved to New York in 1955. After switching to singing she signed with RKO-Point Records where she released an unsuccessful first single, "Wherever You Go." Her second single was a song she wrote, "Come on, Baby," released in 1957 on El Dorado. She recorded several singles for Gone Records and then moved to the majors with ABC-Paramount. In 1959 she appeared in Alan Freed's film *Go, Johnny,*

Go, in which she performed the sassy "Mama, Can I Go Out?" She returned with another film appearance in 1961 alongside Joey Dee in *Hey, Let's Twist.* She finally scored a chart hit in 1962 with the country-flavored "I'm the Girl from Wolverton Mountain," an answer song to Claude King's "Wolverton Mountain." She also made several appearances on Dick Clark's *American Bandstand*. In 1964, she married country singer Troy Seals, and the pair released a few singles as Jo Ann & Troy for Atlantic Records. She retired from music shortly thereafter and lives near Nashville.

Cameron, Britton

After recording two unsuccessful albums with Gainesville band House of Dreams in 1994, produced by John Kurzweg (who later produced several hit albums for Tallahassee band Creed) and one for RCA produced by famed hitmaker Keith Olsen (Fleetwood Mac; Foreigner, .38 Special), Cameron relocated to Nashville to become a staff writer at Warner-Chappell Music, where he worked with another former Gainesville resident, Stan Lynch. Cameron's songs have been recorded by Lonestar, Jack Ingram, Steel Magnolia, Don Williams, Sister Hazel and Jordyn Shellhart. He later became a writer with Super 98 music publishing. Working under the name the Legendary Ballad Junkies and BrittonJack, he and former House of Dreams partner Jack Sizemore (a member of Lonestar) released two albums together.

Cameron also released an album of his own material titled *Working Man*.

Also see *Sizemore, Jack; House of Dreams*.

Campbell, Mike

Born in Panama City in 1950, graduated from Ribault High in Jacksonville in 1968, Campbell moved to Gainesville to attend University of Florida, where he joined Tom Petty's band Mudcrutch in 1970. Mudcrutch was booked throughout Florida and Georgia by Pat Armstrong's agency in Macon. The band moved to Los Angeles in 1974, where they signed with Leon Russell and Denny Cordell's ABC-distributed label, Shelter Records. The band soon broke up, but Petty, Campbell and keyboardist Benmont Tench regrouped as Tom Petty & the Heartbreakers.

In 2011 Campbell was named one of the Top 100 guitarists in a *Rolling Stone* readers' poll. Campbell has also performed with Don Henley, Johnny Cash, Fleetwood Mac, Lone Justice, Roger McGuinn, Tracy Chapman, Warren Zevon, George Harrison, Stevie Nicks, John Prine, Bob Dylan, Patti Scialfa, Brian Setzer, J.D. Souther, Jackson Browne, Robin Zander, and the Wallflowers. Campbell and Petty reformed Mudcrutch in 2007. That band released two albums on Reprise.

Also see *Petty, Tom; Lynch, Stan; Mudcrutch*.

Canova, Judy

Born Juliette Canova in Jacksonville in 1916 (some accounts give her birthplace as Starke and her birthdate as 1913), Canova was a graduate of Andrew Jackson High School. She started out with a family musical comedy act, the Three Georgia Crackers, which had its own radio show in Jacksonville. This led to nightclub engagements in New York, where Canova, known for her hillbilly characterizations, was nicknamed the "Ozark Nightingale." She was spotted by Rudy Vallee, who invited her to appear on his radio show. This led to extensive run of nightclub, Broadway and Vaudeville engagements, which in turn generated offers to appear in films. She signed with Republic Pictures in 1940, where she starred in 13 films. Canova landed her own show on CBS Radio in 1943; it went to NBC in 1946, where it ran until 1955. Canova later became a cabaret singer in Las Vegas. She recorded for several labels including RCA-Victor, Okeh, Mercury, and Varsity Records. Canova died in 1983 after a lengthy bout with cancer and is buried in Los Angeles.

Captain Beyond

Formed in Los Angeles, this band included two members from Jacksonville's seminal psychedelic-rock group the Second Coming. Not long after Second Coming guitarist Larry Reinhardt bolted for Los Angeles to join Iron Butterfly, lead singer Doug Ingle decided to disband the group. Reinhardt and Butterfly bassist Lee Dorman put together a new band they dubbed Captain Beyond—a nickname given to Reinhardt by Yes bassist Chris Squire. They then recruited Tampa Bay-area drummer Bobby Caldwell, who had

worked with the Allman Brothers as well as Johnny Winter. They also recruited former Deep Purple singer Rod Evans. The group moved to Macon, where it signed to Capricorn Records and added keyboardist and former Second Coming member Reese Wynans.

The band split up shortly after their second Capricorn album was released in 1973 but reformed in 1976 and signed with Warner Bros., splitting up again two years later. Reinhardt and Caldwell again reformed the group in 1998 and disbanded in 2003.

Reinhardt died in 2012 as did bassist Lee Dorman. Caldwell, the sole original member, revived the name and began touring in 2015. Wynans is working with blues guitarist Joe Bonamassa.

Also see *Reinhardt, Larry; Wynans, Reese; Second Coming.*

Cameron, Michael

Singer/drummer/percussionist from Pittsburgh; played on Benson's 1971 CTI album *Beyond the Blue Horizon*. Moved to Jacksonville in 1970s where he formed funk band Dynasty of Sound. Later moved to Orlando.

Carlisi, Jeff

Navy brat born 1952 in Queens, N.Y., early years spent in Boston, moved to Jacksonville in while in elementary school. Worked with teen groups the Summer Sons, Marshmellow Steamshovel and

Doomsday Refreshment Committee. Joined up with singer Donnie Van Zant in 1970 to form Sweet Rooster, which included future members of 38 Special. Left for university in Atlanta; upon returning to Jacksonville he joined Van Zant's latest group, 38 Special, previously called Alice Marr. Van Zant had excellent connections through brother Ronnie, and the group was signed to a management deal by Lynyrd Skynyrd's manager, Peter Rudge, who landed them with A&M Records. Carlisi played on all the group's recordings from 1977 to 1997 and co-wrote most of 38's big hits. He also co-wrote "Four Walls of Raiford" with Ronnie Van Zant, which appeared on Skynyrd's compilation album *Legend* (1987) and on the box set *Lynyrd Skynyrd* (1991).

After leaving 38, Carlisi worked with Big People, which included singer Derek St. Holmes from Ted Nugent's band, bassist Ben Orr from the Cars, Pat Travers on guitar and vocals, and Liberty DeVitto from Billy Joel's band on drums. Carlisi later worked with the Brian Howe-led Bad Company. Carlisi and former Atlanta Rhythm Section members Robert Nix and Dean Daughtry later formed the short-lived group Deep South, featuring singer Jimmy Hall of Wet Willie and former Lynyrd Skynyrd guitarist Ed King. He later organized a music camp for kids and is the author of *Jam! How to Run Your Business Like a Rock Star*, published by Wiley. He lives in Destin.

Also see *38 Special; Van Zant (duo); Elson, Kevin; Lynyrd Skynyrd.*

Carn, Doug

Born in New York and raised in St. Augustine, this jazz keyboardist and saxophonist started out playing organ in church. He studied oboe and composition at Jacksonville University and Georgia State. Carn has recorded with Lou Donaldson, Melvin Van Peebles, Stanley Turrentine, Earth Wind & Fire and former wife Jean Carn, an Atlanta native who carved out a successful career on Philadelphia International Records. Has recorded his own albums for Savoy and Black Jazz, most of which have been re-released by Los Angeles-based Posi-Tone Records. He also did a stint as band director at a private school. In 2013 he reunited with Jean Carn for a tour. He lives in St. Augustine and is one of the founders of that city's annual Lincolnville Festival.

Carr, Pete

Renowned guitarist from Daytona Beach, joined Duane and Gregg Allman's group, the Hourglass, who recorded for Liberty Records in 1968. The Hourglass recorded its second album in Muscle Shoals, Ala., where Duane Allman stayed after leaving the group to become a session player at FAME Studios. Carr replaced Allman as studio session player when Allman signed to Capricorn Records and left to form the Allman Brothers Band in Jacksonville. Carr has performed on albums by Joan Baez, Luther Ingram, Bob Seger, Bobby Blue Bland, Paul Simon, Traffic, Joe Cocker, Willie Nelson, Wilson Pickett, Rod Stewart, Barbra Streisand and many others. He is also a successful recording engineer and producer, having co-produced highly successful albums for Bob Seger and Paul Simon among others. Carr recorded for Big Tree Records as half the duo LeBlanc & Carr, who briefly toured as an opening act for Lynyrd Skynyrd. He lives in Florence, Ala.

Also see *Leblanc, Lenny; Allman, Duane.*

Chain of Fools

Funk-rock outfit led by vocalist-songwriter Michael Ray FitzGerald [author of the present volume]; released two albums on Jacksonville-based Rimshot Records, distributed nationally by Chicago-based M.S. Distributing. FitzGerald's songs have been covered by Rowdy Roddy Piper (*The Wrestling Album*, Epic Records, 1985), Americana singer Karen Abrahams, and zydeco singer C.J. Chenier. FitzGerald also worked briefly with the Allen Collins Band in 1985.

Also see *Mike Angelo & the Idols; Collins, Allen.*

Charles, Ray

Born in 1930, in Albany, Ga.; moved to Greenville, Fla. with his family while still an infant. Attended the Florida School for the Deaf and Blind in St. Augustine; performed in Jacksonville in 1945, where he lived at 752 West Church St.

After arriving in Seattle, Charles signed with Los Angeles-based Swingtime Records in 1947. His first big hit, "I Got a Woman," a rehash of an old gospel song, "I've Got a Savior," would not appear until two years after switching to Atlantic Records in 1952.

In 1959, Charles left Atlantic for ABC-Paramount, who offered him his own production deal. At ABC he hit No. 1 with the groundbreaking *Modern Sounds in Country & Western Music* (1962). Later recorded for Columbia and Qwest (Seattle buddy Quincy Jones's label).

Charles had one of the longest and most successful careers of any entertainer, and continued to record and tour actively until his death in June of 2004 from liver disease.

Chill Deal

Seminal bass-music quartet featuring Jacksonville natives Nathaniel Orange and Jay (Johnny) McGowan; originally signed to Fred Frank's Jacksonville-based CTC (Coast to Coast) label; later signed to Quality Records in 1991, where they released four albums.

Orange and McGowan would later form— and have monster hits with—95 South, including "Whoot, There It Is" on Ichiban and the Quad City DJs with "Come On

and Ride" on BigBeat/Atlantic. Orange, as C.C. Lemonhead, released an album on Jacksonville-based Attitude Records. As producers, the Orange-McGowan team scored more hits with rap acts 69 Boyz (featuring Van Bryant), 3 Grand, and Dis-n-Dat.

Also see *McGowan, Johnny; Quad City DJs; 95 South; 69 Boyz; Bryant, Van; Frank, Fred.*

China Sky

Jacksonville-based rock group formed in 1987, led by current Molly Hatchet guitarist Bobby Ingram, featuring former Detroit resident Ron Perry on vocals and guitar and Richard Smith on bass and vocals. The group signed to Pat Armstrong's PARC label, a joint venture with Epic Records, in 1988 and released one self-titled album, which became popular in Europe. However, the group disbanded when Ingram left to join Molly Hatchet and the label became reluctant to support the act.

Perry and Smith reformed China Sky in 2014 with original Hatchet drummer Bruce Crump and former Danny Joe Brown Band guitarist-vocalist Steve Wheeler and signed to UK label Escape Music. After Crump's death in 2015, the members decided to abandon the project.

Also see *Molly Hatchet; Ingram, Bobby; Perry, Ron; Armstrong, Pat.*

Clark, Susan Thomsen

Born in Washington, D.C., the daughter of famed country musician and *Hee Haw* cast member Roy Clark, this multi-instrumentalist spent some time in Nashville and touring with an all-girl band before moving to Jacksonville in 1990, where she worked with many prominent musicians including Chip Miller (Cowboy, Ace Moreland), Artimus Pyle (Lynyrd Skynyrd. APB), Greg Baril, Banner Thomas (Molly Hatchet), Susan Tedeschi and Derek Trucks (Tedeschi-Trucks Band). Her most recent album appeared on Jim DeVito's Last Resort Records and featured appearances by Stan Lynch and Roy Clark.

Classics IV

The original Classics were formed in 1961 by guitarist-bassist Walter Eaton, a Jacksonville native and graduate of Andrew Jackson High School. The first incarnation included Eaton on lead guitar, Burt Norton on rhythm, Glen Futch on bass, Bobby Bowen on drums, and Greg Carrol on saxophone. This group, who played mostly instrumentals, rehearsed at Norton's parents' home in the Lakewood area. Paxon High graduate Robert Nix, from Jacksonville's Westside, replaced Futch on drums. Two members from the Emeralds, James ("J.R.") Cobb and Joe Wilson, both Paxon High graduates, came in as replacements a year later. Nix left in 1963 to join Susan and the Dynamics, a group who would link to the Lowery organization in Atlanta. Nix was replaced by drummer Dennis Yost, another Jackson High graduate, whose family had moved to Jacksonville from Detroit when he was 5. Yost was also an accomplished vocalist who, when singing, would play the drums standing up. Wilson switched to keyboards and Eaton to bass with Cobb remaining on guitar. The Classics soon undertook a fairly heavy schedule, mostly in an around a 100-mile radius of Jacksonville.

In 1966, the Classics were working at the Purple Porpoise, a Daytona Beach hotel lounge (where Daytona residents Duane and Gregg Allman sat in with the group). They were spotted by Paul Cochran, who was working for Bill Lowery's Atlanta music operation. Cochran became the Classics' co-manager along with Alan Diggs. Buddy Buie, Roy Orbison's road manager and manager of Orbison's backup band, the Candymen, came in as a management partner as well.

With Lowery behind the scenes as music publisher and executive producer, the group signed to Los-Angeles based Capitol Records in 1967, where it released two singles, one of which, "Pollyanna," was written by Lowery staff writer Joe South. Despite the involvement of these heavy hitters, both Capitol singles failed to chart—one reason might have been because "Pollyanna" sounded too much like the Four Seasons. To make matters worse, group was notified that there was already an act named the Classics. The group altered the name slightly to "Classics IV" for their next Capitol release, a cover of the Diamond's "Little Darlin'," an anachronism in 1967. Neither record broke *Billboard*'s Hot 100 ("Pollyanna" had peaked at 103).

Undeterred, the group revamped its sound with "Spooky," a rewrite of a funk-jazz instrumental by Atlanta saxophonist Mike Sharpe (also connected to the Lowery organization). Lowery snagged the group a deal with Los Angeles-based Imperial Records, where it scored a hit. The Classics' version of "Spooky," released in September 1967, reached No. 3 in February 1968 and became the group's ticket to stardom. The group followed in May with "Soul Train," which barely cracked the Top 100. But their next record, "Stormy," reached No. 5 in December 1968; then came "Traces" (No. 2, March 1969) and

"Every Day with You, Girl" (No. 19, June 1969). All were recorded at Lowery's Atlanta studio, Mastersound.

The Classics began revamping their lineup. Cobb had left five months before "Spooky" was released to concentrate on writing and producing; he would, however, remain irreplaceable as the group's resident songwriter and studio guitarist. Cobb was replaced in the touring band by Bradenton guitarist Mack Doss, who had played with Larry Reinhardt in Tampa Bay band the Thunderbeats. Doss lasted about a year and was replaced by Auburn Burrell, formerly with Jacksonville's Dalton Gang; Burrell went on to an illustrious career as a session musician. Troy, Ala., drummer Kim Venable was brought in so Yost could move about freely out front (Robert Nix, then based in Atlanta, served as the group's session drummer). Following a 1969 car crash in which he was seriously injured, founder Eaton left and was replaced by bassist Bill Gilmore; Wilson was replaced by Dean Daughtry. Both Gilmore and Daughtry had been members of Roy Orbison's band the Candymen, which also included Nix. Eaton and Wilson briefly served as A&R reps for New York-based Laurie Records; Eaton also produced records for a number of Jacksonville acts.

In 1970, Cobb, Daughtry and Nix formed the Atlanta Rhythm Section but would continue to perform on many Classics IV recordings as session players. In 1972,

Yost, the only longstanding member at this point, signed with MGM and continued to tour as Dennis Yost and the Classics IV with a shifting cast of musicians.

In the 1980s Yost unwittingly signed over the rights to the service mark "Classics IV" to his manager, who resold it to an obscure doo-wop group. Yost had to fight an expensive legal battle to regain the rights. Yost relocated to Nashville in 1993 and continued to tour the oldies circuit.

In 2006, Yost suffered a head injury falling down a flight of stairs. He spent his remaining years in a nursing facility near his wife's home outside Cleveland, succumbing to respiratory failure in 2008 at 65. Eaton left the music business in the 1970s and went into computer networking and security. He worked for Unisys and the City of Jacksonville; after retiring from the city and earning a doctoral degree, Eaton became a professor at Florida State College at Jacksonville, where he teaches cybersecurity. Cobb is retired and lives in Monticello. Ga.

Also see *Cobb, J.R.; Yost, Dennis; Nix, Robert; Burrell, Auburn.*

Clements, Carroll

Bluegrass singer and banjoist born 1926 in Central Florida; worked with the Low Country All-Stars, a group that also featured cousin Vassar Clements, Ricky Scaggs and Tony Rice. Lives in Jacksonville.

Clinton, George

Born Kannapolis, N.C., in 1941, raised in Plainfield, N.J., where he formed vocal group the Parliaments in the late 1950s; the group released a single on Detroit-based Revilot Records in 1967.

Clinton moved to Detroit where he briefly served as a songwriter for Motown Records. After losing the name the Parliaments, Clinton founded another act he called Funkadelic, which included most of the members of Parliament's backing band, and signed with Detroit-based Westbound Records in 1968, later signed to Warner Bros. He re-formed Parliaments in 1970, signing with Detroit-based Invictus Records, later Los Angeles-based Casablanca. In the 1980s he recorded as a solo artist for Capitol as well as for Prince's Paisley Park label.

Clinton has released about 20 albums. He also produced albums for Bootsy Collins and the Red Hot Chili Peppers and wrote "You're Thinking Right," the theme for *the Tracey Ullman Show*. Parliament and Funkadelic, collectively known as P-Funk, were inducted into the Rock and Roll Hall of Fame in 1997.

Clinton moved to Tallahassee a year later, where he maintains a small recording studio; still tours sporadically under the name P-Funk. He is the author of the memoir *Brothas Be, Yo Like George, Ain't that Funkin' Kinda Hard On You?*

Also see *Boyce, Richard.*

Cobb, James ("J.R.")

Born in Birmingham in 1944, Cobb moved with his parents to Jacksonville as a toddler. After graduating from Paxon High School, he joined the Classics as a guitarist in 1962. Cobb found his forte as a songwriter. He co-wrote most of the Classics IV's hits, including their 1968 smash, "Spooky" (actually a rewrite of an obscure jazz instrumental by Atlanta saxophonist Mike Sharpe). He also co-wrote "Be Young, Be Foolish," which became an R&B evergreen for the Tams, another group in Atlanta impresario Bill Lowery's stable.

In 1967 Cobb left the Classics to concentrate on writing and producing and was re-

placed by Bradenton guitarist Mac Doss, who was in turn replaced by Auburn Burrell, formerly of Jacksonville's Dalton Gang.

Cobb co-founded the Atlanta Rhythm Section in 1970 with fellow Paxon High graduate, drummer Robert Nix, and co-wrote much of that group's material as well. Cobb has also co-written successful songs for Sandy Posey and Wynonna Judd.

In 1985 Cobb went to Nashville to work as a session player for producer Chips Moman. He worked as a sideman with country supergroup the Highwaymen, composed of Johnny Cash, Waylon Jennings, Kris Kristofferson and Willie Nelson. Cobb is retired and lives in Monticello, Ga.

Also see *Classics IV; Nix, Robert.*

Cogburn, Dorman

See *Alias.*

Cohen, Jeff

Founder of Jacksonville-based Attitude Records, whose first act, the Lads, produced by musician/engineer Willetta Smith (aka Mamado) in 1987, signed with Motown. Cohen also launched Mamado herself, whose work he licensed to WTG Records, a CBS label, in 1988. Other Attitude acts include D.J. Trans, M.C. Player, Assault & Battery, C.C. Lemonhead, Quad Force, Tik Tak Toe, Party Boyz, 2 Nazty, I.C. Red, Little Ko-Chees, and da Shorties.

Cohen also dabbled in punk rock. In 1996, Cohen plucked punk godfathers Stevie Stiletto from obscurity, licensing the band's album, *American Asshole*, to S&F Records in Germany.

Cohen sold his distribution and one-stop operation, Dolphin Music, in 2007 and operates a leather-furniture store in St. Augustine.

Also see *Mamado; 69 Boyz; Lemonhead, C.C.; Stevie Stilletto.*

Cold

This Jacksonville Beach-based, super-heavy rock band was formed as Grundig in 1992. The original lineup included singer-guitarist Scooter Ward, drummer Sam McCandless, bassist Pat Lally, and guitarist Matt Loughran, replaced by Kelly Hayes. Grundig spent a frustrating, unfruitful stint in Atlanta trying to gain entrée to the big-time.

After returning to Jacksonville, Limp Bizkit front man Fred Durst took an interested in the group. After a quick name change, Cold signed to Jordan Schur's Flip Records, which was then distributed by A&M. The band's self-titled debut, released in 1998, was produced by Ross Robinson, who had produced Bizkit's debut. Cold was later transferred to Geffen; a second album was released in 2000. Both albums were certified gold (signifying sales of 500,000 copies).

Guitarist Terry Balsamo, who had done a brief stint with Limp Bizkit in 1995, joined the group in 1999, allowing Ward to move around out front unencumbered. A third album was released in 2003; however, by this point relations with Geffen were strained. In 2004, the group signed to Lava Records.

Cold officially disbanded in 2006 but reunited in 2009 and released a new album on Eleven Seven Music. In 2015 Cold signed with Austrian label Napalm Records and is still touring. After leaving the group in 2004 to join rock band Evanescence, early member Balsamo returned to the fold in 2016.

Also see *Durst, Fred; Balsamo, Terry.*

Collins, Allen

Born in Jacksonville 1952, a graduate of Jacksonville's Forrest High School, guitarist Collins joined local group My Backyard, an early version of Lynyrd Skynyrd, in 1964. Collins co-wrote one of the group's biggest hits, "Free Bird."

After Skynyrd's 1977 plane crash, Collins co-founded the Rossington Collins band in 1980. After Rossington left, Collins took over and renamed it the Allen Collins Band. The ACB released one album, *Here, There and Back*, on MCA in 1983, but the group fell apart shortly thereafter for various reasons, mostly related to Collins' lack of focus, due in large part to the sudden death of his wife, Kathy. Collins tried to re-form the ACB with a string of local musicians to little avail.

In 1986, Collins crashed his vehicle into a ditch, killing his girlfriend, Debra Jean Watts, and leaving him a paraplegic. Collins pled guilty to charges of driving while intoxicated. He died in 1990 of respiratory failure. He was 37. At Collin's behest, ACB members Wilkeson, Powell and Hall reformed Lynyrd Sknyrd in 1987.

Also see *Lynyrd Skynyrd; Dougherty, Jimmy; Lindsay, Tim; Hess, Derek; Harwood, Barry Lee.*

Conrad, Bill

Conrad attended the prestigious Bolles School where he befriended aspiring folksinger Gram Parsons. He started out in the music biz in 1967 as manager of Palatka band the Illusions, a band who had its own Jacksonville television show, *Let's Go* on Jacksonville's WFGA (Channel 12) and a single on Columbia Records.

After the Illusions split up, drummer Tim Touchton moved to Tallahassee, where he joined a rock group called Plymouth Rock, which Conrad helped get signed to Epic Records. However, Plymouth Rock's debut album never saw the light of day, so Conrad left for Los Angeles, where he became an apprentice engineer at Hollywood Sound Recorders, where he met producer and label head Jimmy Bowen. Conrad became Bowen's chauffeur. He later became a music journalist for *Buddy* magazine and assistant to record producer Ken Mansfield. He then became a publicist for Waylon Jennings, one of Mansfield's clients. Conrad wrote a series of memoirs for alternative-country journal *No Depression*; in 2015 he published this collection as a book titled *Country-Rock Journals.*

Conti, Robert

Jazz guitarist, born 1945 in Philadelphia, moved to Jacksonville in 1966, lived in the area for 22 years. Signed to Discovery Records in 1979; relocated to Los Angeles in 1988, where he recorded with Joe Pass and worked for film executive Dino Di Laurentiis. Conti was a featured performer at Jacksonville Jazz Festival in 1986.

Sidelined by a back injury, Conti returned as house musician at the Irvine Marriott, a gig he held on to for 10 years. He signed with the independent Time Is label in 1990; England's Pinnacle Records has re-released some of his earlier albums. In 2000 he moved to in Las Vegas where he focused on teaching. He now lives in Idaho Springs and makes instructional videos he markets by mail-order. He also has his own line of custom-built guitars.

Coolidge, Rita

Born in Lafayette, Tenn., Coolidge came to Jacksonville as the daughter of a Baptist minister. After graduating from Andrew Jackson High School, Coolidge attended Florida State University in Tallahassee. She then moved to Memphis to pursue a singing career, where she recorded for the Stax-affliliated Pepper label. She relocated to Los Angeles as a backup singer for Delaney and Bonnie and gained prominence working with Leon Russell, Joe Cocker, Bob Dylan, Jimi Hendrix, Eric Clapton, Dave Mason, Graham Nash and Stephen Stills.

In 1973, she married singer-songwriter Kris Kristofferson and recorded a duet album which garnered a Grammy award. The couple was married for eight years. She garnered her own hit in 1977, "Higher and Higher," on A&M, produced and arranged by her sister Priscilla's husband, Booker T. Jones of Booker T & the MGs.

Coolidge lives near San Diego and concentrates on painting. In 2016 she published her memoirs, *Delta Lady*, via HarperCollins, in which she claims to have co-written the song "Superstar," a No. 2 hit for the Carpenters in 1971, officially credited to Bonnie Bramlett and Leon Russell.

Corley, Alfred

Born in Jacksonville in 1940, as a teenager this alto-sax player studied with Cannonball Adderly at Florida A&M University in Tallahassee.

After working the "chitlin' circuit" in the late 1950s, Corley was recruited by James Brown's bandleader, J.C. Davis. The first Brown recording Corley performed on was "(Do the) Mashed Potatoes," recorded in December 1959 at Dukoff Studio in Miami and released under the name Nat Kendrick & the Swans on Henry Stone's Dade label. That record went to No. 8 on *Billboard*'s rhythm & blues chart and landed at 84 on the Hot 100. Corley's next recording with Brown was a cover of Lowman Pauling's "Think," released on King subsidiary Federal Records in 1960; that record went to No. 7 R&B and No. 33 pop. Corley is listed as having performed on approximately 15 singles during his tenure with Brown. Jacksonville trumpeter and trombonist Teddy Washington worked alongside Corley in Brown's band for a time.

Corley left Brown about 1967 and went to San Francisco, where he played tenor with singer Joan Adams. He returned to Jacksonville where he worked with teen R&B band the Lemon Twisters, managed by Tom Register. He died in 1968 in Jacksonville at age 27.

Cowboy

Capricorn Records act featuring Jacksonville musicians Scott Boyer on guitar and vocals, bassist David Brown (later with Boz Scaggs) and drummer/percussionist Chip Miller along with Tampa Bay-area guitarist Tommy Talton. At the rec-

ommendation of Duane Allman, label owner Phil Walden signed the group to Capricorn, where it would record four albums. Boyer and Brown also performed in Gregg Allman's early solo band.

Also see *Bitter Ind; Brown, David; Boyer, Scott.*

Crawfish of Love

"No-wave" ensemble led by Dave Roberts, former psychology teacher at Jacksonville's Terry Parker High School. Members have included Pat Ogilvie on guitar along with former Mike Angelo & the Idols members Alan Close (bass), Andy King (bass) and Scott Sisson (drums). The group backed It's a Beautiful Day founders David and Linda LaFlamme at the Magnolia Festival in 1998. In 2006 the Crawfish backed former Quicksilver Messenger Service guitarist Gary Duncan on a couple of shows as well as performed on his album *Snake Language*, released on San Rafael, Calif.-based Global Recording Artists, released in the UK on Floating World Records. The Crawfish released two albums of their own via GRA, *Darkest Show on Earth* and *Septober-Octember*.

Also see *Mike Angelo & the Idols; King, Andy; Sisson, Scott.*

Crawford, Dave

A church-trained prodigy on piano, Crawford worked with Albertina Walker, Shirley Caesar and the Gospel Caravans while still a teenager. Crawford gained regional recognition as a WOBS radio personality called "the Demon"; he later did the same at WTMP in Tampa. He co-wrote (often with fellow WOBS DJ Willie "Doctor Groove" Martin) several R&B tunes, including "What a Man" for Stax's Linda Lyndell (1968).

In 1969, Crawford, teamed with "Bad Brad" Shapiro, became a staff producer for Atlantic Records, where he co-wrote and co-produced tracks for Wilson Pickett and DeeDee Warwick. The pair also produced the J. Geils Band's 1970 debut for Atlantic. That same year, he brought his cousin, songstress Jackie Moore, a Jacksonville native, to the label. Crawford and Moore co-wrote her Atlantic hit, "Precious, Precious" (No. 12 R&B, No. 30 pop).

Crawford later worked with several hit acts including B.B. King (ABC), Candi Staton (he wrote and produced her 1976 ABC hit "Young Hearts Run Free"), The Mighty Clouds of Joy ("Ride the Mighty High" on ABC, co-written with Willie Martin) and Phyllis Hyman (Arista).

After many years in Atlanta, Crawford moved to Los Angeles in 1974 to form his own label, L.A. Records. He lost money on this venture and moved to Miami to become a gospel-music radio DJ.

Crawford was murdered in 1988 in Brooklyn, N.Y., and was buried—unidentified—in a pauper's grave. His body was later exhumed and interred in Jacksonville with assistance from his cousin Moore. New York City police refused to release details of the case.

Crawford's songs—including a No. 3 version of "Whatta Man" (a remake of Lyndell's 1968 song) by Salt & Pepa in 1993—would earn roughly $500,000 in the decade following his death.

Also see *Moore, Jackie; Martin, Willie; Lyndell, Linda.*

Creed

Just when everyone thought grunge was dead, Creed exploded on the scene in 1999 sounding like equal parts Pearl Jam and Metallica. This Tallahassee band was formed by singer Scott Stapp, guitarist Mark Tremonti, both from Orlando, along with bassist Brian Marshall from Ft. Walton Beach and drummer Scott Phillips from nearby Madison.

Creed's debut album, *My Own Prison*, recorded in producer-engineer John Kurzweg's home studio in Tallahassee and released on club owner Jeff Hanson's Blue Collar label, got regional airplay thanks to WXSR program director Rick Schmidt.

After being remixed and re-released by BMG affiliate Wind-Up Records, the album sold two million units. Creed's follow-up sold a phenomenal 10 million and its third about the same.

The group split in June 2004, with singer Scott Stapp going solo while the other three regrouped as Alter Bridge. Creed reformed in 2009 and returned with a fourth album on Wind-Up; however, work on a follow-up album had apparently been suspended as of 2013. The three members of Creed sans Stapp have reunited as Alter Bridge. Stapp announced that he would be working with heavy-rock band Art of Anarchy. He is the featured vocalist on the band's second album, replacing singer Scott Weiland, who died in 2015.

Also see *Stapp, Scott; Alter Bridge; Kurzweg, John.*

Crowsdell

Early 1990s Jacksonville jangle-rock trio, consisting of vocalist-guitarist Shannon Wright, bassist Paul Croasdale, and drummer Laurie Anne Wall. The group made a name for itself with several singles on various small indie labels. After signing with British indie Big Cat Records, distributed by Sony, in 1994, the group released its debut, *Dreamette*, in 1995, migrated to Manhattan and began touring Europe. It followed with an EP in 1996 and another full-length album in 1997.

After Big Cat was bought out by V2 in 1998, the band was dropped from the roster. Wright went solo a year later and signed with Chicago indie Quarterstick Records.

Also see *Wright, Shannon.*

Crump, Bruce

Born in Memphis, raised in Jacksonville, this 20-year-old drummer was recruited for Molly Hatchet in 1976, just as the group was getting ready to sign with Epic Records and garner a string of hit albums.

In 1982 he left Hatchet and moved to Canada to work with Winnipeg rockers Streetheart. In 1984, he rejoined Hatchet for a seven-year stint. Then he worked with Hatchet spin-off Gator Country and a new incarnation of China Sky, a group that had been signed to Epic in 1988. Plagued by health problems, Crump died in 2015.

Also see *Molly Hatchet; China Sky.*

Dalton Gang

Mid-1960s Jacksonville band notable for including future Classics IV guitarist Auburn Burrell, later to become a sought-after session player. The group was managed by WAPE and WPDQ jock Dino Summerlin and appeared regularly on local television series *Shakin' Up Summer*, of which Summerlin was M.C. The group also released a single on Summerlin's Kimberly-Ann label.

Also see *Burrell, Auburn.*

Dana, Don

A Jacksonville teen-band impresario during the 1960s, Dana managed several regional acts, including, briefly, Ocala's Royal Guardsmen, who had a No. 2 hit on Laurie Records in 1967, the Illusions, who issued two singles on Columbia, and the Bitter Ind, also known as the 31st of February, who recorded for Vanguard and briefly included future Allman Bros. Band drummer Butch Trucks along with Duane and Gregg Allman. Dana was responsible for putting Lynyrd Skynyrd on its first regional tour—which the band dubbed the "torture tour"—opening for Strawberry Alarm Clock, during which the Skynyrd boys met future lead guitarist and bassist Ed King. Dana formed Senior Planners of

America, a financial-consulting firm based in Jacksonville. He died in 2014 at age 68.

Also see *Bitter Ind; 31st of February; Trucks, Butch; Royal Guardsmen; Mouse & the Boys.*

Daniels, Billy

This Jacksonville native (b. 1915) ran away from home at age 17, supposedly stowing away on a freighter to Manhattan, where he landed a gig as a singing waiter. In 1933, bandleader Erskine Hawkins spotted Daniels and added him as the featured vocalist for his orchestra.

Daniels soon became a popular cabaret singer and began appearing in movies in the late 1930s. In 1943, Daniels gave new meaning to the Johnny Mercer show tune "That Old Black Magic"; the single went on to sell a staggering 12 million copies. He began appearing on Broadway in 1945 and was one of the first African Americans to host his own network-television variety show on ABC in 1952. He continued to perform in Broadway and London musicals such as *Golden Boy* (1964), *Hello, Dolly* (1975) and *Bubbling Brown Sugar* (1977). Even after open-heart surgery, Daniels continued performing in night-clubs, right up to his death in 1988.

Danny Joe Brown Band

Band formed in 1980 by former Molly Hatchet singer Danny Joe Brown. Members included Steve Wheeler on guitar and vocals, Bobby Ingram on guitar (now leader of Molly Hatchet), Buzzy Meekins on bass and vocals, drummer Jimmy Glenn and Detroit keyboardist John Galvin. The group recorded one album released in 1981 on Epic Records, helmed by legendary British producer Glyn Johns. Wheeler wrote the band's single, "Nobody Walks On Me," which was featured in rotation on MTV.

Also see *Brown, Danny Joe; Molly Hatchet; China Sky; Armstrong, Pat.*

D'Arby, Terence Trent

Son of a Pentecostal minister and a gospel singer, Darby was born in New York City in 1962; he moved with his parents to De-Land in 1974, where he attended high school. After a short stint at University of Florida, Darby joined the U.S. Army in 1980 and transferred to Germany, where he moonlighted with funk group Touch.

He landed in London, where his extraordinary vocal talents were noticed by Muff Winwood at CBS Records. Darby helped lead the late-1980s British soul revival with his No. 1 hit "Wishing Well" on Columbia. His debut album, *Introducing the Hardline According to Terence Trent D'Arby*, produced by Martyn Ware of British acts Heaven 17 and the Human League, was an instant success, selling a million copies within three days of its release and nine million ultimately.

D'Arby also appeared in two films and a television mini-series, *Shake, Rattle and Roll: An American Love Story*, in which he plays Jackie Wilson.

D'Arby's sophomore album, however, only sold 300,000 units, and he was dropped by Columbia after a third album. After a stint on producer Glenn Ballard's Java label, Darby changed his name to Sananda Maitreya and records for his own label, Treehouse. He lives in Milan and releases his work through his own online store. He is married to Italian television host Francesca Francone; they have two sons.

Davis, Jackie

Jazz organist, born Jackson J. Davis in Jacksonville in 1920, graduate of Florida A&M University. In 1951 he moved to Philadelphia and from there to New York, where he became a sideman with Louis Jordan, Ella Fitzgerald, Sarah Vaughan, Nat "King" Cole, Louie Bellson and others.

Davis is considered a pioneer in jazz organ and was a major influence on Jimmy Smith. As a solo artist and bandleader, Davis signed with RCA in 1952, Capitol in 1956 and Warner Bros. in 1961. He released a comeback album on EMI in 1980. He died in Jacksonville in 1999 following a series of strokes. Jasmine Records has released a retrospective of his work.

December's Children

Not to be confused with an Ohio band of the same name who released an album on Mainstream Records in 1970, this Jacksonville R&B-rock group, formed in 1967, was fronted by Susan Robey, noted for her husky alto. December's Children also included keyboardist Guy Page, drummer Lenny Campbell, bassist Paul Day and guitarist Jerry McKoon.

Robey had hooked up with Atlanta impresario Bill Lowery in 1963 while fronting Susan and the Dynamics, whose drummer was Robert Nix. Lowery used his connections to land December's Children a deal with Capitol, where the group released one single, "Makin' Music." After failing to chart at Capitol, Lowery moved the group to World Pacific, a sister label of Liberty Records (to which the Classics IV were signed) a year later. World Pacific released two singles by December's Children, "Backward and Forward" and "I've Been Hurt," both of which were written and produced by Lowery staff member Ray Whitley, who had written hits for the Tams and the Swingin' Medallions. A third single was released on Liberty in 1970 sans Robey. The group failed to achieve any significant chart success, but Whitley's song "I've Been Hurt" would hit No. 35 a year later, recorded by Bill Deal and the Rhondels.

Also see *Susan and the Dynamics*.

Dees, Rick

Born Rigdon Dees in Jacksonville in 1950, raised in North Carolina. While still in high school, Dees began his career as a radio DJ at WBGB in Greensboro. After earning a degree in mass communication at UNC Chapel Hill he went to WXYC in that city and from there to Raleigh and Birmingham.

Dees' big break happened when he was deejaying in Memphis, where he hooked up with former Stax Records owner Estelle Axton, who issued his "Disco Duck" on her Fretone label in 1976, which became a nationwide hit. It was picked up internationally by Robert Stigwood's UK-based RSO Records, distributed by PolyGram.

From WMPS Dees went over to the RKO Radio chain, which transferred him from Memphis to KHJ in Los Angeles. From there he jumped over to KIIS. He followed up with "Dis-Gorilla" in 1977, "Bigfoot" in 1978. In 1983 he established his own radio show, *Weekly Top 40*, which is still in syndication. In 1985 he released "When Sonny Sniffs Glue," a parody of "When Sunny Gets Blue," on Warner Bros. Records. He also hosted his own late-night television series titled *Into the Night*, which ran on ABC for one season and was a co-host on *Solid Gold*. He has appeared on television series such as *Roseanne*, *Married with Children*, *Cheers*, *Diagnosis: Murder* and in movie versions of *The Flintstones* and *The Jetsons* as well as a small role in *La Bamba*. He splits his time between homes in Los Angeles and a farm near Danville, Ky., where his morning show actually originates.

Deep Six

See *Mouse & the Boys*

DeLaney, Tim

From Champaign, Ill., moved to Tallahassee with his parents as a child. In 1987 he helped form power-pop quartet the Sight-Seers, composed of himself on bass, vocalist Zollie Maynard, guitarist Jason O'Donnell and drummer Brad Lewis. The Sight-Seers issued an independent album produced by Tallahassee studio owner John Kurzweg.

The group relocated to Atlanta in 1992, where it would sign with Brendan O'Brien's Shotput Records, distributed by Sony. The group disbanded after Shotput went defunct.

DeLaney remained in Atlanta, where he joined the Swimming Pool Qs in 2000. He still lives in Atlanta, where he works as a session musician and engineer.

Also see *Sight-Seers; Kurzweg, John.*

Delisco, James

Born James Beeks in Jacksonville, Delisco (his middle name) attended Jacksonville's Douglas Anderson School of the Arts. He moved to NYC in 1996, where he joined the Broadway casts of *Smokey Joe's Café* and *Ragtime: The Musical.* He also toured with the roadshow of *Jesus Christ, Superstar.* Delisco won the 2005 E! Network reality show *The Entertainer* and developed his own tribute, *The Music of Michael Jackson.* In 2015 Delisco won an Akademia Music Award for best children's song. In between stints as a member of the Australian cast of the musical *Kinky Boots,* Delisco tours as an entertainer on several cruise lines.

Delius, Frederick

A 22-year-old British trust-fund rebel whose family sent him off for two years of farming in Solano Grove (on the river in western St. Johns County) in 1880s; Delius later became a prominent European composer.

DeVito, Jim

Son of a physician from St. Augustine, DeVito played in several area bands. He got interested in recording while a student at Stetson University in Deland. While on tour in 1972 with Jacksonville band Mad Hatter, he got to see a real recording studio. He later went to Nashville to become apprentice at Hound's Ear Studio, where he worked with Jerry Reed, Larry Londin and other greats.

In 1978 he returned to St. Augustine, where he built his own studio, Retrophonics. Clients have included Roy Clark, Mofro, Tom Petty and former Heartbreaker Stan Lynch, who produced several tracks there that appeared on Don Henley's album *Building the Perfect Beast.*

DeVito also played guitar with Jimmy Dougherty's early band Sacred Cow, which also included bassist Larry Steele, and currently performs with Walter Parks' group Swamp Cabbage.

Also see *Swamp Cabbage; Dougherty, Jimmy; Steele, Larry; Lynch, Stan; Petty, Tom.*

Diamond Four

Jacksonville group led by Fred Bible; released a pair of singles on RCA, which were produced by Nashville Brass leader Danny Davis, one of which was the song "Anny Fanny" (1968), co-written by Pete Rowland of Mouse and the Boys. Rowland says he "wrote it as a joke" when he was a staff drummer at Sound Lab, on Edgewood Avenue, where the Classics IV launched their recording career.

Also see *Rowland, Pete; Mouse & the Boys.*

Diddley, Bo

Born Ellas Bates in McComb, Miss., in 1928, Diddley joined the exodus to Chicago in the 1950s, where he recorded several novelty-type R&B hits for Chess Records. Although by the late 1960s he had been relegated to the nostalgia circuit in the U.S., he retained monumental status in England, where he had become a huge influence on such R&B-inspired acts as the Rolling Stones (who covered two of his songs), the Animals and the Yardbirds (who included Eric Clapton).

In the 1970s, McDaniel bought a spread in Hawthorne. In 1979, he opened for the Clash on its US tour. He was inducted into the Rock and Roll Hall of Fame in 1987. In 1994, he sat in with the Rolling Stones, performing "Who Do You Love?" on the group's *Voodoo Lounge* tour. Diddley continued to perform in the 2000s. However, after suffering a series of strokes, he succumbed to heart failure at his home in Archer in 2008.

Dixon, Neil

Guitarist and songwriter born in Fitzgerald, Ga., raised in Albany. In 1985 Dixon recorded an album of original material titled *Life's a Beach* in Muscle Shoals with members of the Muscle Shoals Rhythm Section. Dixon lives in Atlantic Beach. Drummer Scott Sisson, formerly of Mike Angelo & the Idols, later of the Crawfish of Love, was a member of Dixon's Sport Woody Band for a few years.

Also see *Sisson, Scott.*

Dixon, Luther

Born in Jacksonville 1931, Dixon as a child moved to Brooklyn, N.Y., where in 1954 he became a member of doo-wop group the Four Buddies. He and leader Larry Harrison wrote several songs, one of which, "Why, Baby, Why," was recorded by Jacksonville native Pat Boone in 1957 and sold more than a million copies.

Dixon also co-wrote songs for Perry Como ("Born to Be Your Baby), Bobby Darin ("All the Way Home" and "Irresistible You"), the Crests ("Sixteen Candles"), Jerry Lee Lewis ("Lovin' Up a Storm"), Gene Vincent ("Big Fat Saturday Night"), Gene McDaniels ("One Hundred Pounds of Clay"), Jimmy Reed ("Big Boss Man") and Chuck Jackson ("I Don't Want to Cry"). Artists such as Elvis Presley, the Beatles, Dusty Springfield, B.B. King, and the Jackson 5 later recorded his songs.

In 1960 Florence Greenberg of Scepter Records brought Dixon aboard as part-owner, vice-president of A&R and in-house producer. At Scepter Dixon produced most of the Shirelles' work, including the Carole King-Gerry Goffin composition "Will You Still Love Me Tomorrow," which flew to the top of the charts. He co-wrote many of the group's hits including "Baby, It's You," written with Burt Bacharach and Mack David under the pseudonym Barney Williams (his brother's name) and "Boys," co-written with Wes Farrell; both were covered by the Beatles on their 1963 debut. Dixon also co-wrote the Shirelles' "Sha La La," which was covered by English group Manfred Mann. As part of his deal with Scepter, Greenberg allowed Dixon a share of the publishing income for the songs he wrote for the label. Dixon also produced recordings for Dionne Warwick, who started out as a background singer at Scepter, and Chuck Jackson at Scepter's sister label, Wand Records. In 1962, Dixon brought the Isley Brothers to Wand and hired writer-producer Bert Berns to work with them, resulting in a huge hit with "Twist and Shout."

In 1964, flush with success, Dixon formed his own label, Ludix (LU-ther DIX-on), a joint venture with Capitol. Ludix, however, did not live up to Capitol's expectations; by 1966 he was again working as a freelance writer-producer, crafting tunes for the fading Platters on Musicor Records ("I Love You 1,000 Times," co-written with his then-wife Inez Foxx, and "With this Ring") and working with with Atlantic

Records artist King Curtis ("Soul Serenade").

In 1973 "Sixteen Candles" was given a new lease on life, featured prominently in George Lucas' movie *American Graffiti*, and in 1984 John Hughes titled a movie after the song, which was also included in the soundtrack, performed by the Stray Cats.

Dixon retired to Jacksonville, where he died in 2009. That year his song "Boys" was included in the video game *The Beatles: Rock Band*.

DJ Trans

Bass-music rapper/producer signed to Jeff Cohen's Jacksonville-based Attitude label in 1995.

Doctor Hector & the Groove Injectors

Jacksonville-based blues/R&B band formed in 1988 by former Grinderswitch singer-guitarist Dru Lombar, signed to Bob Greenlee's King Snake label based in Sanford, Fla., where the group released six albums. Featuring saxophonist Rick "Hurrican" Johnson, the group toured the US, Europe and Japan on a regular basis. Before his death from heart failure in 2005, Lombar ran his own recording studio, Platinum Audio, and record label, New South Records.

Also see *Lombar, Dru; Johnson, Rick; Greenlee, Bob.*

Doss, Mack

From Bradenton, Doss led teen band the Thunderbeats, which included Larry Reinhardt and occasionally Dickey Betts. All three migrated to Jacksonville in the mid-1960s to work as musicians.

While recording demos at Sound Lab, Classics IV bassist Walter Eaton heard Doss and hired him as a replacement for J.R. Cobb. Doss toured with the Classics for about a year and was replaced by Dalton Gang guitarist Auburn Burrell. Doss continued to live and perform in the Jacksonville area until returning to Bradenton in the early 2000s, where he performs occasionally.

Also see *Betts, Dickey; Reinhardt, Larry; Classics IV; Burrell, Auburn.*

Dougherty, Jimmy

Vocalist and drummer with Jacksonville psychedelic rockers Black Bear Angel, Dougherty later became singer for Alias, a band that included four former Lynyrd

Skynyrd members on its debut album, recorded in Orlando in 1979 and released on Mercury Records. Dougherty, who at one time was invited by Ronnie Van Zant to replace him in Skynyrd, later became front man for the Allen Collins Band, which released one album on MCA. He also played drums for Jacksonville new-wave band Mike Angelo & the Idols on their cult favorite "F**k Everybody" and with seminal St. Augustine "cajun-grunge" band Gunga Din, later renamed Crab Grass. Dougherty died of heart failure at his Jacksonville home in January, 2008. He was 56.

Also see *Collins, Allen; Alias; Mike Angelo & the Idols.*

Dowdy, Toby

Born John Adams Dowdy, Abbeville, Ga., 1920. Appeared on Gainesville's WRUF with his group the Jubilee Hillbillies, perhaps best-known for including Lake City fiddler Chubby Wise in 1938. In 1949 Dowdy recorded a single with his band the Dixie Lily Highpointers for Mercury Records. In 1950 he and his brother Charles founded Decatur Broadcasting, which purchased WMGR in Bainbridge, Ga. In 1955, he became a partner in Gainesville's WDVH. About this time Dowdy began commuting to Jacksonville to host popular WMBR television program, *McDuff Hayride,* which included steel player Tommy Durden, who co-wrote "Heartbreak Hotel," Shorty Medlock (Rickey Medlocke's grandfather) and future teen idol Johnny Tillotson. The Saturday-night program was later retitled *Toby Dowdy's Country Frolics* and was picked up by stations in Orlando, Tampa, West Palm and Miami. Dowdy died in Bainbridge in 1985.

Also see *Wise, Chubby; Tillotson, Johnny.*

Drashin, Sidney

A one-time teen-dance promoter, Drashin eventually became the biggest rock promoter in the region under the banner of Jet Set Enterprises. He also managed a couple of bands including Mouse & the Boys and Cowford County.

Dream Weavers

Miami vocal duo composed of Wade Buff and Eugene Adkinson; expanded to a quartet with the addition of Jacksonville musicians Lee Turner (piano) and Eddie Newsom (bass) while students at University of Florida in Gainesville. Landing their own radio show on college station WRUF in 1955, they began using the Adkinson-Buff composition "It's Always Tomorrow" as the show's theme song.

After recording an early version in Jacksonville, the record began receiving heavy airplay in Miami, whereupon the act was signed by Decca Records. The single was re-recorded in Miami and re-released. The Decca version went to No. 2 in the U.S. and No. 1 in England, earning the group an appearance on *The Ed Sullivan Show.*

56

"It's Always Tomorrow" was covered by crooner Jo Stafford.

Driscoll, Phil

Seattle-born trumpeter/keyboardist/vocalist; had own nightclub and recording studio in Jacksonville in late 1970s where he wrote songs for Blood, Sweat & Tears and Joe Cocker. He also briefly played in Cocker's touring band.

In 1980 he moved to Cleveland, Tenn., and became a prominent Christian recording artist; he won a Grammy in 1984 for a duo recording, "Keep the Flame Burning," with Debby Boone. Driscoll has recorded dozens of albums for various labels and has also performed at numerous White House events.

In 2007 Driscoll served a year in federal prison for tax evasion; he wrote and co-produced an autobiographical film about this experience, which featured Danny Glover and Brian Dennehy. After living in Tennessee and northern Georgia for many years, Driscoll returned to Jacksonville in 2017.

Dunaway, Barry

Originally from Miami, this longtime St. Augustine resident is the brother of singer-songwriter Don Oja-Dunaway. A virtuoso bassist, Dunaway has toured and/or recorded with Atlanta singer Paul Davis, Miami-based blues-rocker Pat Travers, and singer Joe Lynn Turner. Dunaway also spent several years as a member of Swedish guitar god Yngvie Malmsteen's band. He is currently a member of .38 Special.

Also see *.38 Special.*

Durden, Tommy

Born 1919 in Morgan County, Ga., son of a sharecropper, Durden moved to Jacksonville with his family as a youth, where he took up guitar, later slide guitar and eventually steel guitar. In the mid 1950s Durden became a regular on Toby Dowdy's weekly *McDuff Hayride* on Jacksonville's WMBR (TV-4). He also performed in nearby Gainesville with Smilin' Jack Herring and his Swingbillies.

Durden had an idea for a song he'd taken from a story in a newspaper about a young man who had killed himself, leaving a note saying, "I walk a lonely street." The story goes that Durden gave some half-written lyrics to Mae Axton in Jacksonville, who helped him finish the song, which became "Heartbreak Hotel." However, others including former WQIK station owner Marshall Rowland stated Durden had been performing the song onstage prior to this meeting.

Axton had a connection to Elvis Presley and decided the song would be perfect for him. They cut an acetate of the song with WPDQ DJ Glenn Reeves singing, doing his best to imitate Presley. She knew Presley's manager, Memphis DJ Bob Neal, and arranged to meet Presley in person at a 1955 DJ convention in Nashville, where she played Presley the acetate and offered him one-third of the songwriting credits. It was the first song Presley recorded under his new deal at RCA. It became his first million-seller, reaching No. 1 on *Billboard*'s Hot 100 in May 1956 as well as No. 1 on the country/western and R&B charts.

Durden and Axton continued to collaborate, placing songs with such artists as Wanda Jackson and Mario Martin. In addition he played steel with Johnny Tillotson (also from Jacksonville), Tex Ritter and Johnny Cash. Durden also recorded two albums of his own. He retired from music and moved to Houghton Lake, Mich., where he became a commercial appliance repairman. Durden died in Michigan at 79.

Also see *Axton, Mae; Reeves, Glenn; Tillotson, Johnny.*

Durst, Fred

Born in Gastonia, N.C., moving to Jacksonville as a youth, Durst made his mark as front man for Jacksonville rap-rock outfit Limp Bizkit. Durst almost immediately began putting his connections to use scouting other acts. After Bizkit's signing with Jordan Schur's Flip Records, Durst convinced Schur to appoint him to an A&R position. His first signing was Jacksonville Beach rock band Cold, now on Flip/Geffen. His second was Springfield, Mass., neo-grunge band Staind, who sold three million on Flip/Elektra. When Limp Bizkit's sales hit the 10-million mark, Durst and Schur were both rewarded with high-level positions at Universal Music Group, who acquired Flip. In 1999, Durst became a senior VP of A&R at Interscope. Durst then unveiled a joint venture with Interscope, dubbed Flawless Records, with the 2001 debut album by Puddle of Mudd, produced by Tallahassee musician John

Kurzweg. PoM's album sold more than five million copies.

Durst resumed touring with Limp Bizkit in 2009 after an eight-year hiatus during which he focused on making movies. Durst and his band left Interscope in 2011; Limp Bizkit since recorded one album for Miami-based hip-hop label Cash Money Records. A new album, *Stampede of the Disco Elephants*, is said to be in the works.

Also see *Limp Bizkit; Cold; Wimmer, Danny.*

Dykes, Doyle

From Jacksonville, this amazing finger-picker was described by music writer Charles M. Young as "somewhere between Chet Atkins and Leo Kottke." After relocating to Nashville, Dykes began touring with Grand Ole Opry star Grandpa Jones as well as the Stamps Quartet.

Dykes released two albums on Nashville-based Step One Records in 1996 and 1997 and one on New York-based Windham Hill Records in 1998.

In 2004 Dykes began to experience health issues including headaches, nausea, and deafness in his right ear as a result of a brain tumor and consequent surgery. Nonetheless Dykes continues to record and perform ably. He signed with New Jersey-based Howling Wood Records in 2004 but now releases music on his own Doyle Productions logo. Guild Guitars

makes a Doyle Dykes signature model. Dykes is also the author of the book *The Lights of Marfa*, published in 2011. He continues to perform.

East Coast Horns

Originally the horn section for Jacksonville funk band Kudu: saxophonist Cloris Grimes, trumpeter Rod McMorries, and trombonist Alan Prater; the trio was spotted in local club by singer Millie Jackson. Later recruited by the Jacksons to play on their 1984 Victory tour; also toured with Cameo. McMorries is now vocalist with Jacksonville band KTG.

Easton, Corbin

Country singer born 1982 in Trenton, former student at University of Florida in Gainesville. In 2005 he participated in a contest as part of the Suwannee River Jam. Moved to Nashville in 2006 where songwriter Reese Wilson and producer Steve Davis took him into the studio to record demos, which they brought to Joe Fisher at Universal Music Group. Fisher signed Easton to Mercury Records in 2009, for whom he has released three albums, his most recent of which hit the No. 1 spot on *Billboard*'s country-music chart in 2015.

Eaton, Walter

See *Classics IV.*

Echoes

This Jacksonville teen group is most memorable for including future Classics IV singer Dennis Yost on drums. Future All-man Brothers Band drummer Butch Trucks also performed with this group while a student at Englewood High. Not to be confused with the doo-wop group of the same name from Brooklyn, N.Y.

Also see *Classics; Yost, Dennis.*

Echo Jet

See *Swirl 360.*

Ellis, Cole

Drummer with several blues and blues-rock groups such as King Snake Records' Eric Culberson (from Savannah), Jacksonville's Doctor Hector & the Groove Injectors and Louisiana's Kenny Neal. He also worked with L.A. Jones and the Blues Messengers backing such stars as Pinetop Perkins, Big Mama Thornton, Otis Rush, James Cotton and others.

Also see *Doctor Hector & the Blues Injectors; Lombar, Dru.*

Elson, Kevin

From the Cedar Hills district of Jacksonville's Westside, this keyboardist worked with rock band Sweet Rooster, which evolved into .38 Special. He later ran live sound for Lynyrd Skynyrd and .38.

After taking on mixing duties with San Francisco hitmakers Journey, Elson became the band's studio producer as well. This led to a career producing albums for

Europe, Mr. Big, Night Ranger, Loud and Clear, Stangeways, Shooting Star and others. Elson also engineered and mixed studio tracks for the Beach Boys and Aerosmith.

He returned to mostly doing live sound and helmed the boards for Aerosmith, Michael Jackson, Don Henley, Van Morrison, Carole King, Foreigner, Bush, Jewel and Kelly Clarkson. Elson recently produced a reunion album for the original members of rock band Mr. Big. He lives in Pasadena.

Evergreen Terrace

Jacksonville metal-core band, formed in 1999 by Andrew Carey (vocals), Josh James (guitar), Josh "Woody" Willis (guitar), Josh Smith (bass) and Christopher Brown (drums). Deriving its name from the TV series *The Simpsons*, the band has

released a total of six albums on the Indianola, Eulogy, Metal Blade and Rise labels. Carey announce his retirement in 2015, but the band continued to perform with longtime guitarist Craig Chaney added to the group in 2000, assuming vocal duties. Carey returned in 2016. Drummer Brown, who left in 2005, also rejoined.

Also see *Lugnut*.

Facemire, Allen

Born in Long Island, moved with family at 11 to St. Augustine, where he played drums in a teen band with guitarist Jim DeVito. Became a freelance cameraman for Jacksonville station WJXT (Channel 4). Also worked as a part-time DJ at radio station WAPE-AM, where he landed his own show, *The Underground Circus*, which featured music from the burgeoning psychedelic scene.

In 1968 he approached Jacksonville band the Second Coming and became its manager. He also produced a single for the group that was released by New Jersey-based Steady records, a cover of Cream's "I Feel Free," sung by Dickey Betts, backed with a cover of Jefferson Airplane's "She Has Funny Cars," sung by Betts' wife, Dale.

When the Second Coming broke up after Betts and bassist Berry Oakley joined the Allman Brothers Band and moved to Macon, Facemire decided to get back into

television and moved to Miami, where he worked at WCKT (Ch. 7). After a year in Miami he moved to Atlanta, where he did freelance work for *ABC News*, *20/20*, CNN and other clients. He worked on several television series including the *Dukes of Hazzard* and *Mega Dens* and has been a cinematographer and director of photography for movies including the *Buddy Holly Story*. He and his wife, Suzan, own Salt Run Productions. They live in Norcross, Ga., and also have a home in St. Augustine.

Felder, Don

Born in Gainesville in 1947, this virtuoso guitarist led his own band, the Continentals, which briefly included fellow Gainesville High School student Steven Stills. In 1965, Felder, along with guitarist

Bernie Leadon, formed the Maundy Quintet, releasing a single on their own Paris Tower label two years later. An employee at Marvin Kay's Music Center, Felder sold guitars and gave lessons; one of his students was a young Tom Petty. Felder himself had gotten pointers on slide guitar from Daytona resident Duane Allman of the Allman Joys.

With two former members of Ocala's Incidentals, Felder formed instrumental group Flow (formerly Ginger Bread) and moved to upstate New York. The group was spotted at the Fillmore East by label owner/producer Creed Taylor. Flow recorded one unsuccessful album for Taylor's CTI Records, released in 1970.

After a stint as a session player in a Boston recording studio, Felder, taking Leadon's advice, moved to Los Angeles, where he performed with David Blue and Crosby, Stills & Nash (Leadon had made the move back in 1967). In early 1974, Felder played a session with the Eagles, adding slide guitar to their song "Good Day in Hell." The next day they asked him to join the group as lead guitarist and fifth member, shortly before Leadon left the band. Felder co-wrote one of the Eagles' biggest hits, "Hotel California." Despite its six-minute length, the single hit the top spot in *Billboard*'s Hot 100 in February 1977, and the Grammy-winning album of the same title remains one of the top-sellers of all time. When the group broke up in 1980, Felder returned to session work, performing on recordings by Pure Prairie League, Joe Walsh, Bob Seger, J.D. Souther, Warren Zevon, Stevie Nicks, Boz Scaggs, the Bee Gees, Barbra Streisand and many others.

Felder rejoined the Eagles in 1994 for their "Hell Freezes Over" reunion tour. However, in 2001 he had a major falling-out with bandleaders Don Henley and Glen Frey, who demanded Felder sell his interest in the corporation to them and work as a salaried sideman, a proposition Felder adamantly refused, even though members Joe Walsh and Timothy Schmit had already accepted it and urged Felder to do so.

Though he no longer toured with the Eagles, Felder remained a shareholder in Eagles Inc. and continued to receive one-fifth of the band's net earnings. His 2008 tell-all book, *Heaven and Hell: My Life in The Eagles* (1974–2001) was published by John Wiley & Sons.

Felder leads his own group, the Don Felder Band, which continues to tour.

Also see *Flow; Maundy Quintet; Leadon, Bernie.*

Fenwicks

Originally a New York-based folk-punk-funk-ska duo consisting of Stephen Schub and Jimmy Corrieri. Schub met former Lynyrd Skynyrd drummer Artimus Pyle, who augmented the act with several musicians, including himself and Chain of Fools rhythm section Ken Nasta (drums) and Ed Richardson (bass).

Briefly based in Jacksonville and managed by *JAM* magazine founder Darrell Massaroni in Orlando (who also handled Atlantic acts Seven Mary Three and My Friend Steve), the Fenwicks garnered one nationally released album on Guitar Acoustic Records (distributed by RED) in the early 1990s. The group disbanded not long thereafter but periodically reunited for concert shows until Corrieri's death in 2013. Schub has put together another band, HaSkaLa, and is also an accomplished film and television actor with many impressive credits.

Also see *Pyle, Artimus; APB; Chain of Fools.*

FitzGerald, Michael Ray

Guitarist, vocalist and songwriter, born in Chelsea, Mass. (in the same US naval hospital as punk legend Ray McKelvey); moved to Jacksonville at age 15. In 1975 he worked with drummer Mike Cameron, former percussionist for George Benson, in Cameron's funk band, Dynasty of Sound.

FitzGerald's first studio gig was as songwriter and arranger at Coconuts Recording in North Miami Beach, where he worked with engineer Hal Hansford.

In 1980 FitzGerald formed punk-funk band Mike Angelo & the Idols with drummer Jimmy Dougherty, formerly of Mercury Records act Alias. In 1985, FitzGerald's punk-funk song "F**k Everybody" was covered by Roddy Rowdy Piper on Epic Records' *Wrestling Album*, which sold about 400,000 units.

FitzGerald used royalties from the *Wrestling Album* to form his own studio and a nationally distributed record label. As an engineer he worked with several major-label acts such as Barry Lee Harwood of Rossington Collins, Swirl 360, Athens, Georgia's Trinket, Orlando's Backstreet Boys, J. J. Grey, and Yellowcard.

In 1990, FitzGerald formed funk-rock outfit Chain of Fools, who released two nationally distributed albums on Rimshot Records.

He is a journalist and also the author of the current volume.

Also see *Mike Angelo & the Idols; Chain of Fools; Allen Collins Band; Cameron, Michael.*

Florida Playboys

See *Grier, Tiny*; also see *Charles, Ray; Rowland, Marshall.*

Flow

Originally known as Ginger Bread, this four-piece instrumental ensemble featured former members of Ocala band the Incidentals: John Winter on keyboards and woodwinds and drummer Mike Barnett. The group also included guitarist Don Felder from the Maundy Quintet (Felder would go on to massive success with the Eagles and as a Los Angeles session musician) along with bassist Chuck Newcomb, from nearby Lawtey. The group was spotted at a gig at New York's Fillmore East and was signed by producer Creed Taylor to his fledgling CTI label, where it released one album, in 1970.

Also see *Felder, Don; Maundy Quintet; Leadon, Bernie.*

For Squirrels

Gainesville modern-rock quartet, formed in 1992 by vocalist Jack Vigliatura, guitarist Travis Tooke, bassist Bill White and drummer Jay Russell, replaced by Jack Griego. After releasing two independent collections and touring incessantly in a beat-up Ford van, the band finally landed a deal with Sony/550 Music, which released an album titled *Example* in 1995, which reached the lower rungs of *Billboard*'s album chart. However, on the way back from a gig at CBGB in New York, the van blew a tire and flipped. Vigliatura and White were killed. For Squirrels' debut album, *Example*, was released a month later. Tooke and Griego decided to continue but retired the name For Squirrels. Sony released another album in 1997, *Never Bet the Devil Your Head*, under the group's new name, Sub Rosa, and the band opened several shows for Tallahassee's Creed.

Sub Rosa disbanded in 2001. The surviving members remain active on the Gainesville scene. Tooke's band, Helixglow, released an album in 2012 on New Hersey-based Indigo Planet Records.

Frank, Fred

From Philadelphia, Frank started out as a warehouse worker at Chips Distributing. From there he went to Atlanta-based Godwin Distributors as a promotion man. In the mid-1960s he became Southeast regional sales and promotion manager for Epic Records, where he spent eight years, working his way up to head of promotions for the CBS-owned label, which relocated him to New York. In 1971 he went to work for Janus Records. In 1972 he and former Epic Records art director Sid Maurer started Roadshow Records, which was initially distributed by Stereo Dimension Records.

In 1974 Frank joined Florence Greenberg's Scepter Records, bringing his Roadshow label with him. At Scepter, Frank struck gold (and platinum) with funk group B.T. Express, whose recordings he later licensed to Columbia/CBS. In 1976 Roadshow went with United Artists and two years later with RCA. Frank purchased Greenberg's trio of labels in 1978, one of which, Hob Records, included top gospel artist Shirley Caesar. He also worked with several prominent artists at Roadshow including Brass Construction, Phyllis Hyman, Enchantment and others. In 1980, Frank and Maurer sold Roadshow to CBS and started a new label, Coast to Coast Music and Video.

Frank married a woman from Jacksonville and moved his operation there, where he founded a recording studio at 1328 Romney St. The house engineer was Bill Ande. Frank and Ande worked on and/or promoted several recordings by Jacksonville acts such as Chill Deal (who appeared on Frank's CTC label before signing with Quality Records), gospel singer Walter Ponder, Mamado and others. CTC closed in 1983. Frank moved his operation, then called Florida International, to Orlando, where he still lives. According to his web site, Frank has overseen the sales of more than 20 million records.

Also see *Cohen, Jeff; Ande Bill; Chill Deal Boyz.*

Garland, Hank

Nashville-based guitar virtuoso and session player, born 1930 in South Carolina. Recorded million-selling "Sugar Foot Rag" in 1949, later performed on sessions with Elvis Presley (1958-1961), Patsy Cline, Brenda Lee, Mel Tillis, Marty Robbins, Everly Brothers, Boots Randolph, Roy Orbison, Conway Twitty, and Hank Williams.

Garland had been a jazz player and had brought a serious jazz sensibility to country guitar (as exemplified on Cline's "Crazy"). He also co-wrote Christmas perennial "Jingle Bell Rock," recorded by Bobby Helms and Brenda Lee. A 1961 auto accident ended his career. He went to live with his brother in Orange Park and died in a local nursing home in 2004. His story is the subject of the 2008 independent film *Crazy*.

Garner, Merlene

Born in 1943, this former Murray Hill Theatre ticket taker and protégé of Jacksonville high-school teacher Mae Axton released several singles in the early 1960s on Hilliard-based Davco Records, two of which were written by Axton and her songwriting partner Glenn Reeves.

Garner briefly toured the West and did a short-lived stint in Las Vegas with the Apollos. In 2002, her first single, "You're It," resurfaced in the rockabilly compilation *Real Gone Girls* on Netherlands-based Collector Records. She lives in Middleburg.

Also see *Axton, Mae; Reeves, Glenn; Walker, Frank*.

Gator Country

In 2005, several former Hatchet members, including founding members Duane Roland, Steve Holland and Bruce Crump, along with later members Riff West and Jimmy Farrar, formed Molly Hatchet tribute band Gator Country (the name comes from a song from Molly Hatchet's 1978 debut album). Even though there were more original Hatchet members in this band than in the official incarnation, all had quit Molly Hatchet and had relinquished their rights to the name.

Roland died at his Jacksonville home in 2006. Bassist West, who had played with rock band White Witch before joining Hatchet in 1981, died in 2014; drummer Crump died a year later.

Also see *Molly Hatchet; Brown, Danny Joe; Ingram, Bobby*.

Geohagan, Ashton

This Jacksonville drummer performed with Middleburg Celtic-rock band Seven Nations from 1997 to 2001. Geohagan has also worked with Jacksonville melodic-rock band China Sky, signed to British label Escape Music. In addition he has performed in a locals bands with former Danny Joe Brown Band and China Sky guitarist Steve Wheeler. Geohagan is a paramedic affiliated with the Jacksonville Sheriff's Office.

Also see *Seven Nations, China Sky; Wheeler, Steve*.

Goldsboro, Bobby

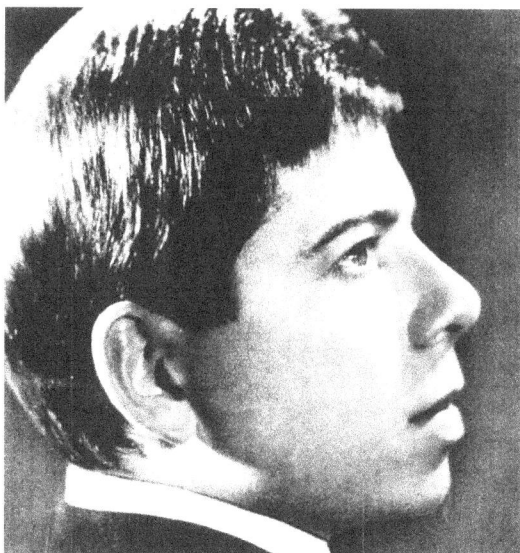

Born in Marianna in 1941, this singer-guitarist moved with his parents to nearby Dothan, Ala., when he was a toddler. While attending Auburn University he hooked up with a group called the Webs, managed by Buddy Buie. When Roy Orbison needed a new band, he hired the Webs, renamed them the Candymen, and brought them to England on a tour with the Beatles.

After two years with Orbison, Goldsboro landed his own deal with New York-based Laurie Records, the same label for which Ocala's Royal Guardsmen recorded. After a few modest successes he scored a monster hit in 1968 with the song "Honey," written by Bobby Russell. Goldsboro himself wrote "With Pen in Hand," which became a hit for Vikki Carr, as well as other hits for other artists. He also recorded for United Artists and for Warner-Curb. In the early 1970s Goldsboro hosted his own

television variety series. In the 1990s he wrote the music for the CBS television series *Evening Shade* and created a children's series called *Swamp Critters of Lost Lagoon.* He lives near Ocala.

Also see *Buie, Buddie.*

Graves, Jim

Guitarist from Lakeland, worked with Jacksonville rock band Cowford County. Also worked with former ABB drummer Butch Truck's jazz-rock ensemble Trucks. One of Derek Trucks' earliest guitar tutors.

Also see *Trucks.*

Green, Bunky

Born Vernice Green in Milwaukee in 1935, this world-renowned alto-saxophonist, jazz artist and session player moved to

New York where he spent several years working with Charles Mingus. Then he relocated to Chicago where he worked with Ira Sullivan, Louie Bellson, Yusef Lateef, Sonny Stitt and Ben Sidran. Recorded fourteen albums for the Exodus, Cadet, Argo, Vanguard, Delos and Apex labels. Also a popular session player, performed on pop and R&B records with Fontella Bass and Maurice White (of Earth Wind & Fire). Taught jazz studies at the University of Chicago, later became head of an award-winning jazz studies department at Jacksonville's University of North Florida until his retirement in 2011. That same year Green was inducted into the Jacksonville Jazz Festival Hall of Fame. He lives in Jacksonville.

Also see Bales, Kevin.

Greenlee, Bob

Born in Daytona Beach in 1944, Greenlee settled in nearby Sanford, where he built a recording studio and nationally distributed record label. He made his first big splash as bassist with the outrageous Root Boy Slim & the Sex Change Band, whose 1978 debut on Warner Bros. Records rivaled the Sex Pistols for audacity.

Greenlee later decided to concentrate on blues and R&B with his own band, the Midnight Creepers, forming the King Snake label to handle Creepers' product. Greenlee found a niche as a producer and label executive as well as songwriter and session player, helping to kick-start and/or

revitalize the careers of Noble "Thin Man" Watts, Kenny Neal, Lazy Lester, Lucky Peterson, Bill Wharton, Ace Moreland, Floyd Miles, Dr. Hector & the Groove Injectors, Eric Culberson and others. Greenlee died in February of 2004 after a two-year battle with pancreatic cancer.

Also see *Root Boy Slim & the Sex Change Band; Midnight Creepers.*

Greer, Billy

From Tennessee, Greer joined second edition of multi-platinum rock group Kansas on bass and vocals in 1986; group currently records for German label Inside Out. Greer lives in Atlantic Beach and occasionally performs as a single act when he is not touring with Kansas. Greer also leads his own rock group, Seventh Key and works with rock group Khymera

Grey, J.J.

See *J.J. Grey & Mofro.*

Grier, Tiny

The 6-ft, 10-inch singer was the leader of the Florida Playboys, a country group who performed regularly on radio station WJHP in Jacksonville, owned by the *Jacksonville Journal*. The group is perhaps best known for including—very briefly—pianist Ray Charles in 1947, not long before Charles left Jacksonville for Seattle. Steel player Marshall Rowland came into the group just after Charles departed.

Also see *Rowland, Marshall.*

Guillory, Isaac

Born on Guantanamo Naval Station in 1947, Guillory moved to Tallahassee with his family in 1958 and then to Palatka three years later, where he became a member of teen band the Illusions. He was a student at St. Johns River Junior College, where he studied cello.

The Illusions garnered their own Jacksonville TV show and released one single on Columbia. However, shortly before the record was released, guitarist-vocalist Guillory left to play bass with Columbia artists the Cryan' Shames in Illinois, who had also signed to Columbia.

In 1970 he moved to England, where he spent six years as a solo performer at Shakespeare's Head folk club in London. His prowess on guitar widely noted, Guillory performed on albums by Donovan, Al Stewart, Elke Brooks, the Buggles and others. He released a self-titled album in 1974 for Atlantic Records. Guillory died of cancer at his home in Wallsend, England, in 2000.

Also see *Illusions.*

Haines, Connie

Born Yvonne Marie Jasme in Savannah, in 1921, Haines moved with her family to Jacksonville at 5. By 9, known as Yvonne Marie, she'd became a regular on local NBC affiliate WJAX.

At 17, she moved to New York. A year later she was performing on comedian Fred Allen's NBC radio show. Soon she would be working alongside crooner Frank Sinatra in both Harry James' and Tommy Dorsey's orchestras. It was James who gave her the name Connie Haines. She later released her own recordings on the Mercury, Coral, Dot, Signature and RCA-Camden labels.

In 1963, she signed with Detroit-based Motown Records, where she recorded a single, "Midnight Johnny," co-written by label honcho Berry Gordy, followed by an album of Smokey Robinson songs. All told, Haines was featured on more than 200 recordings and appeared in six major motion pictures.

Haines was also an ordained minister with the Unity Church. She wrote an autobiography titled *Snooty Little Cutie* and continued to sing until a 2002 auto accident near her home in Clearwater sidelined her. She retired from music in 2006 and died two years later at age 87.

Hall, Al

Born in Jacksonville in 1915, this jazz bassist moved with his family to Philadel-

phia as a youngster. He moved to NYC in 1936 where he would work with Louis Armstrong, Duke Ellington, Johnny Hodges, Billie Holiday, Helen Merrill, Jack Teagarden, Teddy Wilson, Benny Goodman, Hazel Scott and others. He also did regular gigs as a pit musician on Broadway. Hall performed regularly with pianist and songwriter Erroll Garner from 1945 to 1963 and also led his own sessions for Columbia Records. Hall formed Wax Records in 1946, which he sold to Atlantic three years later. He died in New York in 1988.

Hall, Randall

Guitarist/vocalist from Jacksonville who as a member of Running Easy worked with singer Melanie alongside drummer Derek Hess in 1979. He had also been in

Alice Marr with future members of .38 Special.

Hall hit the big leagues in 1983 with the Allen Collins Band on MCA. After that project fizzled he worked with Jacksonville Beach bar band Synergy alongside former .38 Special backup vocalist Carol Bristow and sax player Rick "Hurricane" Johnson and with Jacksonville country singer Larry Mangum. In 1987, Hall was chosen by Allen Collins himself to replace the disabled guitarist in a reconstituted Lynyrd Skynyrd. Hall toured with Skynyrd for seven years and recorded three albums with that band, leaving in 1994 following a financial dispute. He then formed the Randall Hall Band, which has included former Lynyrd Skynyrd/Rossington Collins/Molly Hatchet bassist Tim Lindsay, former Skynyrd drummer Artimus Pyle and former Alias/Allen Collins Band vocalist Jimmy Dougherty. In addition he worked with APB (Artimus Pyle Band) and the Southern Rock All-Stars. Hall currently performs with World Class Rockers alongside legendary drummer Aynsley Dumbar and former members of Journey and Steppenwolf. He lives in Jacksonville.

Also see *Lynyrd Skynyrd; Collins, Allen; Lindsey, Tim; Dougherty, Jimmy.*

Hand, Craig

Country singer-songwriter from St. Augustine, born 1978. In 2005 he landed a deal with Nashville-based Category 5 Records.

He also made a video sponsored by Nex-Tel featuring his song "Direct Connect." Members of his band included Jacksonville guitarist Steve Wheeler, formerly of the Danny Joe Brown Band and China Sky. However, Category 5 soon folded after it was discovered the owner had embezzled the startup capital and subsequently went to prison. In 2008, Hand bounced back with a follow-up album on local label Bling-a-billy Records. In 2012 he joined Nashville-based group Bush Hawg as front man, which released a five-song EP on RCA. In 2018 he recorded a duet of "She's All I Got" with Jacksonville native Gary U.S. Bonds, who wrote the song. Hand is also a member of Jacksonville-based group the Love Rustlers.

Also see *Bonds, Gary U.S.; Wheeler, Steve; Love Rustlers.*

Hansford, Hal

Keyboardist from Palatka; moved to Orange Park in late 1960s, where he hooked up with rock band Richfield, who scored one single on Capitol, the novelty tune "Disco Sucks," released in 1979. After the group fizzled, Hansford opened a recording studio in Jacksonville's Universal-Marion building (now JEA headquarters).

Relocating to Miami, he landed a gig at Coconuts Recording, where he engineered tracks by Blood, Sweat & Tears and the Romantics, including their smash hits, "What I Like About You" and "Talking in Your Sleep." In the early 1980s Hansford discovered budding singer-songwriter Johnny Depp. Hansford produced some demos for the future movie star and brought them to producer-label executive Jimmy Johnson in Muscle Shoals; however, no deal transpired. For many years Hansford operated his own recording service in Miami; he now lives near St. Augustine.

Also see *Richfield*.

Hardy, Oliver

Moved to Jacksonville from Milledgeville, Ga., in 1913; appeared in feature films for the Vim and Metro (precursor to MGM) movie studios. An accomplished singer and drummer, Hardy performed regularly in Pablo Beach bistros before leaving for Hollywood in 1917, where he made 40 movies for Vitagraph. In 1921 he teamed up with British comedian Stan Laurel. The pair would sign with Hal Roach Studios in 1927, where they would go on to make dozens of films together. Hardy made many solo appearance in films but is still perhaps best known for his work with Laurel. In 1956 Hardy had a major heart attack and a series of strokes, from which he never recovered. He died in Los Angeles at age 65.

Hargrove, Linda

Born in Jacksonville in 1949, Hargrove grew up in Tallahassee, where she sang with several groups including country-rock band After All. In 1970 she relocated with that band to Nashville. Soon her songs were being recorded by such stars as Sandy Posey, Michael Nesmith, Leon Russell, Johnny Rodriguez, Lynn Anderson, George Jones, Tammy Wynette, David Allan Coe, Marty Robbins, B.J Thomas, Dionne Warwick and Julie Andrews.

Hargrove signed with Elektra in 1973 where she released two albums, later signing with Capitol (1975-1977). Perhaps her biggest hit was 1975's "Let It Shine" for Olivia Newton-John, which went to No. 5 on *Billboard*'s country chart and No. 1 on its easy-listening chart. She also served as session guitarist and background vocalist for several major acts and on TV and radio jingles. In the 1980s she recorded two Christian albums under her married name, Linda Bartholomew. Leukemia sidelined Hargrove's career, but she managed to release an album of new material in 2005. She died in Tallahassee in 2010.

Harper, Ben

Guitarist from Jacksonville, graduate of Douglas Anderson School of the Arts, founding member of Yellowcard. Formed Takeover Records in 1997 to release Yellowcard's debut album. After moving to Long Beach, Calif., and leaving Yellowcard, Harper expanded the label to include many more acts including Jacksonville skate-punk band Inspection 12.

Also see *Yellowcard.*

Harwood, Barry Lee

Born in North Carolina, this guitarist/vocalist/songwriter moved to Jacksonville with his family as a toddler. Harwood met drummer Derek Hess in seventh grade, and the two later formed a series of groups, one of which was Christian rock band Israel.

Harwood moved to Atlanta in the mid-1970s, where he played on sessions for acts like Joe South, Lynyrd Skynyrd and Paul Davis. When Ed King left Skynyrd, Harwood was offered his slot but declined due to a commitment to tour with singer-songwriter Melanie (Safka), with whom he recorded two albums. Harwood has also recorded with Winterhaven natives Lobo (Kent La Voie) and Jim Stafford.

In 1979, Harwood played on Alias's album, *Contraband* (released on Mercury) featuring singer Jimmy Dougherty along with former Skynyrd members Allen Collins, Gary Rossington, Leon Wilkeson and Billy Powell. In 1980, Harwood and these four formed the Rossington Collins Band, which also included drummer Hess and former .38 Special background singer Dale Krantz. This necessitated a move back to Jacksonville. Harwood co-wrote and sang RCB's hit single, "Don't Misunderstand Me," which reached No. 55 on *Billboard*'s Hot 100.

After the RCB's dissolution, Harwood worked with Collins, Wilkeson and Powell in the short-lived Allen Collins Band alongside singer Jimmy Dougherty and third guitarist Randall Hall. That outfit was even more short-lived than the RCB.

He would form the Hlubek-Harwood Band with former Molly Hatchet guitarist Dave Hlubek in 1988 and TimePiece with bassist Tim Lindsey and former Henry Paul keyboardist Barry Rapp. For a time he played with the worship band at Jacksonville's New Life Christian Fellowship alongside former .38 Special drummer Jack Grondin. At Ed King's behest Harwood came to Nashville, but that project never reached fruition.

Harwood returned to Jacksonville, forming Christian rock band Chariot in 2001. In 2010 Harwood released a solo album titled *The Southern Part of Heaven.*

Also see *Rossington Collins Band; Collins, Allen; Lindsay, Tim; Hlubek, Dave; Hess, Derek.*

Hasselhoff, David

Born in Baltimore, this aspiring actor and musician attended Christ the King Catholic School in the Arlington section of Jacksonville. He and his family moved to Atlanta and then to Illinois. Hasselhof moved to Los Angeles in 1975, where he landed a role on the CBS-TV soap opera *The Young and Restless*.

He launched his singing career on a children's show, *Kids, Inc.* He later became the star of *Knight Rider* (NBC, 1982-86) and *Baywatch* (NBC, 1989).

Hasselhoff's recordings are popular in Germany and Austria, earning multi-platinum status. In 2006 he became a judge on *America's Got Talent*. In 2010 he created the short-lived "reality" series *The Hasselhoffs* with members of his family. He has also appeared in several off-Broadway the-atrical productions. In 2015 Hasselhoff began hosting a TV talk show that airs in Finland while still doing occasional US television roles.

Hawkins, Leslie

Jacksonville singer, former lead vocalist for Donn Finney's progressive-rock group Nolds Bard, later sang backup with Capricorn Records act Wet Willie. In 1975, she joined Lynyrd Skynyrd as a backup singer and was with the band during its 1977 plane crash, in which she suffered multiple injuries. She later worked with Billy Joe Royal alongside fellow Skynyrd backup singer JoJo Billingsley as well as with Jacksonville band Molly Hatchet. She is married to former Exile drummer Bobby Johns. They live in Middleburg.

Also see *Johns, Bobby; Lynyrd Skynyrd; Molly Hatchet.*

Helixglow

Gainesville band founded by former For Squirrels guitarist-vocalist Bill Tooke. Released an album in 2012 on New Jersey-based Indigo Planet Records.

Also see *For Squirrels; Tooke, Bill.*

Henderson, Nancy

Jacksonville singer who sang with several local bands and toured as a backup singer with .38 Special.

Hess, Derek

In the late 1960s Jacksonville native Hess, a drummer, got together with guitarist-vocalist Barry Lee Harwood to form a series of bands, including Christian rock band Israel. Hess later joined Jacksonville group Running Easy, which included future Lynyrd Skynyrd member Randall Hall. Running Easy toured Europe as singer Melanie's backing band in 1979.

In 1983, Hess joined the Rossington Collins Band, which morphed into the Allen Collins Band, both on MCA. In the 1990s, Hess worked with an early version of the Derek Trucks Band as well as notable groups Synergy, the Greg Baril Band and Jethro's Giant Brain.

Also see *Harwood, Barry Lee; Rossington-Collins Band; Collins, Allen; Synergy; Baril, Greg.*

Hinton, Eddie

This Jacksonville native (b. 1944) moved with his mother after she divorced to Tuscaloosa, Ala., where he attended the University of Alabama. He dropped out to tour with a regional rock group called the Five Men-Its.

The Men-Its played the same circuit as Daytona's Allman Joys. In 1967, Hinton got an offer to work as a session guitarist with the house band at Fame Studios in Muscle Shoals. He abruptly quit the Men-Its, leaving the group without a lead singer. The group decided to disband; two of its members joined Duane and Gregg Allman to form Almanac; that band changed its name to Hourglass when it signed with Liberty Records later that year. When Hourglass broke up in 1968, Allman too moved to Muscle Shoals, where Hourglass had recorded its second and final album for Liberty. Hinton and Allman, both hot-shot session players, became roommates.

Hinton performed on records for Aretha Franklin, Otis Redding, Joe Tex, Solomon Burke, Percy Sledge, the Staples Singers, the Dells, Elvis Presley, the Box Tops, Boz Scaggs and many others.

Hinton was also a talented singer and songwriter. He wrote many songs, including "Cover Me" and "It's All Wrong, But It's All Right" for Percy Sledge and "Breakfast in Bed," recorded by Dusty Springfield. In 1977, Hinton recorded his first solo album for Capricorn Records in Macon, which shut down the week of its release. This development apparently set off an emotional tailspin. Unable to cope, Hinton found himself homeless. Muscle Shoals producer Jimmy Johnson helped Hinton get a second album together, which was released in 1982 by Rounder Records' blues subsidiary, Bullseye Blues. Hinton died of heart failure in 1995 while working on an album of new material in Birmingham, where he lived with his mother. The album was released by reconstituted Capricorn Records in 1998.

Also see *Allman, Duane.*

Hlubek, Dave

A navy brat, Hlubek was born in Jacksonville but spent much of his formative years on the West Coast. His family returned to Jacksonville about 1965, where

he attended Lake Shore Middle School, home of several future rock stars, and Forrest High. Hlubek formed rock group Mynd Garden in 1967 and in 1971 became a founding member of Molly Hatchet. Before adding singer Danny Joe Brown in 1976, Hlubek himself was the band's lead vocalist.

After leaving Hatchet in 1987, replaced by Bobby Ingram, he put together a short-lived project with Barry Lee Harwood called the Hlubek-Harwood Band. He later worked with the Southern Jam Band, Southern Rock Legends, and Southern Rock All-Stars alongside former members of Lynyrd Skynyrd and Blackfoot. In 2004 he joined guitarist Mike Estes, formerly of Lynyrd Skynyrd and Blackfoot, in southern-rock band Skinny Molly.

Hlubek rejoined Hatchet in 2005, by this point the band's sole original member. He died in 2017 at age 66 of heart failure.

Also see *Molly Hatchet.*

Hodges, Kenny

Born in Jacksonville in 1936, this bass guitarist joined folk-pop group Spanky & Our Gang in 1968 after that group had already scored two major hit singles. Hodges was with Spanky for two years. He later became session player and part-time country musician in St. Augustine. Hodges died in Papillon, Neb., in 2013.

Hodgson, Mark

Blues-harp (harmonica) player born in Detroit. Grew up in Daytona Beach, where he formed the Rootie Tootie Band in the early 1980s. Later worked with Bob Greenlee's band the Midnight Creepers and Noble "Thin Man" Watts.

Also see *Midnight Creepers; Greenlee, Bob; Watts, Noble.*

Hourglass

See *Allman Brothers Band.*

House of Dreams

Gainesville rock quartet featuring singer-songwriter Britton Cameron. Began as a duo with Jack Sizemore on guitar, vocals and keyboards, later rounded out by Jeff Coffey on bass and Tom Hurst on drums. House of Dreams signed to Naked Language, a division of Atlanta's Ichiban Records, in 1994. Its debut album was produced by Tallahassee's John Kurzweg and recorded in Gainesville at Mirror Image.

After Ichiban folded, the group released another album on its own label, which caught the ear of Los Angeles producer Keith Olsen, who snagged the band a deal with RCA. The band recorded an album with Olsen, which RCA declined to release.

Cameron relocated to Nashville to become a staff writer at Warner-Chappell Music and later Windswept Publishing and

recorded with former Gainesville resident Stan Lynch. Sizemore would also move to Nashville, where he would join country group Lonestar. He and Cameron still collaborate as songwriters.

Also see *Kurzweg, John.*

Illusions

Teen pop group from Palatka consisting of Rob Gardner on organ and vocals, Jim Williams on guitar and vocals, Skip Hewett on bass, and Timothy Touchton on drums. In 1966 the group landed its own TV series on Jacksonville's WFGA (Channel 12) titled *Let's Go*. Managed by Jacksonville impresario Don Dana, the Illusions released a single, "I Know," on Dana's ACP (Atlantic Coast Productions) Records, which garnered heavy airplay on Orlando's WLOF in August 1966 and was picked up by Columbia Records.

Just before the record was released nationally guitarist-vocalist Isaac Guillory left to play bass with Columbia artists the Cryan' Shames from Illinois. Guillory later became a successful folk singer. He died of cancer at his home in Wallsend, England, in 2001 at age 52.

Touchton later joined Tallahassee band Plymouth Rock who signed with Epic in 1969, but no album was released, so several members of Plymouth Rock, including Touchton, became backup musicians for singer Bobbie Gentry. In 1972 Touchton went to Munich, where he landed the role of Pontius Pilate in *Jesus Christ,*

Superstar, later becoming a successful songwriter and producer.

Also see *Dana, Don; Guillory, Isaac; Touchton, Timothy.*

Ingram, Bobby

Guitarist from Jacksonville and co-founder of PARC/Epic act China Sky, formerly known as the Bobby Ingram Project, which briefly included front man Jimmy Dougherty, replaced by Detroit singer-songwriter Ron Perry. He also worked with the short-lived Danny Joe Brown Band who released an album on Epic in 1980.

Ingram left China Sky in 1987 to replace Dave Hlubek in Molly Hatchet and is currently the leader of that group.

Also see *Molly Hatchet; China Sky; Brown, Danny Joe.*

Inspection 12

Formed in 1994, this Jacksonville skate-punk quartet signed with Santa Cruz, Calif.-based Honest Don's (a division of Fat Wreck Chords) in 2000. Despite the tragic death of drummer Scott Shad in 2001, the group carried on. However, the band was dropped after two albums, and guitarist Pete Mosely left to take the bass position in platinum-selling Capitol act Yellowcard, also from Jacksonville. The group released albums through Switzerland's Floppy Cow Records in 2003 and in 2004 on former Yellowcard member Ben Harper's Long Beach-based Takeover Records.

Also see *Yellowcard; Mosely, Pete, McClintock, Dan.*

Ivey, Clayton

Born 1945 in Pensacola, this keyboardist started with his father's western-swing band on a local television program. Ivey did his first session in Nashville in mid 1960s, then moved to Muscle Shoals in 1969 where he became a staff musician at Rick Hall's FAME studio and played on dozens of hit records. In 1972 he went over to Sheffield, to Muscle Shoals Sound, where he worked with the Swampers. While in Muscle Shoals area he performed behind the likes of Wilson Pickett, Clarence Carter, Aretha Franklin, Etta

James, the Emotions, the Osmond Brothers, Gregg Allman, Hank Williams Jr., Roy Orbison, Paul Anka, Liza Minelli and others too numerous to mention.

In 1973 Ivey became a staff musician and producer at Motown Records and worked with Marvin Gaye, the Supremes, the Temptations, Thelma Houston and others. He returned to Muscle Shoals in 1976 where he co-founded Wishbone Studios and a publishing company.

Ivey moved to Nashville in 1987, where he still resides, and remains a prominent session player, working with the likes of Toby Keith, Alan Jackson, Randy Travis, Kenny Rogers and many others.

J.J. Grey & Mofro

Kitschy, down-home "swamp funk" purveyors from Jacksonville, fronted by for-

mer Alma Zuma singer John "J.J." Grey (Higginbotham). Alma Zuma was lured to London, where it had received an offer from a British label. However, the deal fell through, and the rest of the band returned to Jacksonville. Grey and guitarist Daryl Hance stayed in London where they regrouped as Mofro Magic. After adding an Australian and a Frenchman to the lineup, they returned to the states.

Mofro signed with San Francisco's Fog City label in 2001, releasing its first album, *Blackwater*, that same year. A second album, *Lochloosa*, was released in 2004. In 2007 it signed with renowned Chicago-based blues label Alligator Records and released the album *Country Ghetto.*

Hance left 2010 to start his own band. After releasing six albums on Alligator, Mofro signed with Dutch label Provogue Records (headed by former Jacksonville resident Ron Burman) in 2015 and continues its heavy touring schedule. Current members include Todd Smallie (bass), Eric Brigmond (keyboards) and Marcus Parsley (trumpet), but the line-up shifts continuously.

Also see *Parsley, Marcus; Burman, Ron.*

Jackson, Willis ("Gator Tail")

A Miami native, this screaming tenor saxophonist was a pioneer of jazz-funk fusion and what later came to be called "acid jazz." After graduating with a music degree from Florida A&M in Tallahassee at 17, Jackson joined the Cootie Williams Orchestra.

During the 1950s he moved to NYC, where he became a prominent session player and worked with the likes of Dinah Washington, Jackie Wilson and Ruth Brown, whom he married. He recorded many albums as part of a duo with organist Jack McDuff and Pat Martino as well as several of his own for Prestige, Atlantic and others from 1959 through 1984. Willis died in New York in 1987 at age 55, a week after undergoing heart surgery.

Jamal, Khan

Born in Jacksonville in 1946, earned music degrees at Granoff School, Combs College and Temple University. Prominent jazz vibraphonist, based for a time in NYC. Worked with Ronald Shannon Jackson's Decoding Society, Sunny Murray, Archie Shepp, Grover Washington Jr., and many others; also led own groups for various labels like Steeplechase, Stash and Storyville. Currently resides in Philadelphia, where he runs his own label, Jambrio, and teaches at the University of Pennsylvania. Also founded the Philadelphia Jazz Composers Forum Orchestra.

Janick, John

Janick and fellow student Vinnie Fiorello, drummer for Gainesville punk-pop band Less than Jake, founded Fueled by Ramen Records in 1996 while at University of Florida. The label's acts included Less than Jake, Fall Out Boy and Paramore (now signed to Atlantic). Janick and Fiorello sold FBR to Warner Music Group in 2009, whereupon Janick was named co-president of Elektra Records, where he served until 2012. From there he went to Interscope/Geffen/A&M as chief operating officer and is now CEO of that label group.

Also see *Less than Jake.*

Jarrett, Marvin ("Jet")

Guitarist with Johnny Van Zant's 1970s Austin Nickels Band, based in Jacksonville. After leaving that group he moved to Los Angeles where he purchased *Creem* magazine. After *Creem* folded, Jarrett founded *Ray Gun* and was later editor and co-founder of *Nylon*. He lives in Los Angeles.

Also see *Van Zant, Johnny.*

Johnson, James Weldon

Born in Jacksonville in 1871, Johnson became principal of then-segregated Stanton High School in 1900. He and his brother Rosamond co-wrote the song "Lift Every Voice and Sing," later known as the "Negro National Hymn." Johnson was also a practicing attorney, the first black member of the Florida bar, and a poet. He moved to NYC in 1901, where he became a founding member of the NAACP. Pres. Theodore Roosevelt appointed Johnson US consul in Venezuela and Nicaragua. In 1934 he became New York University's first African-American professor and later a professor of literature at Fisk University. Johnson died in Wiscasset, Maine, in 1938.

Johns, Bobby

Drummer from Richmond, Ky., original member of the group Exile. After debuting on RCA-distributed Wooden Nickel Records in 1973, the group signed with Curb/Warner Bros. Records in 1978 and struck gold with producer Mike Chapman's song, "Kiss You All Over." Johns left Exile in 1979, before it morphed into a country group, and joined Indianapolis-based rock group Roadmaster. He moved to Jacksonville in the 1980s, where he married former Lynyrd Sknyrd backup singer Leslie Hawkins and worked with notable musicians Barry Rapp, Barry Lee Harwood and Tim Lindsey in Time Piece.

Also see *Hawkins, Leslie; Time Piece.*

Johnson, Rick ("Hurricane")

Sax player and keyboardist, originally from Jackson, Miss.; moved to Jacksonville Beach in early 1980s, where he worked with bar band Synergy alongside notable players Tim Lindsey (Molly Hatchet, Lynyrd Skynyrd), John Philip Kurzweg, Rocco Marshall (Vision) and Carole Bristow (.38 Special). In 1987, he led a horn section for Lynyrd Skynyrd's reunion tour.

Johnson recorded and toured for more than a decade with Doctor Hector & the Groove Injectors (King Snake Records) and was also a sought-after session player. He appears on albums by the Midnight Creepers, Little Mike & the Tornadoes, Chain of Fools, Tom Lipkins, Sonny Rhodes, J.D. & the Ravens and many others. Johnson died of liver failure in 2017 at 66.

Also see *Synergy; Kurzweg, John; Hall, Randall; Lynyrd Skynyrd; Doctor Hector & the Groove Injectors; Chain of Fools; Midnight Creepers.*

Jones, Bruce

Concert engineer from Tallahassee; started off with the Tallahassee Band; went on to handle front-of-house sound for the likes of the Gap Band, the Kinks, Scandal, David Bowie, Aerosmith, REM, Rick James, Ted Nugent, the Highwaymen (Willie Nelson, Waylon Jennings, Johnny Cash and Kris Kristoffersen), Joe Cocker, Stevie Ray Vaughn, Counting Crows, Huey Lewis & the News.

Jones, Glenn

Jacksonville-born gospel vocalist, turned R&B singer in 1980; worked with producer/jazz musician Norman Connors.

Signed with RCA in 1983, where he had a minor hit with the song "I Am Somebody." He later signed with Jive, where he scored a No. 2 R&B hit in 1987 with "We've Only Just Begun" (not the Carpenters' song). He signed with Atlantic Records in 1992. An album, *Feels Good,* was released in 2002 on Peak Records. Jones lives in Atlanta, where he performs regularly.

Jones, Sam

Jacksonville-born jazz bassist and cellist; moved to NYC in mid-1950s; worked with Duke Ellington, Cannonball Adderly, Oscar Peterson, Cedar Walton, Illinois Jaquet, Thelonious Monk, and others; also led own big band. Died 1981.

Jon Todd

Avante-garde, instrumental rock quartet led by Stripmine Records founder Damien Lee, based in Jacksonville. With Lee on drums, other members included Chris Stow on guitar, Mike Kaiser on bass and Nick Strate, also on bass. Released album titled *Dreamlike* on nationally distributed Magic Eye Records in 1998.

Jourard, Jeff

Son of a university professor, this Gainesville guitarist joined the group Road Turkey with brother Marty on bass, Steve Soar on guitar and Stan Lynch on drums. He also played in an early incarnation of Tom Petty & the Heartbreakers in Los Angeles around 1974. He joined the Motels in 1978. His brother Marty soon joined the group, which signed to Capitol Records a year later. After recording the group's first Capitol album, Jeff Jourard was replaced by singer Martha Davis' boyfriend in 1980. Marty Jourard stayed with the Motels until their dissolution in 1987. Jeff lives in Los Angeles, where he works in computer networking.

Also see *Jourard, Marty; Road Turkey; Mudcrutch*

Jourard, Marty

Born in Atlanta, the son of a psychology professor, Jourard came to Gainesville with his family at age 4 when his father took a teaching position at University of Florida. Jourard, a multi-instrumentalist, played in several Gainesville groups. He played bass in early 1970s rock band Road Turkey which included Steve Soar and Marty's brother Jeff on guitars along with drummer Stan Lynch (who became a member of Tom Petty & the Heartbreakers).

Jourard moved to Los Angeles in 1976, where he joined new-wave band the Motels, a group that already included Jeff Jourard on guitar, two years later (Marty played keyboards and saxophone in this group). The Motels signed to Capitol in 1979, where they released five albums,

83

garnering two Top-10 hits, "Only the Lonely" and "Suddenly Last Summer." Jourard also played sax on recordings for fellow Gainesville native Tom Petty.

Moved to Seattle in 1989 where he ran a recording studio and taught songwriting, rejoining a reunited Motels in 2014. Jourard is the author of *Music Everywhere*, a history of Gainesville's rock scene from 1964 to 1976, published by University Press of Florida.

Also see *Jourard, Jeff; Road Turkey; Mudcrutch.*

Junstrom, Larry

Bassist with early version of Lynyrd Skynyrd from 1964 to 1971. Replaced by Greg Walker (later of Blackfoot), who was replaced by Leon Wilkeson. In 1977 Junstrom replaced bassist Ken Lyons in .38 Special. He performed with .38 until 2014. He is retired and lives in the Jacksonville area.

Also see *Lynyrd Skynyrd; .38 Special; Blackfoot.*

Kelley, Brian

From Ormond Beach, this young guitarist-vocalist (born 1985) moved to Nashville to attend Belmont University, where he met Tyler Hubbard at a campus worship service. In 2010 the two formed a duo they called Florida Georgia Line, which signed to Republic Records and has since became one of the hottest modern-country acts of the decade.

Key, Ryan

Born in Jacksonville in 1979, a graduate of Douglas Anderson School of the Arts; this guitarist-singer joined Santa Cruz-Calif. group Craig's Brother in 1998. Returning to Jacksonville, he worked with pop-punk group Modern Amusement and landed a guest slot on Yellowcard's first album, Midget Tossing, as a backing vocalist. He then replaced Yellowcard's singer Ben Dobson and fronted that group until its demise in 2017. Key now operates a recording studio, Lone Tree Recordings, near Nashville.

Also see *Yellowcard.*

King, Andy

Bassist and vocalist from Jacksonville's Westside. Worked with a reconstituted Allen Collins Band alongside Collins, guitarist Mike Owings and drummer Robert Nix in 1984. Also replaced Alan Close in new-wave band Mike Angelo & the Idols as well as in Dave Roberts' group Crawfish of Love.

Also see *Collins, Allen; Nix, Robert; Mike Angelo & the Idols.*

King Eddie

Born Edward Whitt in New Jersey; moved to Jacksonville in 1964. In 1985 he joined Jacksonville's premiere reggae group, Pili Pili, as bassist.

In 1998, Whitt hooked up with producer Butch Ingram (singer James Ingram's brother) to record a solo album for Ingram's Philadelphia-based Society Hill Records. Still performs in and around Jacksonville with Pili Pili.

Also see *Nasta, Ken.*

Krantz, Dale

Originally from Indiana, Krantz had been a schoolteacher and a backup singer for Leon Russell before coming to Jacksonville in late 1970s to join .38 Special as a backup singer. Later became lead vocalist for Lynyrd Skynyrd spin-off the Rossington Collins Band for whom she sang lead on "Don't Misunderstand Me"; later a backup singer for the reconstituted Skynyrd. Married to guitarist Gary Rossington.

Also see *Lynyrd Skynyrd; Rossington Collins Band; .38 Special.*

Kurzweg, John Philip

Kurzweg, a Tallahassee native and multi-instrumentalist, was signed to Atlantic Records not long after his then-girlfriend was transferred to Jacksonville in 1988. They lived in the San Marco area for about a year.

Disappointed with his Atlantic debut, Kurzweg abandoned the project to join bar-band Synergy, which also featured future Lynyrd Skynyrd members Tim Lindsay and Randall Hall along with Rossington Collins drummer Derek Hess and Vision guitarist-vocalist Rocco Marshall.

He returned to Tallahassee to put together a studio in his house, where he began engineering and producing recordings for area acts like House of Dreams, the Sight-Seers and newcomers Creed. Creed quickly scored a major deal, eventually selling a whopping 24 million records (the group broke up in June of 2004). Kurzweg was a virtual fifth member of Creed, overseeing its arrangements, singing backgrounds and playing keyboards on its recordings.

Kurzweg later produced Puddle of Mudd's debut for Fred Durst's Flawless label, sales of which hit five million, as well as most of the group's follow-up album. Kurzweg. lives in Santa Fe, where he operates a private production studio.

Also see *Synergy; Creed; Sight Seers; House of Dreams.*

Lads, The

Jacksonville bass-music rappers, released one 12-inch single on Jeff Cohen's Attitude Records, produced by Mamado (Willetta Smith). Later signed with Motown.

Lamoureux, Harley

Born in Jacksonville in 1952, possibly the city's first hippie, known as "Coconut Harley" while a student at Central Adult High School because of his pet coconut. Lamoureux is an accomplished harmonica player who has performed with Charlie Daniels and others. After years in Nashville, where he met his wife Carolyn, Lamoureux returned to Jacksonville. Lamoureux often performs in prisons with Shooting Stars Tour and ministers to the inmates.

LaVoie, Kent

See Lobo.

Leadon, Bernie

Born 1947 in Minneapolis, the son of an aerospace engineer/professor, Leadon moved to Gainesville with his family at age 16, where he worked alongside guitarist Don Felder in the Maundy Quintet, playing guitar and banjo. He wrote and arranged the group's only single, "2's Better than 3."

Leadon made the leap to Los Angeles in 1967, where he hooked up with country-rock pioneers Hearts & Flowers and the Dillard & Clark Expedition; he later became a member of Gram Parsons' Flying Burrito Brothers and a sideman along with Don Henley and Glenn Frey in Linda Ronstadt's band. In 1971, he became a founding member of the Eagles. When the group decided to bring in a third guitarist, Leadon suggested former Gainesville bandmate Felder. Leadon left the Eagles in 1976 after they decided to focus on a heavier, rock-oriented sound and was replaced by former James Gang frontman Joe Walsh. In 2013 he rejoined the Eagles, but with the Frey's sudden death in early 2016, the Eagles' future became cloudy. Leadon performed with the remaining Eagles in a tribute to Frey a month after Frey's death. However, in 2017, Don Henley, the only original member of the group, announced a new Eagles lineup sans Leadon.

Leadon lives in Nashville. Leadon's brother, Tom, was a member of Tom Petty's early band Mudcrutch.

Also see *Maundy Quintet; Mudcrutch.*

Leadon, Tom

Gainesville guitarist-vocalist, younger brother of Bernie Leadon. A member of the Epics, one of Tom Petty's early Gainesville bands (Petty played bass). Leadon and Petty co-founded Gainesville group Mudcrutch in 1971, but a year later Leadon left for Los Angeles, where he replaced his brother, Bernie Leadon, in Linda Ronstadt's band after the elder Leadon left to co-found the Eagles. Danny Roberts replaced Leadon in Mudcrutch. In 1975, a song Tom Leadon co-wrote with his brother Bernie, "Hollywood Waltz," landed on the Eagles album *One of These Nights.* Buck Owens also recorded it. In 1976, Tom joined country-rock band Silver, signed to Arista Records, as bassist. In 2007, Petty decided to re-form Mudcrutch and asked Tom Leadon to re-join. Mudcrutch has since recorded two albums for Reprise Records.

Also see *Mudcrutch; Leadon, Bernie; Petty, Tom.*

Leavell, Allan ("Fin")

This multi-instrumentalist/songwriter/arranger/singer, a graduate of Douglas Anderson School of the Arts, along with Mandarin High School grad Luke Walker, formed Jacksonville punk-pop group Start Trouble, who were spotted by Matt Pinfield and signed with Columbia Records in 2001, but their album was not released until three years later, and the group quickly folded. Leavell and Walker then moved to Los Angeles and formed Summer Obsession, who quickly signed to Virgin Records. Neither group sold enough records to establish a career foothold. Leavell leads his own group called Nightswim and lives in Los Angeles.

Also see *Start Trouble; Summer Obsession.*

Leblanc & Carr

Soft-pop duo from Daytona Beach who relocated to Muscle Shoals in the mid-1970s and signed with Atlantic Records, where they scored some minor hits, including 1978's "Falling." After serving as an opening act on Lynyrd Skynyrd's fateful 1977 tour, Pete Carr decided he preferred studio work to touring. The duo disbanded soon thereafter.

Also see *Leblanc, Lenny; Carr, Pete.*

Leblanc, Lenny

Born in Leominster, Mass., in 1951, Leblanc came with his family to Daytona Beach at 3, where he later formed a band with guitarist Pete Carr, who would go on to become one of the top session musicians in the business, based in Muscle Shoals, Ala. Leblanc got a call from his former Daytona bandmate inviting him to join him in Muscle Shoals. Garnering work as a touring bassist, Leblanc performed behind the likes of Hank Williams Jr., Crystal Gayle, Etta James, Shenandoah, Ricky Skaggs, Sawyer Brown, the Supremes, Joan Baez, Amy Grant and Roy Orbison.

Leblanc recorded an album of his own material in 1975, which Carr, who served as its producer, sent to Jerry Wexler at Atlantic Records. Wexler suggested the two form a duo, christened Leblanc & Carr, who scored some minor hits on Atlantic.

The duo disbanded in 1978 after scoring a minor hit with "Falling." Leblanc then garnered a solo deal with Capitol. In 1980 he began recording Christian music for Heartland Records. In 1987 he opened his own Muscle Shoals-based studio. Leblanc has since retired but still lives in the Muscle Shoals area.

Also see also *Carr, Pete.*

Lemonhead, C.C.

Born Nathaniel Orange, a founding member, along with Johnny (Jay) McGowan, of Jacksonville rap pioneers Chill Deal. He and McGowan went on to phenomenal careers: They later founded million-sellers 95 South ("Whoot, There It Is," on Ichiban Records), and the Quad City DJs ("Come On and Ride the Train," on Big Beat/Atlantic), and co-produced club hits for the 69 Boyz and 3 Grand. In addition, Lemonhead was a solo artist on Jacksonville-based Attitude Records. He is also an ex-

pert in computer programming and networking. He lives in Jacksonville.

Also see *Quad City DJs; 95 South; Chill Deal.*

Less than Jake

Formed by University of Florida students Chris DeMakes (guitar and vocals), drummer Vinnie Fiorello (drums) and bassist Roger Lima, these ska-punk revivalists, complete with horn section, signed to Capitol in 1996; later switched to Santa Cruz, Calif.-based indie Fat Wreck Chords. Fiorello also formed Fueled by Ramen label, whose roster once included Jacksonville's Yellowcard. In 2003, Less than Jake signed with Sire Records. Fiorello and his business partner John Janick sold Fueled by Ramen to Warner Music Group in 2006. Fiorello has since formed a new label, Sleep It Off Records. Less than Jake is still actively touring.

Also see *Janick, John.*

Liesegang, Brian

Born in New York, this guitarist, vocalist and songwriter, a graduate of Jacksonville's prestigious Bolles School, met Nine Inch Nails sideman Richard Patrick while at college in Chicago. Liesegang joined NIN in the early 1990s. Liesegang and Patrick left in 1993 to form Filter, which broke through with the song "Hey, Man, Nice Shot" on Reprise Records in 1995. He left Filter in 1997. Liesegang also wrote songs for Nina Hagen and

Veruca Salt and currently works with indie rockers Ashtar Command, with songs featured in feature films, television series, commercials and video games.

Limp Bizkit

Limp Bizkit, whose original lineup was composed of vocalist/rapper Fred Durst, guitarist Wes Borland, bassist Sam Rivers and drummer John Otto, were underdogs on the Jacksonville scene until frontman Fred Durst met bassist Fieldy from rap-metal band Korn after a show at Jacksonville's Milk Bar in 1994. Durst, a tattoo artist, offered to do some free work for the band members, and they went over to his house. Durst gave a demo tape to the Korn members, who passed it on to their producer, Ross Robinson. Robinson shopped it around, which led to a tentative offer from Los Angeles-based Mojo Records, an MCA affiliate. Just before leaving for Los Angeles, guitarist Wes Borland left the group and was replaced by Terry Balsamo. The Bizkit boys traveled to L.A. to showcase for Mojo's owners, but the two parties didn't get along, so the band went

back to Jacksonville and re-added Borland to the lineup.

At another Milk Bar show, Bizkit opened for a band signed to Flip Records, owned by New York real-estate scion Jordan Schur. Schur liked Limp Bizkit and agreed to fund the band's recordings, which, after a year and a $1 million investment by Schur, were picked up by Interscope, another MCA affiliate.

Constant touring and MTV exposure earned the band a double-platinum album. Bizkit's follow-up album sold more than 6 million; its third did more than 8 million. Bandleader Durst used the group's success as a launching pad for his own career as a record exec, overseeing platinum albums by Staind and Puddle of Mudd. Borland left the group again in 2001 but returned in 2004. During a lengthy hiatus, Durst focused on acting and directing movies as well as developing new acts.

Bizkit reunited in 2009 and is still touring. Interscope dropped the act in 2011. The group released four singles on Miami-based Cash Money Records in 2012-2014 with an album reportedly in the works.

Also see *Durst, Fred; Cold.*

Lindsey, Tim

Bassist with Synergy, APB, Rossington Collins Band, Randall Hall Band and Lynyrd Skynyrd; currently a member of Molly Hatchet. Lindsey was actually the original bass player for Hatchet but left before the group got signed to Epic, replaced by Banner Thomas.

Also see *APB* (Artimus Pyle Band), *Rossington-Collins Band, Randall Hall Band* and *Lynyrd Skynyrd*.

Lipkins, Tom

Phenomenal soul singer from Toledo, Ohio; as lead singer of vocal group the Creations Lipkins was one of the earliest acts signed to Motown Records in 1961. He and the group were singing on a street corner in Detroit when Smokey Robinson passed by and decided to sign them. Lipkins died in 2006 after spending much of his life as a truck driver and performing in and around the Daytona Beach area.

Lobo

Born Roland Kent LaVoie in Tallahassee, 1943; moved to Winterhaven, where he played in teen band the Rumors alongside Gram Parsons and Jim Stafford. In 1971, with the assistance of producer Phil Gern-

hard, he would break through as a solo soft-rock act on Big Tree/Atlantic Records with "Me and You and a Dog Named Boo"; two or three more top-ten hits would follow. He also co-produced (with Gernhard) hits for former Rumors bandmate Jim Stafford ("Spiders and Snakes"). Later signed with Elektra; relocated to Nashville and turned toward a more country-oriented direction. He remained popular in Asia, where he toured in 2006 and 2008. He has since retired to his home in Florida.

Also see *Parsons, Gram.*

Lombar, Dru

A fixture on the Jacksonville scene since the 1960s, guitarist-vocalist Lombar led Christian-rock group King James Version, which included bassist Leon Wilkeson, later of Lynyrd Skynyrd. After that he and two other KJV members formed Magi. In the early 1970s, Lombar was invited to join southern rockers Grinderswitch, whereupon he relocated to Macon, and the group signed with Capricorn Records. Grinderswitch, who released albums through Capricorn, Atco and Robox Records, toured worldwide opening for several big-name acts and also served as Bonnie Bramlett's backing band.

After that group dissolved in 1983, Lombar returned to Jacksonville where he eventually formed blues-rock ensemble Dr. Hector & the Groove Injectors, who recorded six albums for Bob Greenlee's

Sanford-based King Snake label. Lombar also ran his own label, re-releasing out-of-print Grinderswitch albums, and operated a recording studio. He died of heart failure in 2005, age 54.

Also see *Doctor Hector & the Groove Injectors*

Lowman, Edmund

Jacksonville guitarist/vocalist Loman was a founding member of Audio Orange, a group who, after his departure, morphed into 3AE and signed with RCA. He was also a member of Ten High, who morphed into Start Trouble, signed with Columbia. He lives in Thailand.

Also see *3AE; Start Trouble.*

Lugnut

Jacksonville Christian-punk band, signed to Calif.-based Screaming Giant Records in 1999. Members included vocalist Steve Park, guitarists Jeremie Faircloth and Dave Luttrell, bassist Owen Holmes (later of Black Kids) and drummer Christopher Brown (founding member of punk-rock band Evergreen Terrace).

Also see *Evergreen Terrace; Black Kids.*

Lundgren, Erik

An early member of the Johnny Van Zant Band, hotshot guitarist Lundgren replaced Marvin "Jet" Jarrett. Recorded several albums with JVZ for labels such as Polydor, Nettwerk and Atlantic Records. Later performed with country duo Van Zant (featuring brothers Johnny and Donny Van Zant).

Also see *Van Zant, Johnny; Van Zant; Jarrett, Marvin; Perpetrators.*

Lynch, Stan

Born in Cincinnati in 1955, Lynch moved with his family in the mid-1960s to Gainesville, where his father was a psychology professor st Santa Fe Community College. At 14 he joined local group Styrofoam Soule as its drummer and later became a member of Road Turkey alongside Marty and Jeff Jourard.

Dreaming of the big time, Lynch lit out for Los Angeles in 1973, where he scuffled for two years until getting together with three former members of Gainesville group Mudcrutch, led by Tom Petty. That group had also relocated to Los Angeles and had signed with Shelter Records but had broken up by this point. Lynch joined Petty's new group, the Heartbreakers.

Between tours with the Heartbreakers, Lynch moonlighted with the likes of Bob Dylan, Jackson Browne, Aretha Franklin, Stevie Nicks, the Eurythmics and the Byrds. Danny Kortchmar introduced him to Don Henley, with whom Lynch would cultivate a fruitful working relationship. He co-wrote several songs on Henley' s 1984 album, *Building the Perfect Beast*

After leaving the Heartbreakers in 1994, Lynch returned to Florida but continued co-writing songs, one with Henley that appeared on the Eagles' *Hell Freezes Over.* He also began co-writing and contributing songs for Toto, the Fabulous Thunderbirds, Eddie Money, Ringo Starr, Matraca Berg, Restless Heart, the Mavericks and Meredith Brooks, Jeff Healey. In 2000, Lynch recorded some instrumental tracks for Henley's comeback album, *Inside Job,* for which he co-wrote nine songs with Henley, at Jim DeVito' s Retrophonics studio in Crescent Beach (musicians included members of St. Augustine group Gunga Din).

He also produced tracks for The Band as well as for Keith Richards and fellow Gainesville rockers Sister Hazel, with whom he co-wrote the song "Lift." In 2004, he co-wrote "Back When," a No. 1 country hit for Tim McGraw. Lynch has homes in Crescent Beach and Melrose.

Also see *Petty, Tom; Road Turkey, Jourard, Marty; Jourard, Jeff; DeVito, Jim; Sister Hazel.*

Lyndell, Linda

Born Linda Rowland in Gainesville in 1946, Lyndell was a country girl who sang R&B. Her first single was co-produced by nightclub owner Dub Thomas and Ocala disc jockey Bob Norris; the B-side was a song written by Jacksonville DJ Dave Crawford, who later became her producer. He brought Lyndell to Jacksonville to record her next single, another Crawford composition; he took the recording to Stax Records in Memphis, which agreed to a deal. Crawford and Lyndell co-wrote and recorded the original version of "What a Man." She improvised the song's verses in the studio.

After the single tanked, Lyndell became disillusioned and retreated from the music business.

Redone by Salt & Pepa, "Whatta Man" became a huge hit in 1993; Lyndell had to sue Crawford's estate, however, to get her share of songwriter royalties. In 2003, she performed the song at the opening of the Stax Museum in Memphis. Now known as Linda Towles, she lives in Crawfordville, Fla.

Also see *Crawford, Dave.*

Lynyrd Skynyrd

Formed in the mid-1960s by Jacksonville Westsiders Gary Rossington, Allen Collins, Bob Burns, Larry Junstrom and Ronnie Van Zant, this group became a fixture on the Jacksonville scene as One Percent. The band changed its name in 1969, spoofing Lee High School physical-education coach Leonard Skinner, who had made them cut their hair.

After the Allman Brothers Band moved to Macon, Skynyrd made the move too. Originally co-managed by Walden's younger brother, Alan, in partnership with Jacksonville's Pat Armstrong, the group recorded an album's worth of material in Muscle Shoals with producer Jimmy Johnson. Even with the combined efforts of Johnson and Alan Walden, the album found no takers, not even at Capricorn, Phil Walden's label.

Soldiering on, the band was later spotted at Funocchio's in Atlanta by producer/musician Al Kooper. Kooper signed the group to his MCA-distributed Sounds of the South label. Manager Walden dumped Armstrong as the deal was being done.

After hooking up with MCA, Skynyrd became one of the biggest and most influential rock acts of all time, thanks mainly to the backlash anthem "Sweet Home, Alabama." The group was devastated by a plane crash in 1977 when its tour plane ran out of gas near McComb, Miss.

After a decade of short-lived side projects, the remaining members band re-formed in 1987, fronted by Van Zant's youngest brother, Johnny. One of Skynyrd's early members, Rick Medlocke, who played drums and sang on their first unreleased Muscle Shoals album, rejoined the band on guitar and vocals in 1996.

Longtime bassist Leon Wilkeson died in 2001 and was replaced by Ean Evans. Lynyrd Skynyrd was inducted into the Rock 'n' Roll Hall of Fame in 2006. Rossington is the sole original member. The group announced its farewell tour in 2018.

Also see *Rossington Collins Band; Van Zant, Johnny; Collins, Allen; Blackfoot; APB.*

McClendon, Lisa

Born Edletha Lorraine Peeples, 1975, in Palatka, McClendon started her singing career as a child in her father's church. In 2002 she signed with Atlanta-based Shabach Entertainment and released her first album *My Diary, Your Life*. Her second album, 2003's *Soul Music*, was a joint venture with Mobile-based Integrity Music and Epic Records. Her next album, *Live from the House of Blues*, was released in 2006 by Integrity through Columbia. McClendon now records for her own Blusoul Worldwide label. She lives in Jacksonville.

McClintock, Dan

Founding member of Jacksonville skate-punk band Inspection 12 in 1994; alternates on guitar and bass but primarily a singer. Left I-12 in 1998 at singer Ryan Key's behest to join him in California Christian-rock band Craig's Brother, signed to Honest Don's, a division of Fat Wreck Chords. McClintock also spent time in California punk band Limp before returning to Jacksonville to re-form Inspection 12, who then signed to Honest Don's. Inspection 12 later released albums through Switzerland's Floppy Cow Records and former Yellowcard member Ben Harper's Takeover label.

Also see *Inspection 12*.

McCormack, Jim

McCormack is a Miami native who grew up in Jacksonville. He was one of the Classics' early drummers (followed by Robert Nix). Through connections with the Atlanta-based Lowery organization, McCormack hooked up with pop singer B.J. Thomas in 1965 and worked with Thomas for eight years. He later worked with a group called the Nightshades, who opened for Roy Orbison. He also recorded an album for VMC Records with a group that included guitarist Jimmy Pitman. McCormack returned to Miami where he became a nightclub DJ. He also served as a radio DJ in Marianna, Fla.

McCormack leads his own group in Jacksonville. Former Richfield drummer Mac McCormack is his cousin.

Also see *Pitman, Jimmy*

McCrae, Gwen

Born in Pensacola in 1943, Gwen Mosley performed in church and with several teenage girl groups before meeting her husband-to-be, sailor George McCrae, in 1963. The two formed a singing duo and moved to West Palm Beach, where they were spotted by singer Betty Wright. Wright referred the duo to Alston Records owner Henry Stone, who signed them as a duo as well as to separate solo contracts. Stone licensed some of her early Alston tracks to Columbia, but she soon returned to the fold on TK subsidiary Cat, where she scored a No. 1 R&B hit, "Rockin' Chair," in 1975.

After TK—and her marriage—folded, McCrae signed with Atlantic in 1980 and relocated to New Jersey. After several successful tours of England, she returned to Florida in 1984 and retired from music. However, inspired by her continued popularity in the UK, she made a comeback in 1996, recording for Memphis-based Goldwax Records. In 1994 she recorded a gospel album. In 2006, she released a live-in-concert album recorded in Paris. While touring England in 2012, she suffered a stroke in a hotel room. However, she continues to work concerts, casinos and corporate events. She lives in Pensacola.

McGowan, Johnny ("Jay")

From Jacksonville, a founding member of Chill Deal along with Nathaniel Orange (aka CC Lemonhead), signed to Fred Frank's CTC (Coast to Coast) label, later to Canada's Quality Records. McGowan and Orange branched out as highly suc-

cessful songwriters and producers for several regional hip-hop and dance acts including 69 Boyz (Rip-It Records), 95 South (Ichiban Records), 3 Grand (MCA), and the multi-platinum Quad City DJs (Big Beat/Atlantic). After several years in Orlando McGowan returned to Jacksonville, where he operates a recording studio.

Also see *Orange, Nathaniel; Chill Deal; 69 Boyz; 95 South; Quad City DJs.*

McGraw, Tim

Son of famed baseball player Frank "Tug" McGraw, who was a pitcher for the Jacksonville Suns in 1966, and 17-year-old Terry Parker High student Betty D'Agostino, Samuel Timothy McGraw was born in Delhi, La., in 1967. When D'Agostino, later Betty Trimble, returned to Jacksonville in 1987, Tim came too. He attended one term at Florida Community College at Jacksonville and sat in with a few local bands.

He bolted for Nashville in 1989. His father introduced him to Curb Records exec Mike Borchetta in 1994. At Curb, he scored a massive hit with "Indian Outlaw"; a string of hits followed. McGraw was voted No. 1 Male Vocalist by the Country Music Association in 1999.

He has also appeared as an actor in several films such as *The Shack, The Blind Side, Friday Night Lights, The Kingdom, Tomorrowland, Four Christmases, Flicka,* and *Country Strong. Forbes* listed McGraw's 2015 income at approximately $38 million. He has been married to singer Faith Hill since 1996. The couple has an $18 million home outside Nashville and also owns an island in the Bahamas.

McKelvey, Ray

See *Stevie Stiletto & the Switchblades.*

McKenzie, Scott

Born Philip Blondheim in Jacksonville Beach in 1939, Scott moved with his parents to Asheville, N.C., when he was only 6 months old. His father died in when he was 2. When his mother moved to Washington, D.C. to work as a civil servant during World War II, Blondheim was more or less raised by his grandmother and other family members.

In suburban Virginia, Blondheim became friends with John Phillips in the mid-1950s, and the two formed a doo-wop group called the Abstracts. After changing their name to the Smoothies, they recorded two singles for Decca. During his tenure with the Smoothies, Blondheim adopted the name Scott McKenzie, which was Phillips' daughter's middle name (actress McKenzie Phillips' first name is Laura). During the folk boom of the early 1960s, the pair formed the Journeymen and recorded three albums for Capitol. When the Journeymen broke up in 1964, Phillips asked McKenzie to help form a new folk-rock group, the Mamas and Papas, but McKenzie demurred. Producer/label owner Lou Adler signed the Mamas & Papas to his Dunhill label, which he later sold to ABC. Phillips helped McKenzie snag a deal with Adler's new label, Ode Records. Phillips wrote, co-produced and performed on McKenzie's 1967 break-through hit, "San Francisco (Be Sure to Wear Flowers in Your Hair)," which became a No. 1 hit in the U.S. and a huge hit worldwide.

Not much else happened for McKenzie until 1986, when he joined a re-formed version of the Mamas and Papas, replacing Denny Doherty. Phillip's ill health forced him to retire from the road, so McKenzie took the lead spot and Doherty returned. McKenzie stayed with the Mamas and Papas for 10 years.

McKenzie and Phillips co-wrote (with Mike Love and Terry Melcher) the Beach Boys' 1988 comeback hit, "Kokomo," which was featured in the movie *Cocktail*. In 2005, McKenzie appeared in the PBS special *My Generation: The 60s Experience* singing "San Francisco." McKenzie died in 2012 at age 73 in Los Angeles. He had suffered from Guillain-Barre syndrome.

McKnight, Mike

Former keyboardist for Jacksonville-based show band Florida, moved to Los Angeles in the late 1980s, where he became a high-profile keyboardist, session player and sequence programmer. He has written programs for a number of acts including U2, Shakira, George Michael, Paul Abdul, Fleetwood Mac, Bruce Springsteen, Whitney Houston, Lenny Kravitz, Celine Dion, Jennifer Lopez, James Ingram and many others. Has has worked as keyboardist for Shakira, Lady Gaga, Madonna, U2, Fleetwood Mac, Mariah Carey, Roger Waters, Don Henley and many others. In addition he was a regular touring member of Earth, Wind and Fire. McKnight has a recording studio in his home of Dana Point, Calif., and writes a monthly column for *Keyboard* magazine.

McPeek, Bob

From Ohio, McPeek moved to Gainesville in 1976, where he and singing partner Ric Kaestner founded popular record store Hyde and Zeke's. McPeek's next venture would be Mirror Image Recording, founded in 1977, which hosted Gainesville bands House of Dreams, Aleka's Attic, Less Than Jake, Sister Hazel, For Squirrels, Hawthorne resident Bo Diddley, Jacksonville's Molly Hatchett, former Eagles member Bernie Leadon and folk singer Tom Paxton. McPeek still plays music, working with a group called the Erasables.

Mamado

Born Willetta Smith in 1958, Mamado (pronounced "Mama-doo") was Jacksonville's first female rapper to achieve fame as well as an accomplished rock musician, recording engineer and producer. Smith took music-theory and engineering courses at Florida State College at Jacksonville and at Edward Waters College.

She signed to Jeff Cohen's Attitude Records, where her 1988 debut, *Wild*, sold more than 40,000 copies before being picked for national distribution by WTG, a CBS Records subsidiary.

She has produced albums for several artists such as the Lads, Assault & Battery, Tic Tak Toe, and I.C. Red. Smith runs her own Jacksonville-based label, Railroad Records and has branched out into video and film production.

Also see *Cohen, Jeff.*

Maple, Mike

Prominent Jacksonville drummer, has toured regularly with the Mark Farner Band and/or Grand Funk Railroad. Also a former member of Vision, along with former Skynyrd members Leon Wilkeson and Billy Powell. Has also toured with country diva Wynona Judd. After leaving Judd he returned to playing in local area bands as well as in church.

Also see *Vision.*

Marshall, Rocco

See Vision.

Marsh, Randall

Drummer for Gainesville's Mudcrutch; also worked with Los Angeles-based rock band Code Blue, a rock trio who released an album on Warner Bros. Records in 1980.

Also see *Mudcrutch.*

Martell, Stan

Virtuoso electric bassist from Kingsland, Ga., worked with several Jacksonville bands including Chain of Fools and 3AE, the latter signed to RCA Records. Operates own studio in Kingsland.

Also see *3AE; Chain of Fools.*

Martin, Willie

Native of Mobile, Ala., former WOBS co-owner and air personality known as "Captain Groovy," Martin co-wrote several hit R&B tunes with Jacksonville native and fellow WOBS DJ Dave Crawford, including "Call My Name and I'll Be There" for Wilson Pickett, "Knock It Out of the Park" for Sam & Dave, "Leanin'" and "Ride the Mighty High" for the Mighty Clouds of Joy. Now a freelance radio consultant and board member of the Northwest Jacksonville Community Development Corp.

Also see *Crawford, Dave.*

Mase

Born Mason Durrell Betha in Jacksonville in 1977; Mase moved to Harlem at age 5, He later returned to Jacksonville to attend Lee High. After moving back to NYC, he won a basketball scholarship to SUNY. More interested in music, however, he traveled to Atlanta to attend a convention, where he hooked up with producer Sean "Puff Daddy" Combs. Mase signed to Combs' Bad Boy label in the late 1990s.

After appearing as a guest rapper on several other artists' albums (including appearances with Brian McKnight and Mariah Carey), his 1997 debut, *Harlem World*, rocketed to double platinum. Greatly disturbed by the shooting of colleague Biggie Smalls (a.k.a. Notorious B.I.G.) in 1999, Mase decided it was an opportune time to retire from music and become a preacher. He did release an album in 2004, *Welcome Back*, on Bad Boy, which sold respectably, but returned to his ministry. In 2005, Mase began working with G-Unit Records owner 50 Cent, but the album was never released as Bad Boy owner Combs refuse to let him out of his contract.

Mase has since returned to his early strategy of making guest appearances on other artists' recordings. He currently does not have a recording contract but appears in the television comedy series *Sandy Wexler*. He lives in Atlanta, where he is pastor at and founder of El Elyon International Church.

Mason, David

Keyboardist from Gainesville. Worked with Tom Petty in teen band the Sundowners, later with Gainesville groups Maundy Quintet, Backlash and the Steve Morris Band. Went on to work with Todd Rundgren, Joe Walsh, Elton John, Jackson Browne, Melanie, George Clinton and many others. Mason died in Tallahassee in 2013 at 63.

Also see *Maundy Quintet*.

Masters Family

This country-gospel act started out in Jacksonville as the Dixie Sweethearts, a husband-and-wife duo featuring Johnnie and Lucille Masters, appearing regularly on country station WPDQ around 1946. In 1947 the duo was joined by their 12-year-old son Owen and became known as the Masters Family. A year later they moved to WJHP, becoming regulars on the *Dixie Barn-Dance Gang*, Jacksonville's most popular radio show, picked up by the Mutual Radio Network for broadcast nationwide.

Having developed a formidable following, the group signed with Mercury Records and moved to Knoxville, where they became regulars on WROL. In 1950 they were signed by Columbia as a gospel act; their prominent recordings included "Gloryland March." The group later added youngest daughter Deanna Masters on vocals and Richard Curley on mandolin.

In the early 1960s the family returned to Jacksonville, playing mostly church venues, and released recordings for Starday, Rich-R-Tone and Decca Records.

Masters, Johnnie

Born in Jacksonville in 1913, Masters was the leader and patriarch of the Masters Family gospel group. Masters wrote several gospel standards, including "Cry from the Cross," popularized by the Stanley Brothers, "Gloryland March," and "That Little Old Country Church House." He also wrote hit tunes for country artists like Hank Snow ("Honeymoon on a Rocket Ship," a top-10 C&W hit), Flatt & Scruggs, Roy Acuff, Don Gibson, Lynn Davis, Molly O'Day, Johnny & Jack and Carl Smith. In the late 1960s Masters took a job as a DJ at a radio station in Jesup, Ga. He died in Jacksonville in 1980.

Also see *Masters Family*.

Masters, Owen

Born in Jacksonville, 1935, the singing son of Johnnie and Lucille Masters, he joined the Masters Family revue in 1947 at age 12. In the early 1950s, Owen spun off as countrified teen idol—basically the model from which Ricky Nelson would be patterned. Masters was badly injured in an auto accident in 1955, which slowed his career considerably. When the family patriarch died in 1980, Masters moved to Nashville, where he died in 1997.

Also see *Masters Family.*

Maundy Quintet

Formerly known as the Continentals, this Gainesville cover band formed in mid-1960s is most notable for the inclusion of two future Eagles members, guitarists Bernie Leadon and Don Felder and future superstar Stephen Stills (he was with the group when it was still known as the Contientals). Other members included vocalist Tom Laughton, bassist Barry Scurran and drummer Wayne "Boomer" Hough, who was also a DJ on Gaineville's WGGG-AM. The group later added a keyboardist, David Mason. Recorded one single on own Paris Tower label, a song titled "2's Better than 3," written by Leadon, which Hough proceeded to play on his radio show. Hough booked the band and scored gigs as far afield as Ondine's in NYC. In 1967,

Leadon moved to Southern California and went to work with Capitol Recording act Hearts and Flowers. He went on to join Dillard & Clark (Gene Clark was a former member of the Byrds), the Flying Burrito Brothers and Linda Ronstadt.

Leadon became a founding member of the Eagles in 1971. Leadon brought guitarist Felder into the Eagles before he quit in 1975. Felder left the Eagles in 2001. Leadon returned to the Eagles in 2013 but has since departed. Mason would later work with Todd Rundgren, Joe Walsh, *Elton John, Jackson Browne*, Melanie, George Clinton and many others.

Also see *Leadon, Bernie; Felder, Don, Stills, Stephen; Mason, David, Flow.*

Medlocke, Rickey

A 1968 graduate of Jacksonville's Paxon High School, this drummer doubled as lead singer for the rock band band Fresh Garbage, which morphed into Blackfoot, for which he switched to guitar. He and bassist Greg Walker left Blackfoot in 1971 to join Lynyrd Skynyrd and recorded an album in Muscle Shoals for which Medlocke wrote and sang two songs. They stayed with Skynyrd for about a year and then reformed Blackfoot in 1974, recording two albums at Muscle Shoals. Blackfoot released material on Island/Antilles, Epic, Atco, Nalli, and Wildcat Records.

Medlocke stayed with Blackfoot until 1996 when he rejoined Skynyrd, this time on guitar. He is also producing and writing music for a new lineup of Blackfoot, with whom he records and sometimes makes guest appearances. He lives in Ft. Myers.

Also see *Blackfoot; Lynyrd Skynyrd.*

Meekins, Buzzy

Born Thomas Meekins in North Carolina, this virtuoso bassist and vocalist moved to the Tampa area where he joined an early version of the Outlaws. He later relocated to Jacksonville and performed with several notable acts including Molly Hatchet, the Danny Joe Brown Band, the Artimus Pyle Band (APB), the Dickey Betts Band, Derek Trucks and Vassar Clements. Meekins died in Jacksonville in 2013 at age 63.

Meices

Formed in 1983 in Orange Park as Three Blind Mice, this modern-rock band was composed of vocalist John Hodges, guitarist Joe Reineke, guitarist Mark Zanandrea, bassist Bill Cohoon and drummer Jimmy Matthews. The group released an independent album, *Who Cut the Cheese?*, in 1988, recorded at Jim De-Vito's studio, Retrophonics.

The band relocated to San Francisco in 1990 and changed its name to the Mice, later to Meices (taken from the 1960s Hanna-Barbera cartoon series *Pixie and Dixie*). In 1993, the Meices released *Greatest Bible Stories Ever Told* on Seattle-based Empty Records and *Pissin' in the Sink* on Perth, Australia's Zero Hour Records. In 1994 the group released *Tastes Like Chicken* on External Records, owned by Dutch conglomerate PolyGram. The group's version of the Billy Idol song "Ready Steady, Go" was included in the 1995 Allan Moyle film *Empire Records* and one of their own songs, "Daddy's Gone to L.A.," in an episode of on MTV's *Beavis and Butthead.*

PolyGram transferred the band to London Records, where it released three singles and the album *Dirty Bird* in 1996. The album didn't sell well, and the group became a casualty of PolyGram's merger with Universal.

Also see *Reineke, Joe.*

Mehldau, Brad

Jazz pianist, born in Jacksonville, 1970. Studied classical piano from ages 6 to 14. The son of a physician, Mehldau moved to Connecticut with his family, where he attended high school. He later attended Berklee College of Music in Boston and the New School in New York. Was a member of the Joshua Redman Quartet and served as a sideman with Michael Brecker, Wayne Shorter, John Scofield, and Charles Lloyd. Formed own trio in 1995; signed to Warner Bros., later to Nonesuch. He is the recipient of numerous awards. Mehldau lives in Los Angeles and maintains a heavy touring schedule.

Midnight Creepers

Electric blues band based in Daytona Beach, formed by former Root Boy Slim & the Sex Change Band members Ernie Lancaster (guitar) and Bob Greenlee (bass), along with former Rootie Tootie Band harmonica player Mark Hodgson. Released several albums on Greenlee's King Snake label through various distributing labels, including Landslide, Ichiban and Select-O-Hits. Also served as backing band for the late Ace Moreland and other King Snake acts. Greenlee died of pancreatic cancer in February 2004. Lancaster too died of pancreatic cancer, ten years later.

Also see *Greenlee, Bob; Moreland, Ace; Hodgson, Mark.*

Mike Angelo & the Idols

Jacksonville punk-funk band, led by Michael Ray FitzGerald [author of this volume]. Other members included drummer (later Alias and Allen Collins Band vocalist) Jimmy Dougherty, "Filthy Phil" Price (bass and keyboards), Alan Close (bass and vocals), Andy King (bass and vocals), Scott Sisson (drums and vocals)

103

Billy Bowers (guitar and vocals), and John Kurzweg (guitar and keyboards).

In 1984 the group issued the cult favorite "F**k Everybody" on Atlanta's Hottrax label. *Rolling Stone* called the record "the furthest-out-there Georgia happening of the year [1985]." As a result of dance-club and juke-box exposure, the group was invited to perform at New York's Peppermint Lounge.

A sanitized version of the song was released by Rowdy Roddy Piper on Epic Records' *The Wrestling Album.* David Lee Roth negotiated its use for his aborted movie, *Crazy from the Heat.* The group followed with an album on FitzGerald's Low Overhead label, distributed nationally by Important Records, in 1987.

Also see *Chain of Fools; Dougherty, Jimmy; King, Andy; Sisson, Scott; FitzGerald, Michael Ray; Kurzweg, John.*

Miles, Floyd

A Daytona Beach soul-music stalwart and favorite performer of Duane and Gregg Allman's, Miles started out playing drums in nightclubs and juke joints with a group called the Universals. After that he was with the Untils. He recorded his first album in 1992, produced by King Snake Records' Bob Greenlee and released through Atlanta's Ichiban label. Miles recorded three more albums, one of which, *Goin Back to Daytona* (2002), featured guest appearances by Gregg Allman and Dickey Betts. He died in 2018 at age 74.

Miller, Harold ("Chip")

Percussionist for Capricorn Records act Cowboy in 1970s, later drummer with Oklahoma funk-rock outfit Smoot Mahootie and the Ace Moreland Band on King Snake Records. Also worked with Greg Baril and Derek Trucks. Died in Jacksonville in 2005 at age 53.

Also see *Cowboy; Boyer, Scott; Moreland, Ace.*

Minor, Laura

Tallahassee native who has also lived in Jacksonville. After earning an MFA in fiction from Sarah Lawrence, she moved to Gainesville in 2001, where she planned on earning a doctoral degree and writing a book.

There she met Jared Flamm of rock band Noah's Red Tattoo, who helped her turn her poems into songs. A demo led to a deal with Oakland, Calif.'s Hightone Records and a tour. Her debut album, *Salesman's Girl,* was recorded in New York with members from NRT and was released in July 2002 to critical acclaim. She has since released two albums.

Minor teaches poetry and songwriting at Pratt Institute in Brooklyn, N.Y., and is working on a collection of short stories. She is also working on her doctoral dissertation at Florida State University.

Mitchell, Jake

Born Arnold Rodriguez in Tampa in 1944, this R&B/soul singer began winning talent contests at an early age and by 1957 was invited to Chicago to record "Darling, Darling Baby," for Chicago's Chess Records (which was apparently not released). In 1959 he moved with his family to Gainesville, where he attended Lincoln High School and formed vocal group Little Jake and the Blenders, who were backed by the Pyramids, a group of white college students who included saxophonist Charles Steadham. In 1960 they were the first black group to perform at the University of Florida's Gator Growl. In 1965 Mitchell relocated to Detroit, where two years later under the name Jock Mitchell he recorded "Not a Chance in a Million" for Impact Records, which hit the UK Top 10 and is considered a classic in England's "northern soul" genre. After that he released several recordings on his own label. Mitchell returned to Tampa in 1992, where he eventually retired. In 2005 he relocated to Gainesville and reunited with Steadham to perform regularly under the name Little Jake & the Soul Searchers.

Mofro

See *J.J. Grey & Mofro*

Molly Hatchet

Jacksonville rock group formed in 1971 by guitarist-vocalist Dave Hlubek, who had earlier led local rock band Mynd Garden. Early members included Steve Holland (from Virginia Beach) on guitars, Tim Lindsey on bass, and drummer Skip Lake. Lindsey left in 1974, replaced by Banner Thomas; drummer Bruce Crump and third guitarist Duane Roland entered the picture in 1975. However, it was not until the addition of dynamic front man Danny Joe Brown in 1976 that the band found its winning formula.

Referred to talent manager Pat Armstrong by members of .38 Special, Hatchet signed a production deal with Armstrong's label, Mister Sunshine Records, distributed by Epic/CBS. Hatchet's sound was similar to Lynyrd Skynyrd's. In fact, Skynyrd singer Ronnie Van Zant was a fan and even supervised Hatchet's early demos, recorded at Jacksonville's The Warehouse studio.

The band's self-titled debut was released via Epic in 1978. After Skynyrd's sudden demise, Hatchet unexpectedly became the bearers of the southern-rock standard, earning themselves four platinum albums in the process.

Brown left in 1980 to form his own group, the Danny Joe Brown Band, also signed to Epic. He was replaced by LaGrange, Ga., vocalist Jimmy Farrar. Thomas left in 1981 and was replaced by bassist Riff West. Detroit native Ron Perry was brought in to replace Farrar in 1982. Perry even began writing for Hatchet, but his addition to the band was aborted by the sudden reappearance of Brown. Crump left in 1982 to join prominent Canadian band Streetheart and was replace by former Mother's Finest drummer B.B. Queen. Crump returned to the band for a short stint in 1984. That same year Holland left and was replaced by keyboardist John Galvin, a Detroit native who had worked with Brown's solo band.

Hatchet signed to Capitol in 1989 and went with German label SPV in 2003. Its most recent release was in 2012 on Brussels-based Mausoleum Records. Molly Hatchet is currently led by guitarist Bobby Ingram, who replaced Hlubek in 1987. Hlubek rejoined the band in 2005. Several former Hatchet members formed a tribute band called Gator Country (the name comes from a Molly Hatchet song). Singer Brown died in 2005. Founding member Duane Roland, also a member of Gator Country, died at his home in 2006. Original leader and guitarist Dave Hlubek died in 2017. Holland lives in Valdosta, Ga., the sole surviving original member. A new lineup of the band continues to tour, led by guitarist Ingram.

Also see *Brown, Danny Joe; Crump, Bruce; Ingram, Bobby; China Sky.*

Moore, Jackie

A Jacksonville native, Moore hooked up with Philadelphia DJ Jimmy Bishop in the late 1960s, who produced two unsuccessful singles for Shout and one for Scepter. She later teamed up with her cousin, Jacksonville native Dave Crawford and his production partner, Brad Shapiro, in Miami. This team hit pay dirt in 1970 on Atlantic with the single, "Precious, Precious" (No. 12 R&B, No. 30 pop), which she co-wrote with Crawford.

In 1975, she went with Shapiro's TK-distributed Kayvette label, where she scored several more R&B hits. In 1978 she and Shapiro went to Columbia with the single, "Personally," which was covered by Karla Bonoff. Moore released one more album on the independent Sunnyview label in 1985. She lives in Ft. Lauderdale, where her husband, Cal Hopkins, is pastor at Williams Memorial CME Church.

Also see *Crawford, Dave.*

Moreland, Ace

A native of Monkey Island, Okla., Moreland came to Jacksonville in 1987 as a member of R&B-rock band Smoot Mahuti, which included former Cowboy percussionist Chip Miller on drums. Moreland quickly attracted the attention of King Snake Records owner/producer Bob Greenlee, with whom he recorded five albums. Moreland lived in Sanford and toured nationwide and in Europe, until his death from stomach cancer in February 2003.

Also see *Greenlee, Bob; Midnight Creepers*.

Morrison, Jim

Born in 1943 in Melbourne, the son of a high-ranking naval officer, Morrison was mostly raised near Orlando and in Alexan-

dria, Va. He attended college at Florida State University in Tallahassee before transferring to UCLA film school. Morrison met keyboardist Ray Manzarek on the beach in Venice, Ca., where the two co-founded legendary rock group the Doors. He died in Paris in 1971.

Morse, Steve

Born in Hamilton, Ohio, in 1954, this virtuoso guitarist attended the University of Miami as a music major, where he became a founding member of a group that evolved into the famed Dixie Dregs, who signed to Capricorn Records in 1976 and to Arista in 1979. In the 1980s Morse joined progressive rockers Kansas and since 1995 has performed with Deep Purple. He lives in Ocala.

Mosely, Pete

Founding member of Jacksonville skate-punk band Inspection 12; left that group in

2002 to join multiplatinum rockers Yellowcard as bassist. After leaving Yellowcard in 2007, Mosley studied music at Jacksonville University and worked with alternative-country group Canary in the Coal Mine.

Also see *Inspection 12; Yellowcard.*

Mouse & the Boys

Formerly known as the Deep Six, these teenage white-soul sensations from Jacksonville featured lead vocalist Maurice ("Mouse") Samples along with guitarist Larry Dreggors, bassist Billy Harden, keyboardist Lester Langdale and drummer Ted Vaughn. With the 1967 addition of horn players Frank Crumpler and Jimmy Moore on trumpets along with saxophonist David Brown (who had played bass in the Bitter Ind and would go on to do the same in several other prominent bands), the band became Mouse, the Boys and Brass. Singer Pete Rowland came in on drums when Vaughn got sent to Vietnam in 1968.

Managed by Sidney Drashin, in 1968 the group scored a regional hit, "Love Is Free" backed with the psychedelic "Excedrin

Headache No. 69"—which sounds like a cross between Blue Cheer and the Rascals —on Rubiyat Records. The band followed with "Dancin' to the Beat," (No. 103, 1968) on Shelby Singleton's Nashville-based SSS International label.

In 1970, the group re-formed as M.O.U.S.E. and recorded for Bell Records, distributed by RCA. In 1972 Samples retreated from pop music to form Christian-rock group Israel, later becoming a minister. Drummer Pete Rowland took over as singer, renaming the group the Boys. Rowland later formed a group called Music Machine (not to be confused with the Los Angeles band of the same name). The original group staged reunions in 2005 and 2007.

Also see *Rowland, Pete.*

Mudcrutch

Gainesville band featuring vocalist Tom Lenahan and bassist-vocalist Tom Petty, included future Heartbreakers Benmont Tench on keyboards and guitarist Mike Campbell along with Gainesville guitarist

Tom Leadon (brother of Eagles member Bernie Leadon) and drummer Randall Marsh. When Lenahan left in 1973, Petty added guitarist-vocalist Danny Roberts, when the two traded lead-vocal roles, each playing bass while the other played guitar and sang lead.

Booked by Macon-based Pat Armstrong & Associates, Mudcrutch began performing throughout the Florida-Georgia region. In 1974 Petty and Roberts, armed with a handful of demos of songs Petty had written, traveled to Los Angeles, where they garnered interest from several labels, including Leon Russell and Denny Cordell's ABC-distributed label, Shelter Records.

Tampa bassist Charlie Souza was brought on board so Petty could stop playing bass and concentrate on singing. Producer Cordell now demanded that the focus be on Petty (and his songs), though Petty and Roberts had been co-lead singers up to this point. Petty quit the group when Roberts and Souza insisted their songs be included on the group's debut album. Petty, however, was retained by Cordell as a solo act and began recording with session players, one of whom was Al Kooper on keyboards.

Petty formed the Heartbreakers with former Mudcrutch members Tench and Campbell, adding Gainesville musicians Ron Blair on bass and drummer Stan Lynch, who had been hanging out in Los Angeles for a year or more.

Mudcrutch re-formed in 2007, signing with Reprise Records. The band released another album in 2016, followed by another tour. Petty died in 2017 of an overdose.

Also see *Tom Petty & the Heartbreakers; Armstrong, Pat; Roberts, Danny; Souza, Charlie.*

Mystics

Rock group from Tallahassee (not to be confused with the doo-wop group of the same name from Brooklyn, N.Y.), their cover of the Night Owls' 1962 R&B hit "Ooh Poo Pah Doo" made a small splash on Black Cat Records in 1965.

Nasta, Ken

A mainstay on the Jacksonville scene since the early 1980s, this hard-hitting drummer has worked with such national acts as Royal Trux (Virgin, Drag City), Greg Garing (Revolution), Shinedown (Atlantic), Start Trouble (Columbia), the Fenwicks (Guitar Recordings), Karen Abrahams (Mozo City), Chain of Fools (Rimshot), the Perpetrators (Rimshot) and King Eddie (Society Hill). Currently performs with Jacksonville reggae band the Dubmasters (featuring King Eddie) and with St. Augustine singer-songwriter Chuck Nash.

Also see *Fenwicks; King Eddie; Chain of Fools; Abrahams, Karen; Perpetrators; Start Trouble; Shinedown.*

95 South

Orlando bass-music group featuring Nathaniel Orange (a.k.a. C.C. Lemonhead) and Johnny (Jay) McGowan, formerly of Jacksonville's Chill Deal. As 95 South, the duo had an immense hit with "Whoot, There It Is" on Atlanta's Ichiban Records. Later recorded for Orlando-based Rip-It Records.

Also see *Quad City DJs; Chill Deal; Mc-Gowan, Johnny; Lemonhead, C.C.*

Nightcrawlers

Led by Charlie Conlon and Sylvan Wells, this teen-pop band was part of a close-knit 1960s Daytona scene that would also spawn the Allman Joys. After receiving airplay on Daytona's WROD and later on Jacksonville's 50,000-watt powerhouse WAPE, the band's second single, "Little Black Egg," got picked up by Kapp Records (a division of Decca/MCA) for national distribution, whereupon it went to No. 85 in *Billboard*'s Hot 100. The song went on to become a "garage-rock" classic and was later covered by the Cars.

After many years as a Daytona Beach attorney and mediator, Wells retired and now lives in Halifax, Mass., where he builds guitars.

Nix, Robert

Born in Blakely, Ga., in 1945, drummer Nix moved to Jacksonville with his family, where he graduated from Paxon High School in 1962 (other famous Paxon alums include Hoyt Axton and J.R. Cobb). As a teenager, he joined an early edition of the Classics, which included J.R. Cobb.

He later worked with Susan and the Dynamics, who landed a two-single deal on Dot Records thanks to Atlanta impresario Bill Lowery. Nix was working with the Dynamics in 1964 at the Golden Gate Lounge on Cassat Ave. when he was recruited by Roy Orbison; his next gig would be opening for the Beatles on a sold-out British tour with Orbison's backing group, the Candymen (Nix, however, did not play on Orbison's recordings; the drummer on "Oh, Pretty Woman" was Nashville session musician Buddy Harman).

In 1966, the Candymen landed their own deal on MGM (and later ABC) and split off from Orbison. Nix left the Candymen around 1968 to pursue a career as a session player and songwriter. He submitted the song "Cherry Hill Park," which he co-wrote with fellow Candyman Billy Gilmore, to Billy Joe Royal, by way of Buddy Buie, who was part of Lowery's

110

vast entertainment empire. "Cherry Hill Park" charted at No. 15 in 1969.

Nix became a prominent Atlanta-based session musician—he played on most of the Classics IV's hits as well as on Lynyrd Skynyrd's "Tuesday's Gone" and a couple of Al Kooper solo albums. In 1970 the studio ensemble he had been working with added a singer, Rodney Justo, and became the Atlanta Rhythm Section and signed to MCA.

Nix left ARS in 1979 and was later appointed head of A&R for Macon-based Capricorn Records. He signed Jacksonville punk-rockers the Attitudes just as Capricorn was folding in 1987. Nix also produced Rick Christian's debut album, recorded at Butch Trucks' Tallahassee studio in 1990, released as a joint venture between Capricorn and Columbia.

He spent several years working with Memphis-based singer Alison Heafner, whom he married in 2008. He later formed short-lived supergroup Deep South with former Skynyrd drummer Artimus Pyle and Wet Willie singer Jimmy Hall. Nix died suddenly in Batesville, Miss., in 2012 at age 67 of complications from surgery.

Also see *Susan & the Dynamics; Classics IV; Cobb, James; Attitudes; Buie, Buddy.*

Oakley, Berry

Originally from the Chicago area, Oakley was playing in a local band that opened for Tommy Roe when he heard that Roe needed a bassist. Oakley had never played bass but landed the gig nonetheless and moved with Roe's band, the Roemans, to the Clearwater area. While there he met Bradenton guitarist Dickey Betts, and the two formed the Soul Children, later called the Blues Messengers.

In 1968, the Blues Messengers were offered a house gig at a Jacksonville club called the Scene, whereupon the group relocated and changed its name to the Second Coming—the name was club owner Leonard Renzler's idea; he thought Oakley looked remarkably like Jesus. Thanks to a series of free outdoor concerts, the Second Coming became Jacksonville's hottest band.

A year later, Duane Allman, who already had a record deal, came to Jacksonville to recruit Oakley for his new band; Oakley joined on the condition that Betts be included as well. The pair then became founding members of the Allman Brothers Band.

The newly formed group left Jacksonville for Macon, where Oakley was killed in a 1972 in a motorcycle accident—only blocks from the spot where Duane Allman had been killed a year earlier.

Also see *Allman Bros. Band; Second Coming.*

O'Malley, Kevin

Real-estate agent in Atlantic Beach who managed St. Augustine band Spider Monkey and Orlando pop-rock group Tabitha's Secret. Atlantic Records' regional promo rep Kim Stephens became interested in Spider Monkey, who was selling out venues all over the Southeast. Stephens came to see Spider Monkey at the Alachua County Music Harvest, and Tabitha's Secret happened to be on the same show. O'Malley's brother, John, had financed a set of demos for Tabitha's Secret. Stephens brought these to Atlantic Records exec Jason Flom, who attended a performance at Potbelly's in Tallahassee (where aspiring singer Scott Stapp was a dishwasher). Flom agreed to sign the group. However, before the deal was done, singer Rob Thomas fired O'Malley and two other members of the band, signed with Atlanta

producer Matt Serletic's label, Melisma Records, who then licensed the act to Atlantic under the name Matchbox Twenty, whose debut album on Melisma/Atlantic, *Yourself or Someone Like You*, went on to sell 15 million units.

Also see *Spider Monkey*.

Oracle

Jacksonville heavy-metal band, originally called Prodigy. Signed to Germany's Massacre Records in 1993 where the group released one album, *As Darkness Reigns*. Drummer Brent Smedley, a UNF grad, later joined Tampa metal band Iced Earth.

Orange, Walter ("Clyde")

Born in Jacksonville in 1947, Orange began playing drums and singing while attending Northwestern High School, forming his own group, the J-Notes.

Orange was a student at Alabama State College in Montgomery, where he majored in music, when he first heard the Tuskeegee-based Commodores, who included saxophonist-vocalist Lionel Richie. The Commodores recruited Orange in 1970 as a replacement drummer and co-lead vocalist and would go on to become one of the biggest names in late-1970s R&B. Orange's voice is featured on many of the group's hits, including the No. 1 single (and bar-band standard) "Brick House."

Orange lives in Coral Springs. He leads the Commodores, who continue to maintain a heavy touring schedule.

Owings, Mike

Jacksonville guitarist who has worked with the Allen Collins Band (1983-84), Molly Hatchet (1999-2002), and David Allen Coe; now with Jacksonville southern-rock group Shanytown.

Painter, Rich

Son of Jacksonville Christian-rocker Rick Painter, Rich Painter formed teen-pop band Rich Creamy Paint at age 19. His uncle, John Painter, of Nashville-based husband-and-wife duo Fleming & John, produced RCP's debut album, on which young Rich played all the instruments himself. John Painter landed RCP a deal with Disney-owned Hollywood Records in 1999. Painter expanded the group to a quartet for touring.

Not much has happened for the group after signing, however. Painter downsized the act, making RCP a duo with his wife Mindy on keyboards. After spending time in Nashville, Rich and Mindy moved back to Jacksonville, where Painter is a licensed marriage and family therapist.

Pantfoeder, Dorman

A veteran drummer and vocalist on the Jacksonville scene, in 2005 Pantfoeder replaced the drummer in Love Arcade, a band signed to Atlantic Records by A&R man Danny Wimmer. After Love Arcade dissolved, Pantfoeder and Jacksonville guitarist Paul Phillips were recruited by Los Angeles-based metal band Operator, who released one marginally successful album on Atlantic in 2007.

Also see *Phillips, Paul; Wimmer, Danny.*

Parker, Bill

Sound man from St. Augustine; currently front-of-house mixer for Bad Company.

Parks, Walter

Jacksonville native, classically trained on viola, studied with guitar instructor Robert Conti, Parks is also an accomplished bassist. Parks worked with a couple of high-society and jazz groups before forming new-wavish rock band Dear John with drummer Ken Nasta in the late 1980s. Parks later formed the Nudes with cellist/vocalist Stephanie Winters. The duo relocated to New York for several years, where

Parks was spotted by singer Richie Havens and recruited as his lead guitarist in 2001. He spent ten years with Havens, with whom he performed at Carnegie Hall and Madison Square Garden.

In 2010, inspired by J.J. Grey, Parks formed Swamp Cabbage, a southern-funk roots-rock trio signed to New York-based ZOHO Roots Records. St. Augustine's Jim DeVito is bassist for that group, which maintains an active touring schedule. Swamp Cabbage's songs, written primarily by Parks, have appeared in many television series such as *American Guns, When Patrick Met Kylie, My Big Redneck Wedding, Man vs. Food, Emeril Green, Extreme Pig Outs, Gene Simmons' Family Jewels, Roadtrip Nation, Samantha Brown Passport, Amazing Wedding Cakes* and *Chasing Classic Cars*. Parks lives in Savannah.

Also see *Swamp Cabbage; Nasta, Ken; DeVito, Jim; Conti, Robert.*

Parsley, Marcus

Trumpeter/vocalist Parsley left Jacksonville for New York City in 2002, where he joined the Lostin Harris Trio, which performed a lengthy stint at the Carlyle Hotel. He has since toured and recorded with Charles Bradley, Ian Hendrickson-Smith, soul revivalists Sharon Jones and the Dap-Kings and others. In 2014 Parsley released his debut recording, *Sunday Strollin'* on Rondette Jazz Records. He also tours with Jacksonville's JJ Grey and Mofro.

Also see *Mofro.*

Parsons, Gram

Winterhaven native, raised in Waycross, Ga., where his family owned a cardboard-box factory, an adjunct operation to their lucrative Florida orange groves. After moving back to Winterhaven in the early 1960s, Parsons played in a series of teen bands including the Rumors, alongside Kent LaVoie (aka Lobo) and Jim Stafford.

Parsons graduated from Jacksonville's prestigious Bolles School in 1965, where he led local folk-rock group the Shilos, who released two singles on Columbia. He also appeared on a Sunday-night folk-music program on WJAX.

While attending Harvard University Parsons formed the International Submarine Band and bolted for Greenwich Village. Then he leapt to Los Angeles, where the ISB recorded one album on Lee Hazlewood's LHI Records, now considered a cult classic.

Parsons left the ISB after meeting Byrds member Chris Hillman and briefly became a member of the Byrds; he performed on and wrote two songs for their 1968 album *Sweetheart of the Rodeo*. He soon quit, however, refusing to perform in apartheid South Africa. He then began hanging out in Europe with Keith Richards until he was chased off by Mick Jagger.

Parsons returned to L.A. and formed the Flying Burrito Brothers with Hillman and former Hearts & Flowers member (and former Gainesville resident) Bernie Leadon. The Burritos would pioneer the California country-rock sound, which became a huge influence on acts like the Eagles, Poco, Firefall, etc., as well as on the Stones. Parsons is now recognized as the father of alternative-country music. Many area musicians, including former Burrito Brothers founding member Bernie Leadon, have participated in Waycross' annual Gram Parsons Guitar Pull and Tribute Festival.

Also see *Shilos; Lobo; Leadon, Bernie.*

Parsons, Longineau, Jr.

Jazz trumpeter and vocalist from Jacksonville; has worked with Nat Adderley, Cab Calloway, Doc Severinsen, Herbie Mann, Archie Shepp Sun Ra, Branford Marsalis and appeared in the musical production *Satchmo.* In 1999, San Francisco label Luv N' Haight Records released a retrospective of Parsons' work from 1980 to 1999.

Parsons is an associate professor and head of trumpet studies at Florida A&M University in Tallahassee. His son, L.P. III, was drummer and founding member of multi-platinum punk band Yellowcard.

Parsons, Longineau ("L.P.") III

Son of trumpeter Longineau Parsons, started off playing in his father's jazz group. In 1997 LP III became the original drummer for Jacksonville skate-punk band Yellowcard, which enjoyed a brief but lucrative stint on Capitol Records in 2003.

Parsons left Yellowcard in 2014, whereupon he and former bandmate Harper

115

formed rock group This Legend. He also reunited with the original members of Yellowcard under the name Where We Stand, having lost the rights to the band's name to second-generation singer Ryan Key. Parsons lives in Hollywood, Calif.

Also see *Yellowcard.*

Perry, Ron

This Detroit singer and guitarist was spotted by Molly Hatchet keyboardist and fellow Detroit native John Galvin and recruited to replace Hatchet's departing singer, Jimmy Farrar, in 1987. Perry wrote one song for Hatchet, "Take Miss Lucy Home," which appeared on the band's 1989 Capitol album, *Lightning Strikes Twice*. However, Perry was displaced by the return of Hatchet's original vocalist, Danny Joe Brown.

Perry later became lead singer for China Sky, which released one album on PARC Records (owned by manager Pat Armstrong and distributed by Epic) in 1988. Perry later worked with funk-rockers Chain of Fools, acoustic trio Cruel Shoes, and the Perpetrators. He also operated Alan Audio recording studio in Jacksonville.

In the 1990s Perry led his own band, the Ron Perry Connection, with one album on nationally distributed Rimshot Records. He and former China Sky bassist Richard Smith re-formed that band in 2014 and snagged a deal with British label Escape

Music. Perry spends a lot of time in Detroit, where he is co-owner of an audio-video production company but maintains a home in Jacksonville.

Also see *China Sky; Molly Hatchet; Chain of Fools; Armstrong, Pat; Perpetrators.*

Perpetrators

This anonymous studio-only band recorded one album, *Porno Rock*, on Jacksonville-based Rimshot Records. The idea came from Attitude Records' owner, Jeff Cohen, who imagined "a rock version of 2 Live Crew." However, with its 1980s hair-metal aesthetic, the group sounded more like an X-rated version of Spinal Tap. The Perps included vocalist Hugh Jorgen, guitarist/bassist/ keyboardist Peter Fitzperfect, drummer Woody P. Ness and guitarist Mike Hunt. Shock-rock radio personality Howard Stern has played cuts from the album on his Sirius Radio show.

Peterson, Bobby

Keyboardist with Jacksonville's Susan & the Dynamics, a group fronted by singer Susan Robey, which included drummer Robert Nix. The Dynamics hooked up with Atlanta's Lowery Organization in 1963 and recorded a couple of unsuccessful singles for Dot Records.

A year later Nix and Peterson would join Roy Orbison's backup band, the Candymen, who also released their own albums (mostly on ABC Records). Peterson left the Candymen to join Rick Derringer's group, the McCoys, in 1965 and was re-placed by Dean Daughtry.

In 1968 Peterson reunited with Robey to form R&B-rock band December's Children, managed by the Lowery organization. That group fizzled after issuing three unsuccessful singles on Los Angeles-based World Pacific/Imperial Records.

Struggling with mental illness, Peterson ended up homeless in Gainesville, where he was struck and killed by an automobile in 1993. He was 47.

Also see *Susan & the Dynamics; December's Children; Nix, Robert.*

Pettis, Pierce

A native of Fort Payne, Ala., Pettis made a name for himself as a staff songwriter at Muscle Shoals Sound in Sheffield, Ala. From 1993 to 2000 he served as a staff writer for PolyGram in Nashville. His big break came in 1979 when Joan Baez recorded his "Song at the End of the Movie."

After releasing an album independently in 1987, Pettis landed a deal with High Street Records, a division of Windham Hill Records, in 1991 (now owned by Sony Music), where he released three albums. Pettis signed with Nashville-based Compass Records in 1996.

His songs have been covered by several artists including Art Garfunkel, Dion, and Joan Baez, but Pettis struck the mother-lode when "You Move Me" was released by Garth Brooks on his No. 1 album *Sevens* in 1997.

Pettis lived for several years in Tallahassee but now divides his time between Atlanta and Nashville.

Petty, Joe Dan

Bassist with Bradenton band the Jokers, led by Dickey Betts. Petty later became a member of Mac Doss' group the Thunderbeats alongside guitarist Larry Reinhardt. Both the Jokers and the Thunderbeats relocated to Jacksonville in the mid-1960s to perform at nightclubs such as the Normandy Club, where they became regulars. When Betts joined the Allman Brothers Band and moved to Macon, Petty went with him as a roadie for the ABB.

In 1972, Petty decided to form his own group, Grinderswitch, based in Warner-Robins, Ga. He recruited Jacksonville guitarist-vocalist Dru Lombar, and the band soon signed with Capricorn Records, where it recorded three albums. Later recorded one album for Atco and one for Atlanta-based Robox Records. After the group's dissolution, Petty went back to the ABB as Betts' guitar tech. Lombar returned to Jacksonville and formed R&B group Doctor Hector and the Groove Injectors. Petty was killed in a plane crash in 2015.

Also see *Betts, Dickey; Doss, Mack; Reinhart, Larry; Lombar, Dru.*

Petty, Tom & the Heartbreakers

Pop-rock legends from Gainesville, originally known as Mudcrutch. Toured the Southeast for Pat Armstrong's Macon-based booking agency. Mudcrutch ventured out to Los Angeles in 1974 and landed a deal with Denny Cordell and Leon Russell's Shelter label, which was distributed by ABC (ABC's music operation was later absorbed by MCA, where Petty would remain until switching to Warner Brothers in 1994).

However, Mudcrutch was dropped by Shelter, who proceeded to sign Petty as a solo act. Petty began recording with session players but decided he preferred the cohesion of a real band. About a year later, he would reunite with former Mudcrutch members keyboardist Benmont Tench and guitarist Mike Campbell, adding Gainesville drummer Stan Lynch and Gainesville bassist Ron Blair, who both just happened to be living in Los Angeles, and formed the Heartbreakers. Former Road Turkey guitarist Marty Jourard was a member of the early lineup but was jettisoned when Petty decided three guitars was too many (Jourard would go on to form the Motels with singer Martha Davis).

In 2007 Petty, Tench and Campbell reformed Mudcrutch along with original members Randall Marsh (drums) and Tom Leadon (guitar), brother of former Eagles member Bernie Leadon. Mudcrutch did another album and tour in 2016.

With the Heartbreakers, touring behind Bob Dylan, performing duos with Stevie Nicks, as a member of supergroup the Traveling Wilburys (with Bob Dylan, George Harrison, Roy Orbison and Jeff Lynne) or as a solo act, Petty had one of the longest and most successful careers in rock, having sold more than 80 million albums. He died in Los Angeles in 2017 of an overdose. He was 66.

Also see *Mudcrutch; Lynch, Stan; Road Turkey; Campbell, Mike; Jourard, Jeff.*

Phelps, Arthur

See *Blake, Blind.*

Philip, John

See *Kurzweg, John.*

Phillips, Paul

Formerly with Jacksonville punk-ska band Happy Hour, this Jacksonville guitarist got a call in 2001 from Fred Durst inviting him to audition for Durst's proteges Puddle of Mudd. Leaving PoM in 2007, Phillips joined Los Angeles-based metal band Operator, who released the album *Soulcrusher* on Atlantic Records that same year. He has also performed with Damien Starkey's rock band Society Red alongside rhythm guitarist Adam Latiff, formerly of PoM. Phillips lives in Jacksonville.

Phoenix, River

See *Aleka's Attic.*

Pickens, Earle

Originally from Oak Ridge, Tenn., this keyboardist joined frat-party combo the Rhondells (not to be confused with Virginia Beach outfit Bill Deal & the Rhondels) in 1961 while a student at Lafayette College in Easton, Pa., and began touring the East Coast.

While performing in Atlantic City, the group was spotted by Nathan Weiss, a US attorney for Beatles manager Brian Epstein. Epstein signed the group, changing its name to the Cyrkle and landing a deal with Columbia Records. The Cyrkle had two hit singles, "Red Rubber Ball" (written by Paul Simon), which went to No. 2 on *Billboard*'s Top 100 in mid-1966, and "Turn-Down Day," which got as far as No. 16 a year later. The group toured as an opening act for the Beatles before disbanding in 1967, whereupon Pickens returned to college and medical school and became a surgeon. He moved to Gainesville in the mid-1970s, where he still resides. He is retired.

Pickering, Nigel

Born Frederick Ray Pickering in Pontiac, Mich., in 1930, this guitarist and vocalist gravitated to Chicago in the late 1950s, where he joined the Folksters, a group that included bassist Kenny Hodges.

In 1965 Pickering met folksinger Elaine "Spanky" McFarlane and formed folk-pop quintet Spanky & Our Gang, signing with Mercury Records a year later. Spanky & Our Gang released three albums and two hit singles on Mercury, most notably "Sunday Will Never Be the Same," which hit No. 9 on *Billboard*'s Hot 100 in 1967 and sold more than a million copies, and "I'd Like to Get to Know You" (No. 17) the following year. Pickering purportedly appeared in two ill-fated motion pictures.

In 1975, Pickering and McFarlane reformed Spanky & Our Gang, signing with Epic, disbanding for good in 1980 (in 1982 McFarlane replaced Cass Elliott in a reincarnated version of the Mamas & Papas).

Pickering and Hodges retired to St. Augustine, where Pickering died in 2011 after a long struggle with liver cancer. Hodges died two years later.

Also see *Hodges, Kenny*.

Pinske, Mark

Born in Arlington, Minn., Pinske moved with his parents to Gainesville in 1966, where he attended University of Florida, studying electrical engineering and playing bass in local bands. This led to an interest in live sound as well as recording.

After graduating he worked for sound companies like ShowCo and Clair Brothers and manned the board for B.B. King, Weather Report, Melissa Manchester and others.

In the late 1970s, Pinske moved to Los Angeles, where he became a sound engineer for Frank Zappa, both live and in the studio. Pinske worked with Zappa from 1980 to '87, whereupon he returned to Gainesville to build Pro Media Services, now Skylab Recording.

Pinske has worked with such acts as Axe (MCA Records) Atheist (Metal Blade Records), Malevolent Creation (Roadrun-

ner Records), Assault & Battery (Attitude Records), Stan Bush (Intercord Records), Demented Ted (Pavement Music) and others. He has returned to Los Angeles.

Piscopo, Joe

Originally from Passaic, N.J; attended Jones College in Jacksonville during early 1970s, became a DJ at several local stations, including WIVY (Y-103).

Later became a standup comic; went on to co-star in NBC's *Saturday Night Live*. Recorded an album of novelty songs, starred in several films. In 1997, Piscopo appeared in the Broadway production of *Grease*.

In 2014 he resumed his career as a radio personality, hosting *Piscopo in the Morning* on NYC's WNYM-AM.

Pitman, Jimmy

Born in Washington, D.C., in 1946, this Jacksonville-bred guitarist and singer is a graduate of Paxon High. Pitman worked briefly with Daytona's the Nightcrawlers of "Little Black Egg" fame.

While that band was opening for the Beach Boys in 1965, Pitman met manager Murry Wilson, who invited Pitman to come to Los Angeles. Pitman took Wilson up on the offer, hitch-hiking west to hang out and hope for the best. Before long he had run into fellow Daytona denizens Gregg and Duane Allman and joined their group the Hourglass, who was already signed to Liberty Records.

Nothing much was happening for that band, so Pitman accepted an offer to join a reconstituted version of Strawberry Alarm Clock, a fading psychedelic-rock band that had scored five chart hits, including the number-one "Incense and Peppermints" (1967). Pitman became SAC's lead singer/guitarist in 1969, whereupon guitarist Ed King (later with Lynyrd Skynyrd) switched to bass.

A year later Pitman left to join Los Angeles rock band Jumbo, which signed to Lou Adler's Ode label, where it recorded an album that was never released. In the mid-1970s Pitman returned to Jacksonville and managed a Jacksonville Beach bar owned by former Comic Book Club owner Art Eisen.

In 1978, Pitman again headed west, settling for a time in Salt Lake City, where he formed his own record label. He returned to Jacksonville to become an auto salesman. He formed blues-rock band Big Bad Wolf in 2007. He is retired but performs occasionally and continues to write.

Ponder, Walter, Jr.

Born 1942 in Washington County, Ga., this virtuoso gospel singer ran his own music ministry while an employee with the City of Jacksonville. He was perhaps best known for hosting his own cable-access television show for more than 20 years. Ponder released several recordings with producer-engineer Bill Ande at Fred Frank's label, Coast to Coast. He died in 2010.

Price, Phil

Born 1949 in Jacksonville, graduate of Andrew Jackson High. Started out as a roadie for the Classics IV, whose lead singer, Dennis Yost, also graduated from Jackson. Price later led several bands, one of which featured singer Pete Rowland, formerly of Mouse and the Boys; another featured lead vocalist Jimmy Dougherty, who would go on to sing with Alias and the Allen Collins Band; yet another featured singer Michael Ray FitzGerald, who with Price would form punk-funkers Mike Angelo & the Idols. Price and FitzGerald also worked in a short-lived 1985 incarnation of the Allen Collins Band. He and Dougherty, along with guitarist Erik Lundgren and drummer Robbie Morris from the Johnny Van Zant Band, would later form Southern Rock Superstars. Price died in 2017 from cardiac arrest.

Also see *Allen Collins Band; Classics IV; Dougherty, Jimmy; Lundgren, Erik; Mike Angelo & the Idols; Rowland, Pete.*

Price, Richard

From Ft. Myers, classically trained cellist, bass guitarist for the Load, also member of the New Second Coming, replacing bassist Berry Oakley. Both these bands featured guitarist/vocalist Larry Reinhardt and were based in Jacksonville, where they were managed by Allen Facemire.

Later moved to Nashville and worked with Vassar Clements, the Outlaws, Billy Joe Shaver, Lucinda Williams, and the North Mississippi Allstars. While in Nashville, he worked with former Second Coming bandmate Reese Wynans in a group called Ultra Fix.

In 2001 he moved to Sarasota and reunited with Reinhardt in a band called Blue Swamp. Still performs occasionally.

Printup, Marcus

Jazz trumpeter from Conyers, Ga.; studied at Jacksonville's UNF jazz program and played locally. There he met world-renowned pianist Marcus Roberts, who introduced him to Wynton Marsalis. Printup moved to NYC in 1993, where became member of the Marsalis-led Lincoln Center Orchestra, which led to his signing by Blue Note/EMI in 1995. He has since recorded for Nagel Heyer Records and Steeplechase. He and his wife live in New Jersey.

Also see *Bales, Kevin; Roberts, Marcus.*

Purify, James and Bobby

R&B-gospel-soul duo consisting of James Lee Purify from Pensacola and his cousin, Robert Lee Dickey from Tallahassee, who was replaced by Ben Moore from Atlanta. The duo had an R&B smash in 1966 on Bell Records with "I'm Your Puppet," produced by Dan Penn at FAME studio in Muscle Shoals. Executive producer was Pensacola radio-station owner "Papa Don" Schroder. The group scored one or two other minor hits, including 1967's "Let Love Come Between Us," disbanding in

1978 after signing with Casablanca Records.

Pyle, Artimus

Drummer for Lynyrd Skynyrd from 1975 to 1977, replacing Bob Burns. Also played with the group from 1987 to 1991. In total he worked on seven Skynyrd albums. Currently lives in Asheville, N.C., where he leads the Artimus Pyle Band.

Also see *APB; Lynyrd Skynyrd; Baril, Greg; Nix, Robert.*

Quad City DJs

Dance/rap outfit featuring Nathaniel Orange (aka CC Lemonhead) and Jay (Johnny) McGowan, formerly of Jacksonville's Chill Deal and 95 South. Scored a massive hit in 1996 with "Come on and Ride" on Big Beat/Atlantic, which hit No. 3 on *Billboard'*s Hot 100.

Also see *McGowan, Johnny; Orange, Nathaniel; Lemonhead, C.C.; Chill Deal; 95 South.*

Rapp, Barry

Keyboardist with Henry Paul Band (Atlantic); co wrote "Grey Ghost," the title track of the band' s biggest-selling album with more than 250,000 copies sold.

After leaving the HPB, Rapp moved to Jacksonville, where he formed One Eyed Jacks with Robert Nix, former member of the Atlanta Rhythm Section. He later joined Barry Lee Harwood's band Time-Piece alongside former (and current) Molly Hatchet bassist Tim Lindsey, former Exile drummer Bobby Johns, and guitarist Steve McNally.

In 2002 he joined Tampa-based Ghost Riders led by guitarist-vocalist Steve Grisham, bassist Phil Stokes, Jacksonville guitarist Jim Sexton and drummer Pug Baker. Ghost Riders are signed to German label Phoenix Records.

Rapp lives near Orange Park and is married to the former Theresa Gaines, widow of Lynyrd Skynyrd guitarist-vocalist Steve Gaines.

Also see *Nix, Robert; Lindsey, Tim; Harwood, Barry Lee; Johns, Bobby.*

Ravens

Seminal doo-wop group led by bass singer Jimmie Ricks. Ricks was born in Adrien, Ga., in 1924 and moved to Jacksonville with his family as a youth. At 21, he relocated to New York, where he became a singing waiter and in 1946 formed the Ravens. They soon signed with the small Hub label and a year later moved to the more mainstream National Records and later recorded for Columbia, Okeh, Mercury and Jubilee. Ricks left the group for a solo career in 1956.

Also see *Ricks, Jimmy.*

Red Jumpsuit Apparatus

Christian-rock band founded by Middleburg High schoolmates Duke Kitchens and Ronnie Winter in 2001. Lineup also included Joey Westwood and Jon Wilkes. Started out playing numerous dates at Jackrabbit's in Jacksonville.

After a couple of independent releases, the band attracted the attention of Virgin Records and was signed in 2005. The group's debut album, *Don't You Fake It*, was released in 2006 and was certified platinum (sales of 1 million or more). The band's song "Face Down" was included in the 2007 movie *Georgia Rule* and its song "False Pretense" was included in 2008's *Never Back Down*. The group's second Virgin release, *Lonely Road* (2009), reached No. 14 in *Billboard*'s Top 200 albums.

The band parted ways with Virgin in 2011 but has maintained a strong grassroots following through social media and released its fourth album independently. RJA maintains a busy touring schedule.

Reeves, Glenn

This radio DJ and country singer from Northwest Texas met Mae Axton while she was on a promo tour. In her autobiography (of sorts) Axton wrote that she helped land Reeves a slot at Jacksonville's country station WPDQ. Reeves also sang on Axton's demo of "Heartbreak Hotel," a song she claimed to have co-written with pedal-steel player Tommy Durden. Axton brought the song to Elvis Presley, who imitated Reeves' demo performance—it was Presley imitating Reeves imitating Presley, said publisher Buddy Killen.

Reeves scored his own 1957 single, "She Traded Her Pigtails for a Toni," on Decca. He later became a prominent Jacksonville concert and events promoter with Mellojean, Inc. Reeves died in 1998 at 67 after a battle with cancer.

Also see *Axton, Mae.*

Rein Sanction

Formed in Jacksonville in the late 1980s by brothers Mark and Brannon Gentry along with bassist Ian Chase, this super-heavy trio signed to Seattle's Sub Pop Records in 1991. Sub Pop issued two albums by the band, which broke up in 1993.

Rein Sanction regrouped in 1996 with an album on Souldier Records and a tour. Although less than successful, Rein Sanction is still considered an important band. The group released a single on Seattle-based Flotation Records in 2006, followed by a set of live recordings in 2009, released independently, and a collection of unreleased material in 2010 under the banner Mark Gentry and Rein Sanction. Chase, who was replaced by bassist Darren Bedford in the mid-1990s, owns the Fox Restaurant in Jacksonville's Avondale district.

Reineke, Joe

Guitarist-vocalist and founding member of St. Augustine punk band the Meices, originally called Three Blind Mice, who released an ill-fated album on London Records in 1996. After that label and the band dissolved, Reineke formed Alien Crime Syndicate, which signed to Revolution Records, distributed by Warner Bros. However, this label was dissolved as result of a corporate shakeup, and ACS's debut was shelved. Reineke went on to a career as an engineer and producer. He lives in Seattle, where he is the founder and senior instructor at Seattle Recording Arts and operates a recording studio, Orbit Audio.

Also see *Meices*.

Reinhardt, Larry

From Bradenton, this virtuoso guitarist nicknamed "Rhino" had been a member of Dickie Betts' Sarasota band the Blues Messengers, who upon leaving for Jacksonville became the Second Coming. He had previously been a member of Mac Doss' Bradenton band, the Thunderbeats.

Reinhardt left the Blues Messengers to form his own power trio, the Load. After doing an extended engagement as the house band at Dub's in Gainesville, the Load followed the Second Coming to Jacksonville, where the two bands shared a house in Riverside; both groups developed large followings in the area.

When Betts and bassist Berry Oakley left the Second Coming to join the Allman Brothers band and relocated to Macon, Reinhardt and bassist Richard Price of the Load merged with former Second Coming members keyboardist Reese Wynans and drummer John Meeks to become the New Second Coming.

However, someone from Los Angeles-based psychedelic band Iron Butterfly called Capricorn's offices looking for a replacement guitarist for Erik Brann. Rhino got the call and began touring with Butterfly.

When singer Doug Ingle left that group, Rhino and Butterfly bassist Lee Dorman formed Captain Beyond, a nickname affectionately bestowed on Reinhardt by Yes bassist Chris Squire. Captain Beyond signed with Capricorn in 1972 and added keyboardist Wynans a year later. Several versions of CB tread the boards throughout the ensuing decades.

Reinhardt also worked as a session player, his most notable client being R&B singer-songwriter Bobby Womack, with whom Rhino recorded an album in 1974. Reinhardt died of liver failure in Bradenton in January 2012, age 63.

Also see *Blues Messengers; Second Coming; the Load; Captain Beyond; Wynans, Reese; Betts, Dickey.*

Rice, Chase

Modern country singer Rice was born in Ormond Beach in 1985 but raised in Asheville, N.C. In 2012 he co-wrote Florida-Georgia Line's hit "Cruise," which went to No. 1 on *Billboard* 's country-music chart. (Bryan Kelley of Florida-Georgia Line is also from Ormond Beach). Rice signed as an artist with Columbia Records shortly thereafter but has since left Columbia for Broken Bow.

Also see *Kelley, Bryan.*

Rich Creamy Paint

See *Painter, Rich*

Richfield

Rock band from Orange Park formed by guitarist Page Matherson and drummer Herbert "Mac" McCormack (cousin of B.J. Thomas' drummer Jim McCormack).

Matherson and McCormack had been members of a local teen band the Daybreakers, who had gotten airplay on powerhouse WAPE-AM. After adding vocalist Archie Valliere, guitarist Jim Harrison and bassist Ricky Powell, Richfield took to the bar circuit.

The group recorded some demos of original songs, one of which was the tongue-in-cheek "Disco Sucks," Richfield's commentary on the then-popular dance-club/DJ craze. The demos were produced and engineered by Hal Hansford, who also played keyboards.

The group benefited from having a Lynyrd Skynyrd connection: bassist Powell was Skynyrd keyboardist Billy Powell's younger brother, plus drummer McCormack had been a neighbor and schoolmate of Skynyrd guitarist Gary Rossington.

Thanks to a recommendation from Rossington, Richfield hooked up with Muscle Shoals producer Jimmy Johnson. Johnson produced a single of "Disco Sucks," which was picked up by Capitol and released in 1979. The record failed to crack the charts, however, and Capitol declined to exercise its option for an album. The group continued touring throughout the South until about 1982. Valliere died in 2018.

Also see *Hansford, Hal.*

Ricks, Jimmy

Ricks was born in Adrien, Ga., in 1924 and moved to Jacksonville with his family as a youth. At 21, he relocated to New York, where he became a singing waiter and in 1946 formed the Ravens. They soon signed with the small Hub label and a year later moved to the more mainstream National Records and later recorded for Columbia, Okeh, Mercury and Jubilee. Ricks left the group for a solo career in 1956 and recorded for Paris, Decca and Signature before signing with Atlantic Records in 1962. In 1971, he revived the Ravens. He later worked with the Count Basie Orchestra until his death in 1974.

Also see *Ravens.*

Riperton, Minnie

Born in Chicago in 1947, this five-octave vocalist landed a job as a receptionist at Chess Records, which led to a stint singing backgrounds for the likes of Muddy Waters, Chuck Berry, Bo Diddley, Etta James, Fontella Bass and Ramsey Lewis. In 1967 she joined rock-soul group Rotary Connection, also signed to Chess. In 1970, Riperton recorded her first solo album for Chess subsidiary Janus Records (the entire Chess operation had been purchased by General Recorded Tape in 1969). That album fell through the corporate cracks.

A year later, Riperton and her husband, songwriter Richard Rudolph, moved to Gainesville, where Rudolph landed a gig as a DJ on WGVL and where their daughter, Maya Rudolph, was born.

Riperton signed with Epic Records and moved to Los Angeles in 1973, where she recorded the album *Perfect Angel*, produced by Stevie Wonder. That album yielded Riperton a No. 1 single, "Loving You," which she wrote. She signed to Capitol in 1978 and died of cancer in Los Angeles a year later. She was 31.

Road Turkey

Gainesville band composed of Jeff Jourard on guitar and vocals, brother Marty Jourard on bass, guitarist Steve Soar and drummer Stan Lynch. Lynch and Jeff Jourard would join Tom Petty's Heartbreakers in 1975 but was quickly ousted because Petty felt two guitarists were enough. Jeff and Marty Jourard went on to form the Motels with singer Martha Davis in 1978.

Also see *Jourard, Jeff; Jourard, Marty; Lynch, Stan; Petty, Tom.*

Roberts, Dave

See *Crawfish of Love.*

Roberts, Danny

Guitarist and bassist born in Lakeland in 1952; moved to Gainesville in 1968. Replaced Tom Leadon in Mudcrutch in 1973, where he served as guitarist, bassist and alternate lead vocalist. Roberts and Tom Petty traded off on bass: each would play guitar on songs they sang.

Roberts drove Petty to Los Angeles in 1974 to scout for connections in the record business, a mission they accomplished. Finally signed to Shelter Records, label owner Denny Cordell felt Roberts' style didn't fit his vision of where the band should be going. Not wanting to play bass anymore, Petty called Charlie Souza, formerly of Tampa bands the Tropics and Bacchus, to fill the slot. Cordell later recruited Roberts to work with Shelter singer Phil Seymour. He also worked with Billy Joe Royal and was in an early version of the Derek Trucks Band. Roberts lives in St. Augustine.

Also see *Mudcrutch; Tom Petty & the Heartbreakers; Souza, Charlie.*

Roberts, Marcus

Born Marthaniel Roberts, son of a Jacksonville gospel singer, in 1963. Attended the Florida School for the Deaf and Blind in St. Augustine. After graduating from Florida State University in Tallhassee. Before signing to Novus, RCA's jazz label, in 1988, he had been a member of Wynton Marsalis' NYC-based band. Later signed to Columbia; now records for his own label, J-Master Records. Roberts has been hailed as one of the most important pianists in contemporary jazz. He teaches at Florida State University and still performs with his jazz trio.

Robey, Susan

Robey was lead singer for Jacksonville's Susan and the Dynamics, whose drummer was Robert Nix. That group hooked up with Atlanta impresario Bill Lowery in 1963, who signed them to Dot Records. After a fairly unsuccessful run, Robey and keyboardist Bobby Peterson regrouped as December's Children, and Lowery was able to land the group a deal with Capitol Records, where the group released one single, "Makin' Music." After failing to chart at Capitol, Lowery moved the group to World Pacific, a sister label of Liberty Records. Disenchanted with the music business, Robey retired not long thereafter. She lives in Orlando.

Also see *Susan & the Dynamics; December's Children.*

Robinson, Phil

Virtuoso drummer from Jacksonville, played in various local funk, soul and R&B bands along with members of the East Coast Horns until joining up with Phil Driscoll in 1979. Later became an early member of the Derek Trucks Band and was in a local bar band with future Lynyrd Skynyrd backup singer Debra Rider. Also worked with famed gospel singer Yolanda Adams and gospel/R&B singer Glenn Jones. Appeared in the 1988 Peter Bogdanovich film *Illegally Yours* (shot in Jacksonville and St. Augustine) in a non-speaking role as a reggae musician.

Also see *East Coast Horns; Driscoll, Phil; Trucks, Derek; Rider, Debra.*

Rogers, Gamble

Born James Gamble Rogers, in Winter Park, 1931, Rogers joined the Serendipity Singers in the late 1960s. After going solo in the early 1970s, Rogers accumulated a strong following as much for his story-telling as for his songs. Hit his stride in the 1980s, appearing on a national PBS-TV special and as a regular on *Mountain Railroad* and as guest commentator on NPR's *All Things Considered.* Rogers also wrote several plays. He drowned in 1991 near his St. Augustine home while trying to rescue a stranger.

Root Boy Slim & the Sex Change Band

Outrageous Daytona Beach ensemble formed in late 1970s, led by North Carolina native Foster MacKenzie aka Root Boy Slim, included future Midnight Creepers guitarist Ernie Lancaster and bassist Bob Greenlee. This iconoclastic (and hilarious) act challenged every convention of its day, rivaling the Mothers of Invention for sheer audacity. In 1978, the group was signed to Warner Bros. by Steely Dan producer Gary Katz.

The band's self-titled debut album became a cult classic, dubbed "one of the most bizarre albums ever made" by the *All Music Guide*. Dropped by Warners, the group's follow-up was released in 1979 on Miles Copeland's UK-based Illegal Records. A couple of reunion albums appeared in the late 1980s on Greenlee's King Snake label and another on Naked Language Records, a division of Atlanta R&B label Ichiban, in 1991. Mackenzie died in 1993. Greenlee died in 2004 of pancreatic cancer; Lancaster died 10 years later of the same malady.

Also see *Greenlee, Bob; Midnight Creepers; Lancaster, Ernie.*

Rossington

Jacksonville-based rock band formed by Lynyrd Skynyrd co-founder Gary Rossington and his wife, Dale Krantz Rossington, after the dissolution of the Rossington Collins Band in the late 1980s. Issued two obscure albums on MCA. The Rossingtons headed a reconstituted version of Lynyrd Skynyrd from 1987 to 2018.

Also see *Rossington-Collins Band; Collins, Allen; Lynyrd Skynyrd.*

Rossington-Collins Band

Short-lived group formed in 1979 by surviving Lynyrd Skynyrd members Gary Rossington, Allen Collins, Leon Wilkeson and Billy Powell, augmented by former .38 Special vocalist Dale Krantz on lead vocals, drummer Derek Hess, and guitarist/vocalist Barry Lee Harwood, who wrote the RCB's lone hit single, "Don't Misunderstand Me," which reached No. 55 on *Billboard*'s Hot 100.

The RCB issued two albums on MCA, the first of which, 1980's *Anytime, Anyplace, Anywhere*, released in 1980, reached No. 14 on *Billboard*'s album chart; a second album, 1981's *This Is the Way*, performed admirably, reaching No. 24.

However, the band was coming unglued largely due to Collin's anguish over the sudden death of his wife, Kathy, while the group was on the road.

Also see *Lynyrd Skynyrd Collins, Allen; Rossington; Harwood, Barry Lee; Krantz, Dale.*

Rossington, Gary

From Jacksonville, this Lee High School graduate is a founding member of Lynyrd Skynyrd, the Rossington Collins Band, and Rossington.

Also see *Lynyrd Skynyrd; Rossington Collins Band; Rossington.*

Rothschild, Michael

Rothschild was born and raised in Jacksonville, growing up in the San Marco area where he attended Landon High School. He later attended Tulane University in New Orleans. After two years in the army, he moved to New York, where he worked for a record distributor that also owned rock magazine *Circus.* He became the publication's business manager.

Rothschild moved to Atlanta in 1973, where he co-produced several films. In 1981, excited by the potential of Col. Bruce Hampton's band, the Late Bronze Age, Rothschild formed Landslide Records, which would become an Atlanta institution, with titles by the Heartfixers (featuring Tinsley Ellis), the Cigar Store Indians, Nappy Brown, New Orleans kingpin Dave Bartholomew, Widespread Panic, former Susan Tedeschi sideman Sean Costello, and Tedeschi's husband, Derek Trucks (Trucks signed with Columbia in 2001).

Landslide also distributed Bob Greenlee's blues label, King Snake Records. Rothschild later became an executive for Fahlgren Entertainment, which specializes in marketing movies. He is retired and lives in Fernandina Beach.

Also see *Greenlee, Bob.*

Rouse, Ervin

Born 1917 in New Bern, N.C., the son of a tobacco farmer, Rouse began playing professionally at age 5. He and his brothers, Gordon and Earl, formed a trio and came to Jacksonville in the late 1920s. There they acquired a manager who had them touring up and down the Eastern Seaboard from Miami to Coney Island. Ervin, a singer as well as a fiddler, even did a few dates with the Glen Miller Orchestra. The Rouse Brothers began recording for American Recording Co. (predecessor of

Columbia Records) in 1934. One of their early songs was titled "Duval County Blues."

In 1938, Ervin and Gordon co-wrote "Orange Blossom Special," which the group released on RCA's Bluebird subsidiary a year later. Lake City fiddler Chubby Wise, a friend of the Rouses, who later performed the song with Bill Monroe and his Blue Grass Boys on Nashville's *Grand Ole Opry,* claimed to have co-written the song and was, according to an account give by Rouse, present at its writing at Union Terminal in Miami during the train line's christening. In 1942, Monroe and his band (with Art Wooten on fiddle; soon to be replaced by Wise) released the song on Bluebird whereupon it became a huge hit and a bluegrass standard. Perhaps the best-known version of the song was recorded by Johnny Cash in 1965 sans fiddle. Rouse and his brother also wrote "Mama's Not Dead" and "Sweeter than the Flowers," the latter of which Cash also recorded.

In the late 1940s Rouse returned to Jacksonville, where he appeared on WJHP-AM alongside Tiny Grier & the Florida Playboys (Marshall Rowland was the group's steel player). Rouse, who suffered from diabetes, mental illness and alcoholism, lived out his later years in a plywood shack on some property he'd purchased near Big Cypress Swamp. He died in 1981.

Also see *Wise, Chubby; Grier, Tiny.*

Rowland, Marshal

Born 1931 in Brunswick, Ga., raised in rural Brantley County; came to Jacksonville in 1947 to play steel guitar with Tiny Grier and his Florida Playboys, who had a daily program on WJHP-AM, owned by the *Jacksonville Journal* (Ray Charles had joined that group briefly before Rowland came aboard). Rowland became a DJ on WJHP and later went into the radio business himself, starting with tiny WFBF in Fernandina Beach in 1955. He later operated several more country stations throughout the region, starting with popular Jacksonville country-music outlet WQIK, which he sold in 1984 for $3.25 million. By 1998 he had sold them all. He was also a successful concert promoter. In the 1970s Mayor Jake Godbold appointed Rowland to the Jacksonville Sports and Entertainment Commission. He is retired and lives in Jacksonville.

Also see *Grier, Tiny; Rouse, Erwin.*

Rowland, Pete

This Jacksonville drummer and vocalist worked with local legends Mouse & the Boys. After Maurice "Mouse" Samples left the band in 1972, Rowland took over lead-vocal chores, and the group shortened its name to the Boys. He was also staff drummer at Sound Lab, where he co-wrote the song "Anny Fanny," which was recorded by the Diamond IV in 1968.

Also see *Mouse & the Boys.*

Royal Guardsmen

This young group from Ocala, consisting of Chris Nunley (vocals), Barry Winslow (vocals and guitar), Tom Richards (guitar), Bill Balough (bass), John Burdett (drums) and Billy Taylor (organ), was performing in a Tampa nightclub when they were spotted by Sarasota producer and songwriter Phil Gernhard. He had co-written a novelty song titled "Snoopy Versus the Red Baron." Gernhard took the band into a small Tampa studio and scored a contract with New York-based Laurie Records. The single went to No. 2 in early 1967. A later version of Guardsmen was briefly managed by Jacksonville agent Don Dana. The group disbanded in 1970.

A new version was formed by drummer Burdett in 2006, touring occasionally.

Also see *Dana, Don.*

Royster, Vermettya

As a teenager in 1958 Royster was spotted singing in Jacksonville's Shiloh Metropolitan Baptist Church choir by gospel legend leader Clara Ward. Ward recruited Royster as lead vocalist for the Clara Ward Singers, which toured the world.

In 1965 she became a member of Ray Charles' backup group, the Raelettes. She is featured on Charles' hits "I Don't Need No Doctor" and "Let's Go Get Stoned." She also recorded with Peggy Lee, Marvin Gaye, the Jackson 5 and James Brown.

In 1968, she and former Raelette Merry Clayton formed Sister Love, who signed with Manchild Records and then A&M. In 1972, the group signed with Motown and opened for the Jackson 5. Sister Love disbanded in 1973.

Royster returned to her gospel roots in 1983 with the group New Spirit, who signed to Savoy Records and included former members of the Clara Ward Singers. UK producer Ian Levine sought Royster in 1989 for his Motorcity Records, where she recorded two albums. In 1996, she joined Ike Turner's Ikettes.

Royster has also appeared in many stage productions such as *Spiritual, Black Folk in Song, I Heard That, Sistuhs, God's Trombone, The Glitter Palace, and Gospel, Gospel, Gospel.* She lives in Los Angeles, where she sings in church.

Rudolph, Maya

Actress, singer and comedian, daughter of Minnie Riperton and Richard Rudolph, born in Gainesville in 1972. She moved to Los Angeles with her parents as a child. In 2000, Rudolph became a cast member of *Saturday Night Live* until 2007 and since then has appeared in several movies including *Grown Ups* (2010), *Bridesmaids* (2011), *Grown Ups 2* (2013) and *Sisters* (2015). She also starred in the sitcom *Up All Night* and co-hosted the variety show *Maya & Marty*. Rudoplph is married to film director Paul Thomas Anderson. They live in Tarzana.

Running Easy

Jacksonville rock band formed in 1971 consisting of guitarist-vocalist Barry Lee Harwood (later with Alias, Rossington-Collins Band and Allen Collins Band); guitarist-vocalist Randall Hall (later with Allen Collins Band and Lynyrd Skynryd); bassist Ken Lyons (later with .38 Special),

replaced by Tim Lindsey (Molly Hatchet, Lynyrd Skynyrd); keyboardist Kevin Elson (later a sought-after sound man and record producer), replaced by Steve Perez; and drummer Joe Kremp, replaced by Derek Hess (Rossington-Collins Band and Allen Collins Band). Several members toured with singer-songwriter Melanie in 1979 as her backup band, with guitarist Harwood recording two albums with her.

Also see *Harwood, Barry Lee; Hess, Derek; Lindsey, Tim; Elson, Kevin; Hall, Randall.*

Ryan, Mark

Born 1945 in Jacksonville; this bass guitarist moved to San Francisco in the late 1960s, where he replaced bassist Bruce Barthol in Country Joe and the Fish, one of the psychedelic era's seminal groups. In 1971 he replaced David Freiberg in Quicksilver Messenger Service, with whom he worked for about a year, later with former Jefferson Airplane members Jorma Kaukonen and Marty Balin.

Sadler, Eric

Programmer/producer from Hempstead, N.Y.; in 1987 began working with production team the Bomb Squad, which produced four albums for seminal hardcore rappers Public Enemy on Def Jam Records. Sadler went on to produce recordings for former PE member Ice Cube; LL Cool J; Bell, Biv, DeVoe; Chaka Khan; Paula Abdul; Vanessa Williams;

Jody Watley; New Edition; the Neville Brothers, Ice T's metal band, Body Count and many others. After visiting former Def Jam record exec Russell Sidelsky in Atlantic Beach in the mid-1990s, Sadler and his wife, video director Karen, decided to move there.

Samples, Maurice

See *Mouse and the Boys.*

Sattin, Lonnie

Son of a pastor, born Alonzo Staton in Jacksonville in 1927, he was raised in Philadelphia, where he sang in his father's church and became a divinity student at Temple University.

Sattin formed a gospel choir that toured the US; during this tour he decided to remain in Los Angeles, where he joined Earl "Fatha" Hines' band. Just prior to the tour he married singer/actress Parthenia Milner, who went by the name Tina Sattin.

He moved to Chicago and in 1956 to New York, where performed at the Apollo Theater, the Blue Angel and at Radio City Music Hall. He also appeared in the musical *The Body Beautiful* with Barbara McNair in 1958 and later replaced Billy Daniels (also born in Jacksonville) in *Golden Boy*. Worked with producer/arranger Burt Bacharach in 1962, but these recordings went unreleased. Recorded for Scepter, Sunbeam, Capitol and Warner Bros. Records. He lives in Manhattan.

Schmidt, Rick ("Mookie")

As a DJ at the University of Florida's WRUF, Schmidt broke Gainesville band Sister Hazel's single, "All for You," which was subsequently picked up by Universal Records. Schmidt also broke Creed's "My Own Prison" while at WXSR in Tallahassee. Later program director at Tampa's 98 Rock. He is currently director of marketing at the St. Petersburg Museum of History.

Schroeder, Don ("Papa Don")

Born in Pensacola in 1940, this popular WBSR radio personality became a singer in 1959, recording for several labels, including Ace, Vee-Jay and Philips (Poly-Gram's U.S. subsidiary). He was also a staff writer in Nashville.

In 1966, Schroeder formed a production company that affiliated with New York-based Bell Records and was responsible for the breakthrough of James and Bobby Purify's "I'm Your Puppet," recorded in Memphis. He then built a recording studio in Pensacola, which he shut down a year later and bought radio station WPNN, which he still operates. He also produced Carl Carlton's hit version of "Everlasting Love" for 20th Century Records, which became a top-ten hit in 1974.

Also see *Purify, James & Bobby; Zig-Zag Paper Co.*

Sciabarasi, Ron

Born 1950 in Scranton, Pa., a child prodigy on piano, Sciabarasi had been playing the circuit in New Jersey before moving to Jacksonville to join his family there at 18. He began hanging out at Art Eisen's Comic Book Club downtown, where One Percent (later known as Lynyrd Skynyrd) served as house band. After sitting in with the band, singer Ronnie Van Zant recommended him for a new group, Fresh Garbage, being formed by drummer-singer Rick Medlocke. That band later became known as Blackfoot.

However, Sciabarasi's tenure with Blackfoot was cut short by a stint in Vietnam. Returning to Jacksonville, Sciabarasi was recruited by former Allman Brothers Band drummer Butch Trucks for his jazz-rock group Trucks. Trucks disbanded the group to rejoin the ABB just as it was about to release an album which included some of Sciabarasi's compositions.

Sciabarasi then formed his own jazz-rock group, Trayn, whose album was recorded at Rick Grant's Homestead Studio, where Sciabarasi served as in-house engineer (he engineered Mike Angelo & the Idols' punk-funk classic, "F**k Everybody"). Sciabarasi also replaced keyboardist Reese Wynans in the Jacksovnille-based trio Ugly Jellyroll.

Sciabarasi later spent a good deal of time working in television production and sales and also performed with several country acts including Suzie Kite. He lives in Middleburg.

Also see *Trucks; Blackfoot.*

Second Coming

Psychedelic band formerly known as the Blues Messengers, from Sarasota. Based in Jacksonville's Riverside district in late 1960s; became one of the most influential bands in North Florida. Led by Bradenton guitarist Dickie Betts; included bassist Berry Oakley, keyboardist Reese Wynans and guitarist Larry Reinhardt along with drummer John Meeks and Betts' then-wife, Dale.

The band was spotted by Leonard Renzler, the owner of Jacksonville nightclub the Forum (later the Scene), who offered them a house gig on the condition they change their name to the Second Coming, reputedly because Oakley looked like Jesus.

WAPE disc jocked Allen Facemire produced a single for the band for the New-Jersey-based Steady label, which he proceeded to play on his radio show. Duane Allman, already signed to Macon-based Capricorn Records, came to Jacksonville a year later to recruit bassist Oakley for his as-yet unnamed band. Oakley insisted Betts be included in the new project. The nascent Allman Brothers band made its debut as a guest act at one of the Second Coming's previously scheduled Jacksonville concerts.

Also see *Allman Bros. Band; Betts, Dickey; Oakley, Berry; Reinhardt, Larry; Wynans, Reese.*

Seven Nations

Originally formed in Middleburg as Clan Na Gael by singer and bagpiper Kirk McLeod, this Celtic-rock band relocated to NYC in 1993. Early members included Neil Anderson (vocals, bagpipes, tin whistle and mandolin), Jim Struble (vocals, acoustic guitar and bass) and Nick Watson (drums). Watson was replaced in 1997 by Jacksonville drummer Ashton Geohagan, who left in 2001, replaced by Christian Miceli. In 2002, Seven Nations signed with NYC-based Razor and Tie records.

The group, which has has sold more than 140,000 albums, has relocated back to Middleburg and is still touring.

Also see *Geohagan, Ashton.*

Shackelford, Mike

Singer-songwriter from Kentucky; came to Jacksonville as a member of folk-rock duo Justin. Formed his own group in 1987, which backed Gary U.S. Bonds onstage and in the studio. Shackelford's band also included members of Mike Angelo & the Idols (Michael Ray FitzGerald and Scott Sisson) along with future Creed producer John Kurzweg.

Also see *Bonds, Gary "U.S."; Kurzweg, John; Sisson, Scott.*

Shay, Dorothy

Singer/comedienne/character actress, born Dorothy Sims, 1921, Jacksonville. Moved to NYC, where she launched a career as the "Park Avenue Hillbilly." A regular on Spike Jones' radio show in 1947; also had a No. 4 hit on Columbia with "Feudin', Fussin' and Fightin'" from the 1947 musical *Laffing Room Only*. Sold over three million records for Columbia. Also appeared in films and TV. Died of heart failure in Santa Monica, Calif., 1978.

Sheldon, Jack

Jazz trumpeter, born in Jacksonville in 1931, moved to Los Angeles in 1947; worked with Art Pepper, Benny Goodman, Stan Kenton, Frank Sinatra, Tony Bennett, Mel Torme, Rosemary Clooney, Gary Burton, the Monkees, Tom Waits and many others, as well leading as own band. Perhaps best known for his solo on Johnny Mandel's 1965 hit, "The Shadow of Your Smile." He was a longtime regular on the *Merv Griffin Show*. Formed his own big band in 1991.

Sometime standup comic, also actor in several TV sitcoms including *What Makes Sammy Run?* and in the 1994 movie *Radioland Murders*. He has also appeared in *The Simpsons* and *Family Guy*. Sheldon lives in Los Angeles.

Shinedown

This group was assembled in 2001 around Knoxville, Tenn., singer Brent Smith, who was already under contract to Atlantic Records as singer for defunct rock band Dreve. Atlantic's Orlando A&R rep Steve Robertson contacted Jacksonville engineer Peter Thornton, who helped Smith find musicians. Original lineup included Jacksonville musicians guitarist Jasin Todd, bassist Brad Stewart and drummer Barry Kerch.

Shinedown's 2003 Atlantic debut, *Leave a Whisper*, made few waves until the group, as a lark, performed an "unplugged" version of Lynyrd Skynyrd's "Simple Man" on a live radio show on Boston's WAAF. Album was re-released in 2004 with a hastily recorded version of the song and ultimately achieved platinum status (sales of 1 million). Shinedown's third Atlantic album, *The Sound of Madness*, was certified gold (sales of more than 500,000) in 2009. Second guitarist Zach Myers, from Memphis, was brought aboard in 2005 and moved over to bass after Stewart's departure in 2007. Todd left in 2008 and has since joined rock band Fuel. Shinedown

has released five albums to date and has sold 10 million units worldwide. The group continues to tour extensively.

Sight-Seers

Power-pop quartet formed in Tallahassee in 1987, composed of vocalist Zollie Maynard, guitarist Jason O'Donnell, bassist Tim DeLaney and drummer Brad Lewis, early recordings produced by Tallahassee studio owner John Kurzweg. The group relocated to Atlanta in 1992, where four years later it would sign with Brendan O'Brien's Shotput Records, distributed by Sony. The group disbanded after Shotput went defunct.

Also see *DeLaney, Tim; Kurzweg, John.*

Singleton, Charlie ("Hoss")

Born in Gainesville in 1913, Singleton moved to Jacksonville with his family as a young child, where he graduated from

Stanton High School. Singleton started out as a singer and dancer, moving to NYC in the early 1950s, where he recorded and sang with Joey Thomas for Decca Records and cut a couple singles of his own for Atlas. He also recorded for RCA with songwriting partner Rose Marie McCoy as Charlie & Rosie. As a lyricist, Singleton would go on to co-write more than 1,000 songs, many of them hugely successful, including "Mama He Treats Your Daughter Mean" for Ruth Brown.

He is perhaps best remembered for co-writing the English lyric to a German instrumental hit composed by Bert Kaempfert, which became Frank Sinatra's 1966 No. 1 single, "Strangers in the Night." Singleton also wrote lyrics to Kampfert's "Moon over Naples," changing it to "Spanish Eyes," which became a major hit for Al Martino. Singleton's songs have also been recorded by Pat Boone, Ella Fitzgerald, Nat "King" Cole, Bill Haley, Peggy Lee, Johnny Mathis, Wayne Newton, B.B. King, Elvis Presley and the Beatles. He returned to Jacksonville in 1973, where he died twelve years later at 72.

Sisson, Scott

Drummer-singer from Vidalia, Ga.; came to Jacksonville in 1985 to join punk-funk band Mike Angelo & the Idols. Later worked with many area bands, most notably the Crawfish of Love, who recorded an album with guitarist Gary Duncan in 2006 and released two albums of their own through Global Recording Artist Records. Sisson and bassist Andy King backed Atlantic Records artist John Philip (Kurzweg) as well as bluegrass fiddler Vassar Clements (from Kissimmee). Sisson also worked with David and Linda LaFlamme of It's a Beautiful Day and with Gary U.S. Bonds.

Also see *Mike Angelo & the Idols; Crawfish of Love; Shackelford, Mike; Dixon, Neil.*

Sister Hazel

Formed in 1993 and named after a missionary who ran a Gainesville homeless shelter, the lineup included Ken Block on lead vocals, acoustic guitar; Jett Beres, bass and vocals; and Andrew Copeland, guitar and vocals. Sister Hazel released its debut album in 1994 on its own Croakin' Poet label. Guitarist/vocalist Ryan Newell and drummer Mark Trojanowski were added after the record's release.

A second album, *Somewhere More Familiar*, was released in 1997 and thanks in part to regional airplay generated by WRUF's Rick Schmidt, was picked up by Universal Records, spawning a top-10 hit, "All for You," eventually selling more than one million units. In 2003 the group left Universal and in 2005 signed with Nashville-based Rock Ridge Music. Sister Hazel's music has also been included in movie soundtracks such as *Major League: Back to the Minors*, *The Wedding Planner*, *Clay Pigeons*, *Bedazzled* and *Ten Things I Hate About You*. Sister Hazel released a

country album in 2016 and maintains a heavy touring schedule.

Also see *Schmidt, Rick.*

69 Boyz

Protégés of producers Johnny McGowan and Nathaniel Orange (Chill Deal, 95 South, Quad City DJs), headed by Jacksonville native Van Bryant, who now operates HomeBass Records in Orlando. Bryant was more recently a DJ on an Orlando-area R&B station.

Also see *McGowan, Johnny; Orange, Nathaniel; Chill Deal.*

Smedley, Brent

Born in Alexandria, Va., in 1971, this University of North Florida graduate worked with Jacksonville rock group Oracle, signed to German label Massacre Records. Smedley now performs with Tampa metal band Iced Earth, signed to Century Media, a German label acquired by Sony. The group maintains a heavy touring schedule.

Also see *Oracle.*

Smith, Arvid

See *Tammerlin.*

Smith, Donnie

Jacksonville guitarist and songwriter who became sound man for .38 Special, Austin Nickels Band (early version of Johnny Van Zant Band), Henry Paul Band, Danny Joe Brown Band. Also managed Limp Bizkit's early career; later served as LB's sound mixer and road manager. After several year living and working in Nashville, Smith retired to Jacksonville.

Smith, Rex

Born in Jacksonville 1955, raised in Atlanta. In the early 1970s, Smith became singer for Athens, Ga., band Phaedra. In 1978 he appeared in the Broadway production of *Grease*. He also appeared in the Central Park production of *Pirates of Penzance* with Linda Ronstadt as well as in the 1983 movie version.

A year later he scored a top-10 hit on Columbia Records, "You Take My Breath Away," from the movie *Sooner or Later*. Later became co-host, alongside Marilyn McCoo, of TV series *Solid Gold*. He appeared in long-running soap opera *As the World Turns* from 1990 to 1992. He has also appeared in *Street Hawk, The Love Boat, Baywatch, Caroline in the City* and *JAG*.

His brother Michael Lee Smith is the singer for rock band Starz, who signed to Capitol Records in 1976.

Smokehouse

Blues band formed in 1998 by harmonica player and singer Anthony "Packrat" Thompson, Gary Bavis, and Ture Hayes in New Smyrna Beach. The group has also included saxophonist Noble "Thin Man" Watts. Recorded four albums with producer Bob Greenlee, released on his King Snake label in association with Atlanta's Ichiban Records. The group is still active and tours regularly.

Sneed, Troy

Born in Perry in 1967, a graduate of Florida A&M, Sneed became FAMU's gospel choir director. He came to Jacksonville to teach elementary school but was recruited by Savoy Records to become director of the Georgia Mass Choir in Atlanta. Sneed and the choir appeared in the Denzel Washington-Whitney Houston movie *The Preacher's Wife*. Later produced debut albums for Henrietta Telfair and Rudolph McKissick's Word & Worship Mass Choir. In 1999 he recorded for Jackson, Ms., label Malaco Records and in 2001 for Savoy.

In 2005 he founded the Emtro Gospel-music label. Sneed and his family live near Orange Park.

Also see *Telfair, Henrietta.*

Souza, Charlie

A founding member of popular Tampa band the Tropics and later Bacchus, Souza toured vigorously with those groups throughout Florida, performing often in Gainesville and Jacksonville.

When Mudcrutch settled in Los Angeles and Tom Petty decided to switch from bass to guitar full-time—Petty and former member Danny Roberts had been switching off on bass and guitar—Petty called Souza to fill the slot. Souza met the band at Leon Russell's studio in Tulsa and cut three demos with them, including an early version of "Don't Do Me Like That." After moving to Los Angeles, Souza, along with drummer Randall Marsh, was unceremoniously dumped when he urged the band to include his own songs on the project.

Souza went on to work with several other successful groups including Cactus, White Witch, Gregg Allman, Bill Lordan,

Fortress and others. He lives in Tampa. Souza is the author of a book titled *Live Your Dream.*

Also see *Mucrutch; Roberts, Danny.*

Spider Monkey

In 1992, Canton, Ohio, high-school pals Todd Horn (vocals), Randy Looman (drums), and Tony Gialluca (bass) moved to St. Augustine, where they added guitarist Garrett Coleman, forming Spider Monkey. They hired Atlantic Beach real-estate agent Kevin O'Malley as their manager, who hooked them up with Ft. Lauderdale's Cellar Door Productions, a booking agency and concert promoter. Spider Monkey became a regional sensation, packing club and concert venues throughout the Southeast. The group recorded several albums at Jim DeVito's St. Augustine studio, Retrophonics, which they released on their own Ambassador label, independently selling approximately 20,000 units. After failing to land a major-label deal, the group disbanded in 1999 but has reunited at various points and returned to the studio in 2015.

Also see *O'Malley, Kevin; DeVito, Jim.*

Stanley Brothers

Famed bluegrass duo from Bristol, Va.; Ralph and Carter Stanley were already legends by the late 1950s, when they moved to Live Oak and built the Spirit of the Suwannee Music Park. After brother Carter died in 1966, Ralph headed for Nashville and continued to perform. In 2000, his voice was featured in the Coen Brothers' film, *O Brother, Where Art Thou?* and in 2012, Stanley was featured on the soundtrack of Nick Cave's film, *Lawless*. Ralph Stanley died in 2016 at age 89.

Also see *Masters, Johnnie*.

Stapp, Scott

Born Anthony Scott Flippen in Orlando in 1973, Stapp met guitarist and future bandmate Mark Tremonti while both were students at Highland Preparatory School. The pair reunited while students at Florida State University, adding bassist Brian Marshall from Ft. Walton Beach and drummer Scott Philips from Madison to form rock band Creed, which became hugely successful.

Creed disbanded in 2004 due in large part to Stapp's increasingly erratic behavior. After Creed's (first) breakup Stapp recorded a solo album supervised by Creed's stalwart producer, Tallahassee native John Kurzweg. The other three members re-formed as Alter Bridge and achieved a modicum of success but nothing like Creed's. The four original members reunited in 2009. However, the group disbanded again in 2013 with the other three members going back to their previous project, Alter Bridge.

Stapp had been working on another solo recording with Miami producer Desmond Child, but it was shelved. His next album, produced by Howard Benson, was released in 2013. In 2014, Stapp had a highly publicized meltdown and was diagnosed with bipolar disorder in addition to his substance-abuse problems.

In 2016, Stapp replaced singer Scott Weiland in hard-rock group Art of Anarchy, which has released two acclaimed albums to date, the second featuring Stapp. Stapp wrote an autobiography titled *Sinner's Creed*, published in 2012 by Tyndale House.

Also see *Creed*.

Starling, Gary

Jazz guitarist, started out working with Doug Carn in a Northside Jacksonville lounge. He went on to perform with such acts as Bob Hope, Diahann Carroll, Rita Moreno, Skitch Henderson, the Jacksonville Symphony Pops Orchestra, Eddie Harris, Nat Adderley, Joshua Breakstone, Carla White, Jim Snidero, Ben Tucker and Clarence Palmer.

Starling has performed with his own group at the Hilton Head Jazz Society, Gainesville Friends of Jazz and has made 15 appearances at the Jacksonville Jazz Festival. Became an instructor at Jacksonville University in the 1980s. Also recorded one album with singer Rebecca Zapen.

Also see *Carn, Doug*; *Adderly, Nat*; *Zapen, Rebecca*.

Starkey, Damien

Born in Cincinnati, moved to Jacksonville area as a child. At age 15 he fronted Jacksonville "nu-metal" band Burn Season, a group who signed to Elektra and then Bieler Bros. Records. Later worked as bassist for multiplatinum rockers Puddle of Mudd (2007-2011). Currently lives near Jacksonville Beach, where he writes music for film and television.

Also see *Burn Season*; *Amaru, Bobby*.

Start Trouble

Jacksonville pop-punk quartet formed as Ten High by Mandarin High schoolmates vocalist-songwriter Luke Walker and guitarist Terry Case; lineup later included former Audio Orange guitarist/vocalists Edmund Lowman and Allan "Fin" Leavell along with Mike Crews on drums.

The band signed to Columbia Records in 2001 after WPLA DJ Flounder played its recordings on *Native Noise,* a local-music show. The song was heard by Columbia A&R rep and former MTV personality Matt Pinfield, who happened to be in Jacksonville with his wife visiting her parents. Drummer Ken Nasta played drums on the Columbia sessions and briefly toured with the band.

Start Trouble released its debut, *Every Solution Has Its Problem*, on Columbia in 2004 and disbanded shortly thereafter, whereupon Walker and Leavell formed the group Summer Obsession, relocated to Los Angeles, where they signed with Virgin Records in 2006. Walker is an established songwriter with over 50 cuts to his

145

credit; Leavell leads his own group called Nightswim. Both live in Los Angeles. Lowman lives in Thailand.

Also see *Walker, Luke; Leavell, Allan; Audio Orange; Summer Obsession; Nasta, Ken.*

Steadham, Charles ("Blade")

Gainesville saxophonist, worked with several R&B/soul acts including Linda Lyndell, Little Jake and the Soul Searchers, Founded one of the most successful booking agencies in the Southeast, the Blade Agency.

Steele, Larry

Born in Atlanta in 1952, raised in Jacksonville's Lake Shore district, graduate of Forrest High School. One of his earliest bands, the Mods, formed in 1964, included 12-year-old Allen Collins on guitar. Later played in psychedelic band Black Bear Angel with drummer Jimmy Dougherty and guitarist Skip Veahman. Was recruited for Lynyrd Skynyrd in 1973, but after learning the group's material, Steele discovered the band had opted to use former Strawberry Alarm Clock member Ed King instead (Wilkeson soon returned to the fold, however).

A founding member of .38 Special, Steele dropped out in the group's formative stage and was replaced by bassist Ken Lyons but returned in 1980 as stage manager, a position he occupied for seven years. Steele also co-wrote several songs with .38 Special members.

In 1987 he began working in wholesale electronics until his retirement. Steele died in 2017. He is the author of a memoir about the Jacksonville southern-rock scene titled *As I Recall.*

Also see *.38 Special.*

Stewart, Brad

Jacksonville bass guitarist; original member of Atlantic Records act Shinedown. Stewart left Shinedown in 2007 and has worked with Jacksonville bands Amaru and Society Red. In 2010 he became bassist for Epic Records' act Fuel. He left Fuel in 2015 and became bassist for Memphis-based rockers Saliva, which includes Jacksonville native Bobby Amaru on lead vocals. Stewart also co-wrote the song "Control" for rock band Puddle of Mudd. Stewart lives in Jacksonville and, according to *Wikipedia*, works at Bacardi Bottling when not touring.

Also see *Amaru, Bobby; Shinedown.*

Stiletto, Stevie & the Switchblades/ Stevie Ray Stiletto

Jacksonville punk icons, formed in 1982 by Ray McKelvey on vocals, Stevie "Stiletto" Gallagher on guitar (replaced by Thom Berlin), Michael Butler on bass, and Rob Akk (Acocella) on drums. The group relocated to San Francisco in 1989, where the band, still unsigned, was featured on the cover of *Maximum RocknRoll.* However, the group soon returned to Jacksonville, with the exception of Butler, who remained in San Francisco, where he hosts a local radio show.

McKelvey quit the group on the trip back to Jacksonville, where he formed a series of subsequent bands with names like Continental Ray-Ray. In 1996, after more than a decade of do-it-yourself releases and scuffling including starting their own nightclub, McKelvey and his crew, now known as Stevie Ray Stiletto, with former Attitudes guitarist Frank Phillips, bassist Pat Lally and drummer Neil "Crash" Karrer, were offered a deal by Jacksonville rap label Attitude Records.

The two Attitude releases, *American Asshole* and *Back in Arms*, were distributed in Europe by German label S&F. Phillips and Lally were replaced respectively by Donni Patterson and Lorne Mays.

After more years of scuffling, dealing with drug addiction, alcoholism, liver disease and finally cancer, McKelvey, the undisputed godfather of the Jacksonville punk scene, died in 2013 at age 56.

Also see *Cohen, Jeff; Butler, Mike.*

Stills, Stephen

Born in Dallas in 1945, Stills first came to Gainesville with his family at 8, where he attended Sidney Lanier Elementary School. Stills subsequently attended Saint Leo College Preparatory School, outside Tampa, and Admiral Farragut Naval Academy in St. Petersburg.

He returned to Gainesville in the early 1960s, where he attended Gainesville High, played in the school band and sang with folk ensemble the Accidental Trio. Stills also worked with future Flow and Eagles member Don Felder in Felder's band, the Continentals.

Stills split for New Orleans in 1964, spent some time in Miami's Coconut Grove and wound up in New York City, where he hooked up with fellow folkie Richie Furay. The pair joined a nine-piece outfit called the Au GoGo singers and recorded an album for Roulette Records. Reorganized under the name the Company, the group did a tour of Canada where they met folk-rocker Neil Young of the Squires.

After a modicum of success, Stills and Furay left for Los Angeles in 1965, where Stills purportedly auditioned unsuccessfully for the Monkees. Stills and Furay, along with Young, formed semi-psychedelic folk-rock band Buffalo Springfield, who signed to Atlantic Records' subsidiary Atco, where the group released three acclaimed albums. Springfield scored several hits, including "For What It's Worth," which in March 1967 went to No. 7 on *Billboard*'s Hot 100.

After Buffalo Springfield's dissolution in 1968, Stills made a name for himself with the jam album *Super Session*, recorded with Al Kooper.

In 1969 he formed the trio Crosby, Stills & Nash, who under the guidance of manager David Geffen soon signed with Atlantic and became astonishingly successful.

Stills, an accomplished multi-instrumentalist who has enjoyed one of the most enduring and successful careers of any musician of his generation, alternates between touring with members of CSN and as leader of his own band. He has also performed alongside guitarist Kenny Wayne Shepherd and keyboardist Barry Goldberg in blues band the Rides, signed to Provogue Records.

Strickland, Jimmy

From Jacksonville's Northside, this country-pop singer hosted a local television show, *The Jimmy Strickland Show*, which originated on WJXT (Ch. 4) in Jacksonville and was syndicated to five other stations in the region. Strickland released three singles on Hilliard-based Davco Records in the early 1960s; however, no national hits ensued. In 1964 he released a single on WAPE general manager Jim Atkins' Arlingwood Records. In the 1970s Strickland hosted a cable-access show called *River City Country Jamboree*.

Also see *Garner, Merlene*.

Sub Rosa

See *For Squirrels*.

Summer Obsession

Pop-rock band formed in 2004 by Jacksonville musicians Luke Walker and Allan "Fin" Leavell, both former members of Start Trouble. Relocated to Los Angeles where they snagged a deal with Virgin Records and released one album titled *This Is Where You Belong*, in 2006. Group fizzled shortly thereafter; Leavell founded his own act, Nightswim. Leavell and Walker both live in Los Angeles.

Also see *Walker, Luke; Leavell, Allan; Start Trouble*.

Susan & the Dynamics

Fronted by Susan Robey, this group included drummer Robert Nix, guitar-playing siblings Shink and Charlie Morrison, Jud Walrath on bass, and keyboardist Bobby Peterson. The group appeared regularly at Jacksonville's Tropical Teen Club in the early 1960s alongside Dennis Yost's band the Echoes.

In 1963 the Dynamics linked up with Atlanta publisher Bill Lowery, who landed them a deal on Dot Records, where they released two obscure singles in the Brenda Lee/Skeeter Davis vein, "Happy Birthday to Julie" and "Someday."

Nix was working with the Dynamics at Jacksonville's Golden Gate Lounge (on Cassat Ave.) when Roy Orbison recruited him to join his backup band, the Candymen. Keyboardist Peterson also joined the Candymen but in 1965 left that group to join Rick Derringer's band the McCoys.

In 1968 Robey formed blue-eyed-soul group December's Children, also represented by the Lowery Oganization and included Peterson. Shink Morrison later attained success as a songwriter for the likes of Jerry Reed and Dr. Hook. Struggling with mental illness, Bobby Peterson ended up homeless in Gainesville, where he was struck and killed by a car in 1993. Robey lives in Orlando.

Also see *December's Children; Morrison, Shink; Robey, Susan.*

Swamp Cabbage

A southern-funk roots-rock group formed in 2010 by Jacksonville vocalist-guitarist Walter Parks. Signed to New York-based ZOHO Roots Records. St. Augustine's Jim DeVito is bassist for that group, which maintains an active touring schedule. The group's songs, written primarily by Parks, have appeared in many television series such as *American Guns, When Patrick Met Kylie, My Big Redneck Wedding, Man vs. Food, Emeril Green, Extreme Pig Outs, Gene Simmons Family Jewels, Roadtrip Nation, Samantha Brown Passport, Amazing Wedding Cakes* and *Chasing Classic Cars.* Parks lives in Savannah.

Also see *Parks, Walter; Nasta, Ken; DeVito, Jim.*

Swedien, Bruce

Noted recording engineer from Minneapolis. Got his start working with the Four Seasons in the late 1960s, later with legendary producer Quincy Jones on Michael Jackson's breakthrough albums, most notably *Thriller*. Also worked with Natalie Cole, Roberta Flack, Mick Jagger, David Hasselhoff, Jennifer Lopez, Paul McCartney, Diana Ross, Chaka Khan, Barbra Streisand, Lena Horne, Donna Summer, Sarah Vaughan, Muddy Waters and Diana Ross. Owns a horse farm near Ocala.

Swindle, Phil

Guitarist and songwriter from Muscle Shoals, Ala.; moved to Jacksonville in the 1990s where he worked with Leslie Hawkins (Wet Willie, Lynyrd Skynyrd) as well as other prominent musicians. Recorded an album in Muscle Shoals with Jacksonville musicians Derek Hess (Rossington-Collins Band, Allen Collins Band) on drums, bassist Tim Lindsey (Molly Hatchet), keyboardist Barry Rapp (Henry Paul Band), saxophonist Rick Johnson (Lynyrd Skynyrd, Dr. Hector & the Groove Injectors) and Wet Willie singer Jimmy Hall, released on Synesthesia Records.

Swirl 360

Born in Brunswick, Ga., twin siblings Kenny and Denny Scott moved to Orange Park with their military dad, where they began forming bands such as Dream in Color. After passing some demos recorded in Jacksonville Beach to teen-pop group Hanson's manager, the duo signed with Mercury and released its major-label debut in 1998. Unfortunately, Mercury's rock acts were dropped shortly after the PolyGram/Universal merger.

In 2000, one of the Scott brothers' songs, "Summer of Love," was covered by the Baja Men, whose debut album sold more than three million copies.

In 2007, the brothers renamed their group Echo Jet and signed with Machine Records, but no hits ensued. In 2014 Kenny Scott opened 18 Below recording studio in St. Petersburg; Denny Scott returned to Jacksonville and started a new act called Rock Paper Pistols.

Synergy

An outgrowth of acoustic duo consisting of Rick Block and Jason Chase, this top-40 band was notable for its addition of some of Jacksonville's finest musicians, including Randall Hall (guitar, vocals), John Philip Kurzweg (guitar, vocals), Rocco Marshall (guitar, vocals), Tim Lindsay (bass), Derek Hess (drums) Rick Johnson (sax and keyboards) and Carol Bristow (vocals).

Also see *Lynyrd Skynyrd; Rossington Collins Band; Dr. Hector & the Groove Injectors; Vision; Hall, Randall; Lindsay, Tim; Kurzweg, John; Bristow, Carol; Johnson, Rick.*

Tammerlin

Folk-rock-Celtic duo from Jacksonville, consisting of Arvid Smith and Lee Hunter, formed in 1992. The duo recorded three albums, two of which were released by Baton Rouge-based Binky Records. The duo disbanded in 2014. Smith continues to perform as a solo act. Hunter and guitarist-vocalist Walter Parks opened shows for Emmylou Harris in 2015. She also has her own band, Lee Hunter & the Gatherers.

Taylor, Bob

Drummer, born 1928 in Phoenix, became a key figure in the Western-swing scene with Bob Wills, Lefty Frizzell, and Merle Haggard. Worked with guitarist Duane Eddy ("Rebel Rouser") in 1960s; later led own band, the Rogues, for many years. Taylor came to Jacksonville in 1994, worked locally with Larry Mangum's Cowboy Orchestra. Died in 2001.

Tedeschi, Susan

Boston-born blues rocker, graduate of Berklee College of Music; signed to Boston label Tone-Cool (distributed by Artemis/RED); her first nationwide release sold 600,000.

Tedeschi moved to Jacksonville in 1999 to live with boyfriend (now hubby) Derek Trucks, whom she met while opening for the Allman Brothers Band. Her third album was recorded in Jacksonville Beach with veteran producer Tom Dowd and engineer Pete Thornton. In 2009, Tedeschi signed with Verve Forecast Records. She and Trucks now tour together as the Tedeschi-Trucks Band.

Also see *Trucks, Derek; Allman Brothers Band; Tedeschi-Trucks Band.*

Tedeschi-Trucks Band

Jacksonville-based blues-rock band formed in 2010, fronted by singer Susan Tedeschi and featuring her husband, Derek Trucks, on guitar. Other members include Oteil Burbridge, formerly of the Allman Bros. Band, on bass guitar and Kofi Burbridge on keyboards and flute. Trucks himself is a former ABB member. The Tedeschi-Trucks Band released an album in 2011 through Sony Masterworks.

Also see *Tedeschi, Susan; Trucks, Derek; Allman Bros. Band.*

Telfair, Henrietta

Born in Jacksonville in 1955, this gospel singer is the winner of numerous awards. Troy Sneed of Emtro Music produced her debut album in 2002. She lives and preaches in Jacksonville.

Also see *Sneed, Troy.*

.38 Special

Originally led by Donnie Van Zant, younger sibling of Lynyrd Skynyrd vocalist Ronnie Van Zant, this Westside Jacksonville band had its beginnings as Sweet Rooster, later Alice Marr. Members included Don Barnes on guitar and vocals, Jeff Carlisi on guitar, Ken Lyons on bass, and dual drummers Jack Grondin and Steve Brookins. After signing to A&M in 1976, where it experienced a slow start, the band's 1981 album *Wild-Eyed Southern Boys* became its breakthrough, scoring platinum status (more than 1 million copies sold). Lyons left in 1979, replaced by former Lynyrd Skynyrd bassist Larry Junstrom, who was already touring with .38 as a roadie. In the 1980s the band scored more than 10 major hits, including "Hold on Loosely," "Caught Up in You," "If I'd Been the One," and "Back Where You Belong."

.38 remains the area's all-time biggest-selling act. Barnes left the group in 1987, replaced by singer Max Carl, who sang .38's hit "Second Chance." Barnes returned in 1992, whereupon Carlisi left.

Since leaving A&M .38 Special has released records through NYC label Razor & Tie and North Carolina label CMC International. Van Zant left the group in 2012 due to hearing problems. Junstrom retired in 2014, replaced by St. Augustine bassist Barry Dunaway, who previously worked with guitarist Yngvie Malmsteen. The group still tours regularly though it only has one original member, Barnes, who sang on most of the band's hits.

Also see *Van Zant; Elson, Kevin; Dunaway, Barry; Steele, Larry.*

31st of February

Formerly folk-rock trio the Bitter Ind, this group, composed of singer-guitarist Scott Boyer, bassist David Brown and drummer Butch Trucks, expanded to a quintet with the addition of Duane and Gregg Allman. The group's debut album was released on Vanguard, produced in Miami by Steve Alaimo. Its second album, declined by Vanguard, was later issued as *Duane & Greg Allman* on Alaimo's Bold label.

In 1969, Trucks would help form the Allman Brothers Band. Boyer would form Cowboy, and Brown would become a busy session musician, later a member of Cowboy and Boz Scaggs' band.

Also see *Allman Brothers Band; Bitter Ind; Trucks, Butch; Brown, David.*

152

Thornton, Pete

Jacksonville native Thornton graduated from Bishop Kenny High and earned a degree from Full Sail School of Recording in Orlando in 1994. While working as an engineer at Jasmine Recording in Jacksonville, Donnie Smith, former sound man for the Outlaws, brought Thornton an unknown band he was managing named Limp Bizkit. Thornton engineered the group's early recordings.

At singer Fred Durst's behest, Thornton produced successful demos for Jacksonville Beach hard-rock band Cold. Thornton moved from Jasimne to Judy Van Zant's studio, Made in the Shade (now defunct), where he worked with blues-belter Susan Tedeschi and rap-rockers Superfly Rodeo. He also helped Atlantic A&R rep Steve Robertson put together a band for Knoxville, Tenn., singer Brent Smith called Shinedown. Thornton worked on Shinedown's demos alongside Orlando producer Tony Battaglia (Mandy Moore, N'Sync). He and Battaglia later developed Jacksonville rock band 3AE, which signed with RCA Records in 2002.

Thornton later ran the Fort studio in Winter Springs and established a studio in St. Augustine.

Also see *3AE; Audio Orange; Durst, Fred; Limp Bizkit; Cold; Shinedown; Tedeschi, Susan.*

3AE

Jacksonville modern rock band, formed in Jacksonville in 2000 as Audio Orange. Original members included Jacksonville guitarist/vocalist Edmund Lowman, guitarist/vocalist Chris Gill, bassist Stan Martell (from Waycross, Ga.) and drummer Mitch Watson.

Upon hooking up with Orlando-based producers Pete Thornton (from Jacksonville) and Tony Battaglia, Lowman and drummer Watson left the group, replaced by former Denizens singer Christopher Rice from Orlando, and drummer Matt Brown, also from Central Florida. At this point the band changed its name to 3AE and signed with RCA Records in August 2002. The group disbanded when singer Rice was killed in an auto accident. Lowman resurfaced with Jacksonville band Start Trouble (formerly Ten High), which signed to Columbia Records in 2002.

Also see *Thornton, Peter; Audio Orange; Start Trouble.*

3 Grand

Protégés of producers Johnny McGowan and Nathaniel Orange (Chill Deal, 95 South, Quad City DJs), this Jacksonville bass-music trio signed to MCA in 1991, later switching to Ichiban's Wrap subsidiary in 1992, where they had a huge club hit with "Daisy Dukes."

Also see *Chill Deal; McGowan, Johnny; Orange, Nathaniel.*

Tillis, Mel

Born 1932 in Tampa, Tillis was working for the Atlantic Coast Line railroad when he met Nashville music publisher Wesley Rose of Acuff-Rose Music, where he began writing hits for Webb Pierce, Stonewall Jackson, Ray Price and Brenda Lee, among others. His songwriting success gave him the leverage to snag his own deal with Columbia Records in 1958. In 1963 Bobby Bare covered his song "Detroit City." Tillis also cut the original version of "Ruby, Don't Take Your Love to Town," covered by Kenny Rogers in 1969 and "Mental Revenge," covered by Waylon Jennings, Linda Ronstadt, Barbara Mandrell and others. Tillis eventually became a best-selling country-music star in his own right, recording for MGM, Elektra, RCA, Mercury and Curb Records. He also branched out as a character actor in motion pictures. In the 1990s he built a theater in Branson, Missouri, where he performed regularly until 2002. He owned a ranch near Ocala, where he lived until his death in 2017 at age 85. Country singer Pam Tillis is his daughter.

Tillotson, Johnny

Born in Jacksonville in 1939, Tillotson straddled the line between country and pop. His father, Jack Tillotson, was a country-music disk jockey.

Tillotson moved to Palatka in 1948 to live with his grandmother but made regular trips to Jacksonville. As a youth he appeared on Herb Young's *Young Folks Revue* on Palatka's WWPF-AM and as a student at Palatka High School landed his own radio show on that station.

In her book *Country Singers as I Know 'Em* songwriter Mae Axton claims Tillotson landed on her Murray Hill doorstep one day looking for career advice. Impressed with his talent and clean-cut good looks, she contacted Toby Dowdy, host of TV-4's *McDuff Hayride* and landed

Tillotson a semi-regular spot. Soon he was offered his own show on TV-12.

In 1957, while Tillotson was studying broadcast journalism at University of Florida, Gainesville DJ Bob Norris (who would later figure prominently in the career of Gainesville songstress Linda Lyndell) submitted a tape of a Tillotson performance to talent contest in Nashville. Tillotson didn't win the contest, but he was spotted by music publisher Lee Rosenberg, who took the tape to Archie Bleyer, owner of New York-based Cadence Records, also home to the Everly Brothers. Bleyer signed Tillotson to a three-year contract. In 1958, while he was still in college, Cadence released Tillotson's first single, a self-penned ballad, "Dreamy Eyes" (Tillotson wrote much of his own material, an unusual accomplishment for a pop singer in the pre-Beatles era). In 1959, Tillotson moved to NYC to pursue his career full-time.

He broke through in 1960 with his sixth single, "Poetry in Motion," recorded in Nashville with top session players. It went to No. 2 in the US and hit the top spot in the UK. He scored again in 1962 with "It Keeps Right on a-Hurtin'," which he wrote and which landed on both the pop and country charts ("Hurtin'" was covered by Elvis Presley and in 1989 became a No. 1 country hit for Billy Joe Royal). It would be Tillotson's last recording for Cadence. After being drafted, Tillotson returned to find Cadence out of business. He managed

to snag a new deal at MGM. Between 1958 and 1967, he racked up no fewer than 14 top-40 hits. Tillotson's hits slowed during and after the British Invasion, yet ironically he maintained a huge following in England. In 1969, he shed his teen-idol image and reinvented himself as a cabaret crooner, landing regular spots in New York, Miami Beach, and Vegas.

In 1973, Tillotson signed with Columbia Records' Nashville division as a full-fledged country artist, something he said he'd always wanted to be. However, by this point his recording career had pretty much run its course.

He still tours regularly, however, and remains popular in Las Vegas, Australia and the Pacific Rim. Tillotson's voice was heard on reruns of *Gidget*: Tillotson sings the show's theme song, "Wait Till You Meet My Gidget." Tillotson lives in the San Fernando Valley with his wife, Nancy. He is still touring the oldies circuit.

Also see *Axton, Mae.*

Todd, Jasin

Guitarist from Jacksonville Beach; early member of Shinedown; worked with Epic/Sony-signed rock group Fuel from 2010 to 2011. Todd is currently working with acoustic artist Trista Mabry. The couple lives in Nashville.

Also see *Shinedown.*

155

Tolliver, Charles

Born in Jacksonville 1942, this jazz trumpeter studied pharmacy science at Howard University in Washington, D.C. Tolliver moved to NYC in early 1960s to pursue a full-time career as a musician, where he joined alto saxophonist Jackie McLean's band. He has also worked with Max Roach, Roy Haynes, Hank Mobley, Willie Bobo, Horace Silver, McCoy Tyner, Sonny Rollins, Booker Ervin, Gary Bartz, Herbie Hancock, Roy Ayers, Art Blakey & the Jazz Messengers and others.

Tolliver also led his own bands for Impulse and Black Lion Records. In 1968, Tolliver received *Downbeat*'s Critic's Choice award. He formed his own label, Strata-East Records, in 1970. His big band, dubbed Music Inc., released an album on Blue Note in 2007, for which he won a Jazz Journalists Association award.

Still tours regularly with that group, mostly in Europe.

Tooke, Bill

Gainesville guitarist-vocalist, founding member of For Squirrels. Leader of Helixglow, who released an album in 2012 on New Hersey-based Indigo Planet Records.

Also see *For Squirrels; Helixglow.*

Touchton, Tim

From Palatka, original member (drummer) of the Illusions. In 1966 the group landed its own TV show, *Let's Go,* on Jacksonville's WFGA (Channel 12). Managed by Jacksonville impresario Don Dana, the Illusions issued a single, "I Know," on Dana's ACP (Atlantic Coast Productions) Records, which garnered heavy airplay on Orlando's WLOF in August 1966 and was subsequently picked up by Columbia Records. After the Illusions split up, Touchton moved to Tallahassee, where he joined a rock group called Plymouth Rock, which signed to Epic Records in 1969, but no album was released, so several members of Plymouth Rock, including Touchton, became backup musicians for singer Bobbie Gentry. In 1972 Touchton went to Munich, where he landed the role of Pontius Pilate in *Jesus Christ, Superstar,* later becoming a successful songwriter and producer.

Also see *Illusions.*

Travolta, John

Born in Englewood, N.J., in 1954, Travolta started out in musical theater. He was in the touring company of the musical *Grease* as well as in the Broadway production of *Over Here* before moving to Los Angeles, where he became a TV and film star. He lives near Ocala.

Trucks

Short-lived jazz-rock instrumental group formed in 1978 by former Allman Brothers Band drummer Butch Trucks. Included keyboardist Ron Sciabarasi, who had been with an early version of Blackfoot, guitarist Jim Graves, former Outlaws bassist Buzzy Meekins and second drummer Jimmy Charles. Sciabarasi and Charles went on to form jazz-rock outfit Trayn.

Meekins went on to join the Danny Joe Brown Band and an early version of the Derek Trucks Band.

Also see *Bitter Ind,; Allman Brothers Band; Danny Joe Brown Band; Meekins, Buzzy.*

Trucks, Butch

Jacksonville-born drummer, played with teen bands the Vikings and the Echoes while a student at Englewood High, where he also played with the school band.

While a student at Florida State University, Trucks formed folk-rock group the Bitter Ind with schoolmates Scott Boyer and David Brown. The group relocated to Daytona Beach, where it met the members of the Allman Joys. The trio released a single under the name Tiffany System on Nashville-based SSS International Records, a cover of Dino Valenti's "Let's Get Together."

The group then signed to Vanguard, where it released one album under the name 31st of February in 1969. In an effort to garner another album release, the group added two former members of the Allman Joys, Duane and Gregg Allman, to record demos in Miami with producer Steve Alaimo.

Trucks joined the original lineup of the Allman Brothers Band later that year and stayed with that group for its entire career. However, during the ABB's many hiatuses, Trucks formed several side projects including the jazz-rock fusion group Trucks, jam band Frog Wings and others.

In 1986 he moved back to Tallahassee where he built a state-of-the-art studio, Pegasus Recording. Trucks continued to work with the Allman Brothers Band until his suicide in his Palm Beach home in 2017. He was the uncle of slide guitarist extroaordinaire Derek Trucks. Another nephew, Duane Trucks (Derek's brother), is drummer for Widespread Panic.

Also see *Allman Brothers Band; Bitter Ind; Trucks; Sciabarasi, Ron.*

Trucks, Derek

Nephew of Allman Brothers Band drummer Butch Trucks, slide guitarist since age 9. Started out performing with Jacksonville's Greg Baril Band. Became a guest performer with the Allman Brothers Band, later added as a full-time member.

In 1996 he formed the Derek Trucks Band, which signed to Columbia/Sony and lasted until 2010. The group's album *Already Free*, released by Sony's Legacy division, won a Grammy Award in 2010 for Best Contemporary Blues Album.

Trucks has also toured with Eric Clapton, Joe Walsh, Stephen Stills, Buddy Guy and Bob Dylan and has been listed twice in Rolling Stone's "100 Greatest Guitarists of All Time." Currently tours with wife Susan Tedeschi in the Tedeschi-Trucks Band.

Also see *Allman Brothers Band; Trucks, Butch; Baril, Greg; Tedeschi, Susan.*

Van Zant

This duo consisting of Van Zant brothers Donnie (of .38 Special) and Johnny (of Lynyrd Skynyrd), recorded two albums for CMC International in 1998 and 2001. In 2005, the duo signed with Columbia/Sony as a country act; two singles off the duo's Columbia debut album, *Get Right with the Man*, hit the country Top 10. The album went gold (sales of 500,000 or more units). A second album, *My Kind of Country*, was released by Columbia in 2007, but the act soon parted ways with the label.

Donnie Van Zant has retired due to hearing problems. However, during one of Skynyrd's hiatuses, the duo reformed along with guitarists Erik Lundgren and Bobby Ingram to do a benefit for Clay County victims of Hurricane Irma.

Also see *.38 Special; Lynyrd Skynyrd; Van Zant, Johnny.*

Van Zant, Donnie

The second of three Van Zant siblings to become a rock singer, Donnie Van Zant fronted hitmakers .38 Special for most of that band's career. He retired from performing in 2012.

Also see *.38 Special; Van Zant.*

Van Zant, Johnny

Youngest of the three singing Van Zant siblings. Originally a drummer; formed Austin Nickels Band in late 1970s, which signed to Polydor in early 1980s, later with Nettwerk/Elektra.

In 1987, Johnny replaced deceased brother Ronnie in the re-formed Lynyrd Skynyrd. Also records with brother Donnie in a duo called Van Zant, which has recorded two albums for CMC International and two for Columbia/Sony.

Also see *Lynyrd Skynyrd; Van Zant.*

Van Zant, Ronnie

See *Lynyrd Skynyrd.*

Velvet, Jimmy

Born James Tennant in Jacksonville, Velvet was a Paxon High student of Mae Axton's; she arranged his appearances on Toby Dowdy's *McDuff Hayride* TV show alongside fellow Axton protégé Johnny Tillotson.

Through Axton, Velvet became a friend of Elvis Presley's and a collector of Presley memorabilia; he later founded the Elvis Museum, which was located across from Graceland in Memphis. As a recording artist for ABC-Paramount in the early to mid-1960s, Velvet remade sappy ballads like "Blue Velvet," "(You're Mine and) We Belong Together," and "Teen Angel."

Velvet left music to join the US Air Force; returned in 1968 with an album on United Artists. Later acquired Chips Moman's American Recording studio in Memphis, where Elvis had recorded his comeback hits.

159

In 1992, Velvet recorded a Presley tribute album in Nashville with producer/co-writer David Allen Coe, titled *Did You Know Elvis?*, released on Velvet's Music City label. He reportedly sold his collection of Elvis memorabilia for $2.4 million. He became curator of the Legends Collection of showbiz memorabilia in Nashville that includes many priceless artifacts of pop culture. He has since relocated to Las Vegas, where he sells copies of his memoir at the Auto Collections Museum in the LINQ Hotel and Casino.

Also see *Axton, Mae.*

Vinson, Teraesa

Jazz vocalist born St. Louis 1975; spent eight years in Gainesville earning her PhD in counseling and teaching at University of Florida. She bolted for the Big Apple in 2003 and in about a year snagged a contract with Amplified Records, for which she recorded three albums. She also served a two-year residency at Langan's in Times Square with the Quincy Davis Trio. Vinson moved to Los Angeles in 2013, where she is a licensed psychologist.

Vision

Jacksonville Christian-rock band; released three independent albums. The original lineup included guitarist/vocalist Rocco Marshall, drummer Mike Maple (later with Mark Farner and Wynonna), keyboardist David Jinright, and multi-instrumentalist Leonard Jones. Vison's self-titled debut was released in 1985 on Heartland Records.

Later members included former Lynyrd Skynyrd members Leon Wilkeson on bass and Billy Powell on keyboards; Wilkeson and Powell left in 1987 to form a new version of Lynyrd Skynyrd. Vision released two new albums through Iowa-based Born Twice Records, one of which was a re-release of a set the group recorded in 1984. Marshall died in early 2018 as a result of renal failure and cardiac arrest.

Also see *Lynyrd Skynyrd; Synergy.*

Walker, Greg T.

Bassist for southern-rock band Blackfoot; also played briefly with an early version of Lynyrd Skynyrd alongside drummer Rick Medlocke during that group's recordings made in Muscle Shoals, Ala., in 1971. After re-forming Blackfoot, Walker served as that group's bassist until singer/guitarist Rick Medlocke took control of the name in 2012 and assembled a whole new lineup. In 2014 Walker recorded an EP with French group the Lloyd Project.

Also see *Blackfoot; Lynyrd Skynyrd; Medlocke, Rick.*

Walker, Frank

Founder of Jacksonville's Davco Records, which in the early 1960s released singles by singers Johnny Folkston, Jimmy Strickland and Merlene Garner.

Walker, Luke

From Jacksonville, this Mandarin High graduate began recording demos of songs like "Chemical" and "Let's Get Fucked Up," which garnered airplay on WPLA's Sunday-night local-music show, *Native Noise*. In town visiting his wife's parents, MTV VJ Matt Pinfield, then a Columbia Records A&R executive, heard the recordings and expressed interest. A band was formed that included Allan "Fin" Leavell and quickly signed to Columbia after one or two name changes. However, the group's 2001 album, *Every Solution Has Its Problem*, got lost in the corporate shuffle and foundered.

In 2004, Walker and Leavell, along with drummer Chris Wilson, formed the Summer Obsession. The group relocated to Los Angeles where they snagged a deal with Virgin Records. An album titled *This Is Where You Belong*, was released two years later. However, that group was short-lived as well. Summer Obsession reunited in 2007 and released an independent EP.

Walker lives in Los Angeles where he is focusing on a career as a songwriter and producer.

Also see *Start Trouble, Summer Obsession; Leavell, Allan.*

Washington, Teddy

Born in 1930, this Jacksonville native graduated from Stanton High School in 1949. As an aspiring trumpeter he worked with area pianist R.C. Robinson, later known as Ray Charles. Washington also played trombone. After graduating, Washington was drafted into the army, where he served as conductor of the U.S. Army Band, in Saltzburg, Austria. He also did a couple of tours with blues artist B.B. King.

Around 1963, Washington was spotted performing at the Palms, a Moncrief nightclub, by singer James Brown. Washington spent seven years with Brown's band. He also played on sessions for Louis Armstrong, Dizzy Gillespie, Frank Sinatra, Nancy Wilson and Patti LaBelle. In the 1970s he moved to Miami to become a session player at TK Records. He assembled a house band at the Fontainbleu Hotel that included future members of KC & the Sunshine Band.

In 1979 he suffered a serious auto accident after which he had to learn to play left-handed. After living for several years in Atlanta, Washington returned to Jacksonville in 1981, where he led his own smooth-jazz group and hosted a local cable-access show. He performed at the Jacksonville Jazz Festival 19 times. Washington, who wrote an autobiography titled *Life: The Puzzle*, died in Jacksonville in 2009 at age 78.

Waterford, Charles "Crown Prince"

Born 1917 in Jonesboro, Ark., Waterford started a career as a blues singer in Oklahoma City in 1936. He soon lit for Chicago, where he became a fixture on the scene. Moved to Los Angeles in 1945, where he briefly worked alongside singer Jimmy Witherspoon in Jay McShann's band, then returned to Chicago. Recorded for Capitol and King.

Came to Jacksonville in mid-1960s to attend Edward Waters College and Luther Rice Seminary and became a minister at Greater Hope and Mt. Zion AME churches. Recorded spiritual music in early 1970s.

Waterford was convinced to come out of retirement and made a successful appearance at the 2002 *Springin' the Blues* festival backed by the After Hours Band. Waterford died in February 2007 in Jacksonville. Some of his early works have been re-released.

Watts, Noble ("Thin Man")

Native of DeLand, grad of Florida A&M University (Watts was in the FAMU marching band with both Adderly brothers.) In the 1940s through the 1950s, he played tenor sax with Charles Brantley & the Honeydippers; pianist Ray Charles was also a member of that ensemble. Watts went on to work with such notables as Dinah Washington, Amos Milburn, Ruth Brown, Lionel Hampton, Jerry Lee Lewis, Chuck Berry and many others. Also recorded as a solo artist on various labels, including DeLuxe, Cub, Enjoy and Vee-Jay; later signed with Bob Greenlee's Sanford-based King Snake Records. Watts died in 2004 in Deland at age 78.

Also see *Greenlee, Bob; Charles, Ray; Adderly, Julian; Adderly, Nat.*

Wells, Sylvan

See *Nightcrawlers*.

Wharton, Bill

Tallahassee singer and blues guitarist perhaps best known for his special hot sauce, which he promotes at his appearances. Has recorded for Kingsnake and Ichiban Records.

Wheeler, Steve

Electric guitar virtuoso, worked with several Jacksonville rock bands such as Money with Larry Steele and Jimmy Dougherty and Bonnie Gringo with Tim Briggs before joining former Molly Hatchet singer Danny Joe Brown's band, which released an album on Epic in 1981. Wheeler wrote the DJBB's first single, "Nobody Walks On Me," which appeared on video via MTV. Later became a member of the re-formed China Sky, signed to UK label Escape Music in 2015. Now retired.

Also see *Danny Joe Brown Band; China Sky; Steele, Larry; Dougherty, Jimmy, Briggs, Tim.*

Where We Stand

Band formed by founding members of Yellowcard (Ben Harper, Ben Dobson, Warren Cooke, and Longineau Parsons Jr) after Ryan Key took over Yellowcard. Now defunct.

Also see *Yellowcard.*

Whitman, Slim

Born Otis Dewey Whitman in Tampa in 1923, yodeling Slim Whitman was already a top-rated country performer with 30 top-50 country singles and 19 gold albums when he bought a spread near Middleburg (southwest of Jacksonville, in Clay County) in 1957.

Extremely popular in England, at one point he even surpassed the Beatles on the

163

Swamp Music

British charts. George Harrison cited Whitman as an early influence. Whitman made a comeback in the mid-1980s with a greatest-hits set released via mail order, which was picked up by Cleveland International/CBS.

His yodeling song, "Indian Love Call" (from the 1924 musical *Rose Marie*), released in 1952, was featured in the 1996 Tim Burton film *Mars Attacks!* In the movie the song is used to drive off alien invaders. "I killed the Martians," he quipped in a 2008 interview. Rob Zombie included Whitman's version of "I Remember You" in his 2003 movie *House of 1,000 Corpses*. Whitman released a final album in 2010, *Twilight on the Trail*, produced by his son Byron Whitman. He died in an Orange Park hospital in 2013 at 90.

Wilkeson, Leon

Born 1952 in Newport, R.I., raised in Jacksonville, this bassist grew up in the Cedar Hills district of Jacksonville's Westside. In 1966 he met singer Ronnie Van Zant and briefly joined Van Zant's band the Collegiates. He later joined Christian-rock outfit King James Version, led by guitarist-vocalist Dru Lombar, who would go on to work with Grinderswitch (on Capricorn Records).

In 1973, Wilkeson was invited by Van Zant to replace bassist Greg Walker in Lynyrd Skynyrd. He worked with the band until the recording of its debut album on Al Kooper's Atlanta-based Sounds of the South Records. Wilkeson got cold feet, returning to Jacksonville to work in a refrigerated warehouse at FarmBest Dairy. He was briefly replaced by guitarist and bassist Ed King, formerly of Los Angeles psychedelic-rock band Strawberry Alarm Clock. However, Wilkeson rejoined the group by the time of its next release.

After Skynyd's 1977 plane crash Wilkeson and three other former Skynyrd members worked with JoJo Billingsley in the short-lived group Alias, who released one album on Mercury. Those same members then formed the Rossington-Collins band, who scored a couple of hits on MCA. After Gary Rossington and singer Dale Krantz left the RCB to form their own group in 1983, Wilkeson, Powell and guitarist Allen Collins carried on for a brief period as the Allen Collins Band, also on MCA.

In 1986 Wilkeson and Powell joined guitarist-vocalist Rocco Marshall to form Christian rock band Vision, who released two albums. Wilkeson (and Powell) rejoined Skynyrd in 1987 and toured regularly with that band until Wilkeson was found dead of heart failure in a Ponte Vedra Beach hotel room in 2001.

Also see *Lynyrd Skynyrd; Alias; Lombar, Dru; Vision.*

Wilson, Wesley

Pianist/vocalist/songwriter, born in Jacksonville in 1893; worked with Sidney Bechet, Fletcher Henderson, and Coot

Grant; his songs have been performed by Billie Holiday, Lavern Baker, Dr. John, Louis Jordan, B.B. King Nina Simone, Diana Ross and others. Died in New Jersey in 1958.

Wimmer, Danny

Former co-owner of Jacksonville's Milk Bar, went to work for Fred Durst's Interscope-distributed Flawless label in 1988, later for Epic. From there he went to Atlantic Records as a senior VP of A&R. Wimmer is now a concert promoter, creating some of the biggest outdoor music festivals in the country with the participation of Alliance Entertainment Group.

Wise, Chubby

Born Robert Russell Dees in 1915 in Lake City; Wise, who took his stepfather's surname, came to Jacksonville at 15 to pursue a career as a fiddler. He scuffled around Jacksonville for a few years performing at area nightclubs while driving a taxi during the day. While in Jacksonville he became friends with the Rouse Brothers. In 1938 he landed a regular gig on Gainesville's WRUF with Toby Dowdy and the Jubilee Hillbillies. In 1943 Wise traveled to Nashville for an unscheduled audition with Bill Monroe's Bluegrass Boys, whose fiddler Art Wooten had joined the navy. Wise was hired on the spot. As a member of the Blue Grass Boys, Wise frequently performed the Rouse Brothers' "Orange Blossom Special."; he claimed to have contributed

to the song and was in fact present at the time of its writing, according to Ervin Rouse, the song's main writer. After leaving Monroe in 1948, Wise enjoyed an illustrious career with the likes of the York Brothers, Flatt & Scruggs, Hank Snow, Red Allen, and the Stanley Brothers (who lived near Live Oak in the 1960s). In 1947 Wise recorded several songs with Hank Williams including "Honky Tonkin'" and in 1970 played on Merle Haggard's album, *The Fightin' Side of Me*. The writer or co-writer of 93 published songs, Wise recorded his own albums for the Starday and Stoneway labels. Wise lived in Virginia before settling in Glen St. Mary (Baker County, Fla.) in 1984. He died of congestive heart failure in Bowie, Md., in 1996 while visiting relatives.

Also see *Rouse, Ervin; Stanley Brothers.*

Wright, Shannon

Former lead singer of Jacksonville modern-rockers Crowsdell, moved to NYC with that band after signing with Big Cat, a small British label distributed by Sony, in 1995.

Upon Big Cat's demise in 1998, Wright relocated to rural North Carolina, where she honed her songwriting skills, eventually landing a deal with Chicago indie Quarterstick Records, for which she released four critically acclaimed albums. She later signed with Chicago label Touch and Go and has recorded several albums supervised by famed Nirvana producer Steve Albini.

Currently based in Atlanta, Wright maintains a significant following in Europe and is signed to French label Vicious Circle.

Also see *Crowsdell*.

Woody, Bill

Nashville-based country-pop singer, born in Jacksonville 1959. A singles deal with Roy Acuff's Hickory Records led to a joint venture with ABC in 1977 and then to MCA/Curb in 1979, but no major hits ensued. Many of Woody's recordings have be re-released on independent Red Bus Records.

Wynans, Reese

Organist in late-1960s Sarasota band the Blues Messengers, which came to Jacksonville to become the Second Coming. Upon that group's merger with the Allman Brothers, Wynans formed Jacksonville trio Ugly Jellyroll with vocalist Gary Goddard.

He later moved to Macon to rejoin former Second Coming guitarist Larry Reinhardt in Capricorn act Captain Beyond. Doing session work at Capricorn's recording studio, Wynans hooked up with Texas rocker Delbert McClinton, with whom he would relocate to Texas. While in Texas, Wynans began performing with bluesmeister Stevie Ray Vaughan. He has also worked with Joe Cocker.

Wynans has also played with blues artists Buddy Guy, John Mayall, Kenny Wayne Shepard. He lives in Nashville where he has worked with acts such as Brooks & Dunn, Trisha Yearwood, Martina McBride, and Hank Williams Jr. Wynans is currently touring with blues guitarist Joe Bonomassa.

Also see *Blues Messengers; Second Coming; Captain Beyond; Betts, Dickey; Reinhardt, Larry; Oakley, Berry; Allman Brothers Band.*

Yanique

Jacksonville "quiet-storm" R&B singer; released one album on EMI-distributed Bellmark Records (owned by former Stax CEO Al Bell), co-produced by Mamado (Willetta Smith). Now sings gospel music under her real name, Rosa Banks, reunited with Smith as co-writer and producer. Banks is a minister with Shield of Faith Global Dimension Vision Ministry, headed by her husband, Robert Banks III.

Yellowcard

In 1997, these Douglas Anderson high-school students recorded their debut album, *Midget Tossing,* at Michael Ray FitzGerald's Music Factory in Jacksonville Beach. Drummer Longineau Parsons III is the son of jazz trumpeter Longineau Parsons.

After replacing original singer Ben Dobson with Ryan Key of local band Modern Amusement, the group relocated to California in 2000, where they signed a one-off deal with Santa Barbara-based Lobster Records. Later signing with Gainesville-based Fueled by Ramen Records, for which Yellowcard released an EP, the group was picked up by Capitol.

Yellowcard's major-label debut, *Ocean Avenue,* wound up selling more than two million units. The group's second Capitol album, *Lights and Sounds*, went gold (at least 500,000) units, and its third, *Paper Walls*, came in at 358,000.

By 2005, two of the band's founding members, guitarist Ben Harper and bassist Warren Cooke had left the group. Cooke's replacement, Pete Mosely, was a founding member of Jacksonville punk-rockers Inspection 12. The original members, including singer Ben Dobson, having lost the rights to the name Yellowcard, briefly reunited under the name Where We Stand (from the title of the band's second album).

Key and Parsons regrouped in 2012 and signed with Los Angeles-based Hopeless Records, through which it released three albums. However, Parsons, the only original member by this point, left in 2014. That same year the group signed to New York label Razor & Tie but returned to Hopeless in 2016. Key announced Yellowcard would be disbanding and the group gave its final performance at the House Of Blues in Anaheim in March 2017.

Key lives near Nashville, where he is building a recording studio and label, Lone Tree Recordings. He also produced an album for Swedish group Like Torches. Ben Harper lives in Long Beach, where he operates Takeover Records. Longineau Parsons III lives in Hollywood, Calif. Dobson lives in Jacksonville.

Also see *Where We Stand; Inspection 12; Parsons, Longineau ("L.P.") III.*

Yost, Dennis

Born in Detroit in 1943, Yost moved to Jacksonville with his family at 5. As a student at Andrew Jackson High he began playing drums with local groups like the Echoes. In 1963 he placed Robert Nix in Water Eaton's Classics IV. In addition to playing drums, Yost was an outstanding singer and learned to play standing up so audiences could watch him sing.

The Classics were spotted in Daytona Beach by Paul Cochran, who was working for Bill Lowery's Atlanta operation. Cochran brought in Alan Diggs, and the pair became the group's co-managers. Diggs and Cochran brought the Classics to Atlanta and with Lowery's assistance landed a deal with Capitol.

The Classics' first two singles, including "Pollyanna," written by Lowery staff songwriter Joe South, flopped. The group moved to Imperial Records in 1968, where it would score a No. 2 nationwide hit with "Spooky," a song adapted from a jazz instrumental by Atlanta saxophonist Mike Sharpe.

Yost, as lead singer, decided to move up front and was replaced on drums by Alabama musician Kim Venable while Robert Nix became the band's studio drummer. The Classics IV scored three top-10 hits. After a period as Dennis Yost and the Classics IV, Yost went solo and signed with Liberty Records in 1969 and with MGM three years later.

Yost was based in Nashville for several years. He died in a Cleveland nursing facility in 2008, age 65, of respiratory failure, complications from a head injury received in a fall.

Also see *Classics IV; Echoes.*

Yo-Yos

From Jacksonville; had one national release in 1966, "Leaning on You," on Memphis-based Goldwax Records.

Also see *Mouse & the Boys.*

Zapen, Rebecca

Singer/songwriter/violinist and multi-instrumentalist from Jacksonville; has issued four albums of her own and appeared on two with guitarist Gary Starling. In 2007 Zapen was selected as a finalist in Disc Makers' Independent Music World Series showcase in Nashville, co-sponsored by *Billboard* magazine. She also wrote original music for Laura Newman's 2007 film *Sexy Clown Bitch*, an official selection at the Avignon Film Festival. Zapen has also toured Europe and performed onstage with the Indigo Girls. She appeared on NPR's *Whad'ya Know* in 2009. She lives in Tampa.

Also see *Starling; Gary.*

Zig Zag Paper Company

Despite its psychedelic-sounding moniker, this Pensacola group made its bread and butter backing R&B duo James and Bobby Purify. Released two unsuccessful singles on Bell, produced by Papa Don Schroeder.

Also see *Schroeder, Don; Purify, James & Bobby.*

Photo Credits

Cover photograph of Michael Ray FitzGerald by Richard Levine.
Al Hall by William P. Gottlieb.
Aleka's Attic by oliviasloan.
Allman Brothers Band by Linda Oakley Miller.
Alter Bridge by albes83.
Bernie Leaden – Flying Burritos by Rob C. Croes.
Bill Wharton by David Spitzer.
Blackfoot by Jack.
Bo-Diddley by David Spitzer.
Brad Mehldau by Björn Milcke.
Bunky Green by David Spitzer.
Burnseason by Matt Swig.
Charles Tolliver by Gene Jackson.
Charlie Hoss Singleton courtesy of the Florida Photographic Collection.
Charlie Souza by Laurie Pipper-Souza.
Dave Hlubek by Alberto Cabello Mayero.
David Hasselhoff by Jonas Mohr.
Derek and Susan Trucks by Carl Lender.
Dickey Betts by Sala Bikini.
Don Felder by Ralph Arvesen.
Evergreen Terrace by Mike Vance.
Fenwicks by Bennett Miller.
Fred Durst by David Shankbone.
George Linton by Spector1.
Jack Sheldon by David Spitzer.
James Weldon Johnson by Laura Wheeler Waring.
John Travolta by Georges Biard.
Johnny-van-zant by Spc. Patrick A. Ziegler.
King Eddie by King Eddie.
Limp Bizkit by Carlos Varela.

Lobo by Toppop.
Longineau Parsons Jr. by Longineau Parsons Jr.
Marty Jourard by Marty Jourard.
Maya Rudolph by Mingle Media TV Network.
Mike Campbell by Davidbaker.
Noble Watts by David D. Spitzer.
Oliver Hardy by RKO Pictures.
Pete Carr by Charlotte Price.
Phil-Driscoll by Phil Driscoll.
Pierce Pettis by Pierce Pettis.
Randall Hall by Randall Hall.
Ray Charles by Maurice Seymour.
Rebecca Zapen by James Zambon.
Red Jumpsuit Apparatus by 3/4 of zer0.
Rick Dees by Rick Dees.
Rick Johnson by Rick Johnson.
Rita Coolidge by Lauren.
Road Turkey by Jody Marcil.
Rodgers Gamble courtesy of the Florida Photographic Collection.
Root Boy Slim by Frederic Gleach.
Royal Guardsmen by the Royal Guardsmen.
Sananda Maitreya (Terence Trent D'Arby) by Danielle Belton.
Shinedown by GirloftheGoats.
Slim Whitman by Fabry.
Stephen Stills by Davidwbaker.
Steve Morse by Stephan Birlouez.
Tedeschi Trucks Band by Carl Lender.
Tim McGraw by Steve Kwak.
Troy Sneed by Emily Sneed.
Waltetr Orange by Carl Lender.
Walter Parks by Suzanna Mars.
Wes Borland by queenkwong.

Every effort has been made to credit images. Unaccredited images are in the public domain. Contact the publisher at richie@hiddenowl.com for any corrections or if you have an image you would like to offer for future editions.

INDEX

173

174

175

179

183

Biography

Michael Ray FitzGerald is a freelance writer, journalist, media historian, teacher and musician. He has written hundreds of articles for local, regional, national and international publications, including several scholarly journals. His book *Native Americans on Network TV* was a top seller in Rowman & Littlefield's Film & History line. Yoko Ono praised his collection, *Mixed Metaphors*. He has also co-written a screenplay based on a story he wrote for *Southern Cultures* and is a writer and associate producer for a documentary television series in development called *GuitarTown*.

FitzGerald has a bachelor's in journalism from Jacksonville University, a master's in mass communication from University of Florida and a doctorate from University of Reading (UK). His primary research area is film and television history. He has taught communication courses at University of North Florida in Jacksonville as well as at Flagler College, College of Coastal Georgia, Art Institute of Jacksonville and at the College of Journalism and Communication at University of Florida, Gainesville. Before going into academia he led several bands based in Jacksonville and operated two recording studios along with two nationally distributed record labels. In his spare time he enjoys reading, watching films and riding his bicycle.

FitzGerald has written for the following publications:

- *American Indian Culture and Research Journal,* University of California, Los Angeles
- Associated Press, Miami bureau
- *Atlanta Business Chronicle*
- *Bangkok Post*
- *Both Sides Now,* Jacksonville
- *Canopic Jar,* Woodstock, Ill.
- *Cow Ford,* Jacksonville University
- *Film and History,* Oshkosh, Wisc.
- *Film Locations: Paris,* Intellect Books, Manchester, UK
- *Folio Weekly,* Jacksonville
- *Free Inquiry,* Amherst, N.Y.
- *Historical Journal of Film, Radio, and Television,* London
- *Howard Journal of Communication,* Howard University, Philadelphia
- *Jacksonville Business Journal*
- *Jacksonville Business Quarterly*
- *JAM,* Orlando
- *Journal of Popular Culture,* East Lansing, Mich.
- *Lede,* Jacksonville University
- *Left Curve,* Oakland
- *Merge,* Adelaide, Australia
- *Musician's Trade Journal,* Nashua, N.H.
- *Orlando Business Journal*
- *Southeast Entertainer,* Jacksonville
- *Southern Cultures,* Chapel Hill
- *Southern Fried,* Nashville
- *The Campus Voice,* Florida State College at Jacksonville
- *The CommuniGator,* University of Florida
- *The Humanist,* Washington, D.C.
- *The Navigator,* Jacksonville University
- *The Notebook,* Jacksonville
- *Thursday Night,* Halifax
- *Utne Reader,* Topeka

www.ingramcontent.com/pod-product-compliance
Lightning Source LLC
Chambersburg PA
CBHW062041090426
42740CB00016B/2982